Plutocracy and Politics in New York City

D0470641

Urban Policy Challenges

Terry Nichols Clark, Series Editor

Cities are critical. From the Los Angeles riots of 1992 to the Hong Kong reversion of 1997, cities represent in microcosm the problems and potentials we face at all governmental levels.

Focusing on cities can help clarify our most challenging issues. Most key decisions affecting our lives are made locally. Although national governments collect the majority of funds, most welfare state programs around the world are provided by local governments. Urban leaders play key roles in encouraging economic development, maintaining quality public services, and mandating reasonable taxes.

And they are pressed to do more: provide attractive physical environments, improve amenities such as bike paths, help encourage recycling, assist disadvantaged groups to achieve broader acceptance and access to public facilities, keep streets safe, and fill the gaps in health and social services.

Books in the *Urban Policy Challenges* series will explore the range of urban policy problems and will detail solutions that have been sought and implemented in cities from around the world. They will build on studies of leadership, public management, organizational culture, community power, intergovernmental relations, public finance, citizen responsiveness, and related elements of urban public decisionmaking.

These approaches to urban challenges will range from case studies to quantitative modeling. The series will include monographs and texts as well as edited volumes. While some works will target professional and student audiences, many books will elicit attention from thoughtful public leaders and informed citizens as well.

Plutocracy and Politics in New York City

Gabriel A. Almond

Stanford University

Westview Press

A Division of HarperCollins*Publishers*

Urban Policy Challenges

Copyright © 1998 by Westview Press, A Division of HarperCollins, Inc.

Published in 1998 in the United States of America by Westview Press, 5500 Central Avenue, Boulder, Colorado 80301-2877, and in the United Kingdom by Westview Press, 12 Hid's Copse Road, Cumnor Hill, Oxford OX2 9JJ

Library of Congress Cataloging-in-Publication Data
Almond, Gabriel Abraham, 1911–
   Plutocracy and politics in New York City / Gabriel A. Almond.
      p.   cm. — (Urban policy challenges)
   Originally presented as the author's thesis (Ph.D.)—University of Chicago, 1938.
   Includes bibliographical references and index.
   ISBN 0-8133-9983-1 (pb)
   1. New York (N.Y.)—Politics and government.   2. Democracy—New York (State)—New York—History.   3. Elite (Social sciences)—New York (State)—New York—History.   4. Politicians—New York (State)—New York—Social conditions.   5. Social classes—New York (State)—New York—History.   I. Title.   II. Series.
JS1225.A55   1998
320.9747'1'09041—dc21   97-27164
                                                                                          CIP

The paper used in this publication meets the requirements of the American National Standard for Permanence of Paper for Printed Library Materials Z39.48-1984.

10   9   8   7   6   5   4   3   2   1

Contents

Part Three
Politicians Under Democratic Conditions

Part Four
Plutocracy and Insecurity

Tables

Foreword

The publication of Gabriel Almond's doctoral study, *Plutocracy and Politics in New York City,* is a significant event. It takes us back to 1938, seedtime for what became the behavioral revolution, but also a time when American political science was still closely tied to European political sociology. Almond's analysis reflects this European tradition. He depicts the American landscape, not as a pluralist competition among a myriad of groups, but as a place in which there is ongoing tension between the plutocracy, that is, the wealthy classes, and the forces of democratization channeled through professional politicians elected from and by the middle and lower classes.

Relying on extensive analyses of the social background of office-holders, Almond shows the shift away from domination by individuals of wealth and prestige, in the early days of the nation, to a more diverse set of officeholders as democratization takes hold. Almond combines quantitative analyses of social backgrounds with detailed historical narratives, in this way directing the reader's attention to the recurring tensions between social classes. Writing in the midst of the New Deal effort to cope with the economic insecurity and hardship of the business cycle, Almond sees American politics as "animated by an intensifying struggle between the wealthy classes and those elements seeking a greater share in the fruits of our economy and technique." Yet, Almond argues, the United States is no arena of conventional class struggle. He puts forward instead his own version of American exceptionalism.

Accurately forecasting that the nation would have neither a revolution of the left nor a takeover by the authoritarian right, Almond offers us a different scenario to think about, albeit one that still offers little cause for celebration. Almond describes what we now label as a regime, and he pictures it in clear political economy terms. In this regime there is a division of labor between economic activity, directed by the principal holders of private wealth (the plutocracy), and political activity, directed by office-holders who are increasingly professional politicians. Though professional politicians must be attentive to the mainly lower and middle class constituencies that elect them, these professional politicians are not champions of class struggle. Far from it, as, Almond argues, they are not animated by general causes, but by self-aggrandizement and by the advantages of attending to particular constituent interests.

Almond teaches us an important lesson: democracy is not a sham behind which the plutocracy rules, but *elected office is an insufficient power base for governing society.* The holders of private wealth must be reckoned with to a special degree. To be sure, the plutocracy is not of one mind, even in attitude toward democracy. However, Almond shows, any crisis of consequence to the wealthy classes, from world war to municipal corruption, evokes heightened political participation. Thus, rather than simply withdrawing from the political arena in the face of rising democracy, social and economic notables changed strategy and cultivated the kind of personal connections appealing to self-aggrandizing politicians. Thus, while the withdrawal of the notables was substantial, they did not surrender influence. When direct control could no longer be sustained, indirect influence became the fallback.

At the same time, crises, including popular discontent with the privileges of wealth—indeed, any threat to the power balance between various classes —spurs the wealthy to resume direct participation in political life. But the plutocracy, Almond notes, does not sustain a high level of direct participation. Once the crisis is diminished, the social and economic notables return to mainly indirect influence. Of course, some particular business executives do engage in direct participation of a narrow kind, that is, participation in pursuit of profit opportunities for their own businesses or industries. Lacking, however, is the kind of general involvement in the process of governance that characterized the early days of the nation. Democratization has altered the regime since then.

By not attributing control of society to the business class, Almond invites us to think through the nature of the regime that has taken shape. What is it, if it is neither an oligarchy of private wealth nor democratic pluralism? The economic sector is an independent force in governance. It enjoyed that status in 1938, and it still enjoys that status today despite all of the changes brought on by the New Deal, World War II, the Cold War, and the Great Society. Public office-holding provides little control over the economic order, especially at the local level.

As Charles Lindblom so forcefully argues, control of the economy is part of the governance of society.[1] Writing in 1938, Almond subscribed to this same view, but he made a broader point as well. Major policy change requires the involvement of at least some elements of the economic sector. Why? Without some plutocratic involvement, government is too weak, public office-holding lacks the luster of high prestige and full legitimacy, and needed resources are unavailable. How do we know this? As Almond shows, crises "make apparent the actual power situation." When crises emerge, the division of labor between economics and politics lessens. Governance becomes a matter of joint action.

This account of the American regime of necessity simplifies Almond's detailed and historically grounded analysis, but it highlights the basic dynamics he describes. By using a long historical sweep, Almond is able to put the spotlight on the emergence of a division of labor between economic and political actors while showing that political actors have limited capacity to act independently on broad issues. Therefore they have little motivation to build their careers around such concerns. If one cannot pursue broad aims as a public office-holder, except in time of crisis, when general-minded allies from the plutocracy are more readily available, then it should not be surprising that politicians would protect narrow constituencies and engage in self-aggrandizing behavior. This behavior has consequences, however— low regard for professional politicians.

As we look at Almond's analysis from the perspective of the 1990s and a transition to the twenty-first century, we gain understanding of the present lack of confidence in the American politician. Term limitations and the appeal of personalities who depict themselves as political outsiders are phenomena that bespeak an extraordinarily low standing for politicians. The 1990s represent only a change in degree, not a change in direction, from what Almond found in 1938. Contemporary politicians are seen in much the same way that Almond sees them historically—self-aggrandizing, little concerned with problem-solving for society at-large but much concerned about personal privileges and their own individual network of contacts. Not every politician fits this mold, and Almond makes no such claim. He does suggest, however, that there is a systemic tendency toward politicians who are not guided by general issue concerns. Much observable behavior squares with that characterization of the American regime.

The genius of Almond's analysis lies in the attention he gives to the context within which politicians operate. They are part of a division of labor in which government is often unable to act in a broad way *without the participation of business interests.* Much of the direct involvement of business stems from narrow profit-oriented concerns. As Almond points out, when the plutocracy retreated from broad and direct participation in political life, social irresponsibility surfaced. Disconnected from a direct role in governing America, the wealthy became self-indulgent and displayed a tendency toward frivolous social activity. This, however, is no inconsequential fact. With great power—of the kind bestowed by the top economic positions—comes great responsibility. To fail to act on that responsibility for whatever reason is to withhold from society a capacity to confront and act on its problems.

In Almond's scenario, America acts governmentally only when crisis driven. That scenario fits the post-1938 picture as well as it did the earlier period examined by Almond. The governing capacity of the nation is only selectively and sporadically mobilized to confront society's problems. Few business executives wear the mantle of social responsibility in anything other than a rare instance. Civic involvement too often is a matter of show without substance.[2] As a consequence, governance falls well short of the need to act. A wide gap between potential power and its realization thus characterizes the American regime—it has in the past and the gap promises to continue for the foreseeable future.

It is especially appropriate that Almond's analysis focuses on New York City, the nation's largest city. It is in urban America that the disjuncture between power and responsibility is most acute. The pattern of selective business involvement in city affairs offers some painful, albeit still inadequately learned, lessons. As we look back over the past half-century at multiple efforts to revitalize the nation's cities, we need to ask what went wrong and why cities suffered a deteriorating quality of life and a consequent declining appeal to the middle and working classes. Why has democracy in the nation's cities not worked better?

Urban decline is linked with selective business participation in the affairs of the city. Slum clearance, expressways, mass transit, mega-convention centers, expanded airports, tax abatements and special tax districts, festival market places, aquariums, downtown stadiums, and much more have not prevented an escalating crime problem and deteriorating schools. Why? Because cities have been enabled to do only those things that were directly profitable and appealing to business interests. When Robert Salisbury wrote about the "new convergence of power" that came to the forefront in American cities in the post World War II period, he was describing a set of public-private partnerships.[3] But these were partnerships with a limited domain of action and responsibility. They were partnerships dedicated to the physical restructuring of the city, not to the incorporation of urban masses into a changing economy. They paid little attention to schools or to broad policies of human investment. A qualified workforce, urban business interests assumed, could be found simply by building more expressways and expanding the labor pool deeper and deeper into the suburbs. Alternatively, the gates of immigration could be opened more widely.

Thus public-private partnerships did not confront the changing job market as a barrier to economic inclusion. Instead, public-private partnerships converged mainly about the very kind of land deals, construction contracts, and retainer-generating projects that Almond saw as the central link between the plutocracy and the professional politician. In this way, business interests were only selectively involved in public affairs and maintained relatively low profiles. Instead of assuming a role in governing the whole urban community and facing all of its problems, business leaders played a narrow role and confronted only part of the city's problems. They did not foresee the extent to which crime and social disorder would grow as a result of increasing social and economic fragmentation. Nor did they appreciate the depth of challenge faced in incorporating urban minorities into a changing economy.

In the immediate rush to restructure land use, business elites gave little attention to the long-range consequences of social inaction. Others were more heedful. Philanthropic foundations, for example, displayed significant social awareness. As early as the 1950s, the Ford Foundation aimed its Grey Areas projects at turning around urban decline, broadly understood. Foundation staff and others who were paying attention could see a deteriorating job market, failing schools, ineffective welfare programs, and other danger signals about the urban future. Their specific responses can be faulted, but they, at least, had their eyes open.[4]

Why, then, did businesses with a stake in the central city not see what others could see? Perhaps their isolation from public accountability enabled them to believe what was comforting to believe, that is, to believe that short-term business prosperity would filter down to everyone and automatically create an inclusive America. In any event, the "new convergence of power" identified by Salisbury was highly selective in what it chose to address. It apparently suffered from an acute form of social myopia.

As the twentieth century comes to a close, business is awakening to a wider urban reality, a realization that central city revitalization requires more than a physically restructured landscape. There is an emerging consensus that deteriorating schools and rising crime are among the prime threats to past and future investments in the city. Slowly awareness grows that past inattention to social needs has consequences, and these consequences have not left the business sector unscathed.

Why have the consequences of social neglect received recognition only belatedly? Answering this question calls for a further examination of the nature of regimes.

A regime is a form of social learning. It focuses attention on some issues and possibilities more than others. A regime learns through what it does and through the relationships it promotes.[5]

Because cognition is limited, even those with significant stakes at issue may fail to appreciate distant consequences. Certainly urban-based businesses were selective in what they saw. Perceptions stem from activities, and the regime that Gabriel Almond describes was engaged in a restricted form of activity—projects that brought together business interests with politicians and their supporters who were seeking highly particularistic benefits. In New York City, this phenomenon is durable enough to be labeled "the permanent government."[6] This was the system that New York's Robert Moses learned to manipulate so skillfully. And as the biographer of Moses shows, the "master builder" and his allies were very selective in the consequences they gave attention to.[7] What the regime concept teaches us, then, is that a public-private partnership is not necessarily a means through which governance is broadened, and a partnership may in fact render governance narrow and selective.

Gabriel Almond's 1938 study of "Plutocracy and Politics in New York City" predates the public-private partnerships that formed after World War II in pursuit of central city redevelopment. Even so, Almond's study anticipates their weakness. If the power of business is used to attend only to its profit needs and its class interests, government will be unable to confront and act on many of society's problems. Urban democracy will be hobbled accordingly.

A pattern of incomplete governance bequeathed today's problems and fed the view that government is helpless to solve social problems. Politicians are the targets of resentment that, as Almond shows, are more properly directed at the regime. Business escapes blame from the public, but escaping blame does not diminish the city's problems or diminish urban disinvestment.

The most exposed partners in the modern regime are the professional politicians. They are vulnerable on the grounds that Almond identifies, that they tend to neglect big issues and focus on narrow, self-serving concerns. What is the alternative to the professional politician? There is no ready answer to that question. Almond's analysis stands as a caution that the capacity to govern is broader than what elected officials are able to do alone, and this is the case whether the elected office-holder is a professional politician or a citizen activist. Until business executives are accountable for a wide range of social consequences, elected officials will face frustrations. They will be tempted to narrow the range of their own concerns. As was true of the period in which Almond did his study, so it is now: political reform without a larger regime reform will amount to very little. In 1938, Almond exposed a weakness in American democracy. Today we are still struggling to overcome it, and the urgency of that challenge has grown.

Clarence N. Stone
University of Maryland

Notes

1. Charles E. Lindblom, *Politics and Markets* (New York: Basic Books, 1977).

2. Michael Bernick, *Urban Illusions* (New York: Praeger, 1987).

3. Robert H. Salisbury, "Urban Politics: The New Convergence of Power," *Journal of Politics,* vol. 26 (November, 1964): 775–97.

4. Peter Marris and Martin Rein, *Dilemmas of Social Reform* (Chicago: Aldine Publishing Co., 1973).

5. Clarence N. Stone, *Regime Politics* (Lawrence: University Press of Kansas, 1989).

6. Jack Newfield and Paul DuBrul, *The Permanent Government* (New York: Pilgrim Press, 1981); see also Jim Sleeper, *The Closest of Strangers* (New York: Norton, 1990).

7. Robert A. Caro, *The Power Broker* (New York: Knopf, 1974).

Preface: Remembrance of Things Past

The research for this dissertation was done in New York City in 1935–36. The Great Depression supplied the background events and themes. The stock market crash of 1929 happened during my sophomore year at the University of Chicago. I recall a seminar one cold winter morning in 1930 when the economist Frank Knight spoke apologetically of his privileges as a university professor with a secure salary of $8,000 per year. He offered his help to those of us unable to buy the required text or who might in other ways be needy. The Depression led me to change my major to political science from English literature and composition. Teaching and research seemed more practical and relevant than the cultivation of *belles lettres*.

I had a direct confrontation with the unemployed—then one-fourth of the nation's labor force—just before entering graduate school in 1933. I worked as a "complaint aide" in the Stockyards District of the Unemployment Relief Service in order to accumulate enough money to cover my expenses in my first graduate year. I stood a daily watch for eight months as angry, hungry, mostly Slavic unemployed stockyard laborers demanded to see their social workers to get larger food allowances, rental payments, shoes for children, and the like. I had the power to permit or deny them access to their social workers who would have to approve their requests.

My first scholarly publication came out of this experience. Though not yet enrolled in graduate school, I interested Harold Lasswell in the possibilities of research on the responses of the "American working classes to the capitalist crisis," as manifested in the Stockyard's office of the Unemployment Relief Service. Our "Aggressive Behavior of Clients on Public Relief,"[1] reporting on the social characteristics of the "proto-revolutionaries" among the Chicago south side unemployed, was published in the *American Political Science Review* in 1934 and committed me once and for all to a professional political science career emphasizing "field research."

Class and class conflict were dominating themes in the larger political and media world, as well as in the more intimate university life of the early 1930s. The Communists, Trotskyites, and socialists had chapters on the University of Chicago campus. One heard their class struggle analyses and polemics in the Reynolds Club, in the University Commons and Coffee Shop, or in the open-air demonstrations around the campus.

In the larger world the New Deal had come to power in America, and the National Socialists had come to power in Germany. Around the time of my fellowship year the Social Security and the Wagner Labor Relations Acts were being debated and enacted, at the same time that the radical populist voice of Father Coughlin was being heard over the radio. The Liberty League was raising funds from the business and financial community to combat the "threat to freedom" mounted by the Roosevelt administration. Some said that "it (fascism) can happen here."

The ideas being broached in the graduate seminars of Charles Merriam, Harold Lasswell, Harold Gosnell, Frederick Schuman, and others that I attended in 1933 and 1934 reflected a much more complex structure of causality including personality and culture, as well as class and status. Merriam took us beyond class and class conflict into the emerging concept of a "perfectable" and "perfecting" pluralist democracy, rather than a perfect one. He was intrigued by the theme of political leadership; a group of his graduate students wrote dissertations on particular American political leaders (Gosnell's *Boss Platt*[2] was the first one). My first research papers done for Lasswell's seminars were empirical studies of the Chicago industrial, financial, political, and social elites. I was seeking to test, in the immediate world about me, the diagnoses and remedies of the Marxists. When I presented my dissertation plans to Merriam—to make a quantitative study of the relation between wealth and politics in New York City from colonial times until the then present day of the 1930s—he gave his assent along with a gentle and ironic warning that "the desert is full of bones."

My dissertation year in New York was supported by a pre-doctoral field fellowship from the Social Science Research Council, the first year such fellowships were granted. It was in the infancy of the social science movement in the United States, before it came to be called "behavioralism." The emphasis was on field research, on "empirically grounded" work, on quantification, on sociological and psychological explanation. The social science departments at the University of Chicago were of great importance in these developments. Charles E. Merriam chaired the Department of Political Science at the University of Chicago, as well as the university's Social Science Research Committee; and in the 1920s and '30s, he chaired the Board of Directors of the national Social Science Research Council. He was very much a part of the New Deal as well, a middle western *eminence grise*, a close confidant of Interior Secretary Harold Ickes, a member of the National Resources Planning Board, and the President's Committee on Administrative Management. Some of us were enabled to make a little money on the side by doing some of the research and drafting of the reports made to the president by these boards and commissions. The graduate students of my generation had a sense of being linked to the metropolitan, national, and international setting.

My first dissertation supervisor, Harold Lasswell (Harold Gosnell finished the job after Lasswell left the university early in 1938), set no limits on what I had described as a study of the elites of New York City. Large topics were still permissible in these early years. The terms of reference of my award as a "pre-doctoral field fellow" obligated me, I thought, to engage in participant observation. And so in the fall of 1935 for a month or two I visited among the elite on the East Side of Central Park and interviewed a number of social secretaries and guardians of upper class manners such as Emily Post. This search for the values of the New York rich turned out to be more exhausting and less illuminating than I had anticipated, and by the winter I had settled down to hard work in the New York Room of the great New York Public Library.

This large high-ceilinged room with long tables and well-worn wooden chairs, surrounded by cabinets full of old volumes—directories, yearbooks, memoirs, diaries, and the like—became my home for eight months or so. This was the precopier, precomputer age. Day after day, week after week, month after month, I recorded in handwriting on slips of paper the data that were to produce the percentages in the 68 tables of my doctoral dissertation and computed in the following year on an old adding machine on the top floor of the Social Science Research Building at the University of Chicago. Most of these tables appear in a number of appendices in the dissertation which, for reasons of economy, are not reproduced in this book.

Harold Gosnell paced me through the process of data presentation, interpretation, and oral defense. By a coincidence I was notified by Westview Press that they would publish the dissertation on the very day that Gosnell's obituary appeared in the *New York Times,* reporting his death in his 100th year. He may have been the only one of my three mentors who really read the dissertation all the way through. My adversary at my dissertation defense was L. D. White, who thought that I had bitten off more than a doctoral candidate should and who was troubled by my disrespect for the elites. I dedicate this book to the memory of Harold Gosnell, who took me in hand in 1938 and helped me to my doctorate.

Time and place had much to do with the origins of this dissertation and the shape it took. I studied for my degree at the University of Chicago at the time that Merriam, Lasswell, Gosnell, Quincy Wright, Leonard D. White, and Frederick Schuman were at the height of their productivity. In their seminars one was exposed to the powerful literature of European political sociology and psychology—the ideas of Marx and the Marxists, Freud and his followers, Max Weber, Vilfredo Pareto, Gaetano Mosca, Roberto Michels. But the strongest message was an empirical, pragmatic one. Ideas were brought down to earth in American accents and tested against American experience.

The influence of Max Weber on my intellectual development was especially strong. In 1933 and 1934 I shared an office in the Social Science Research Building with Edward Shils who was then collaborating with Louis Wirth in a translation of Max Weber's methodological essays. He introduced me to Max Weber's *Wirtschaft und Gesellschaft*[3] (*Economy and Society*) and to his two classic lectures—*Wissenschaft als Beruf* and *Politik als Beruf*[4] (Science as a Calling and Politics as a Calling). I was awed by Weber's enormous learning and his moral authority. I laboriously translated *Politik als Beruf* in preparation for my German language examination. Weberian concepts and, I blush to acknowledge, some of his Germanic sentence structure entered into the prose of this dissertation.

I was similarly fortunate in New York City, arriving there at the same time that refugee scholars from Germany and Italy were arriving and forming the Graduate Faculty of the New School for Social Research. The intellectual historian Albert Salomon gave me a reading course in Max Weber's political sociology. In that same year I also encountered Franz Neumann and Otto Kircheimer freshly arrived in New York from the Frankfurt Institute of Social Research. Hans Speier helped me understand the finer points of theoretical difference among the various neo-Marxist trends represented in the newly arriving academic refugees.

The title I gave to the dissertation, *Plutocracy and Politics in New York City,* needs a bit of explaining. I believed it was an error to speak of the American political system as a democracy, a "rule of the people." Although the "demos" participated, it surely did not rule. Under the influence of Max Weber I felt obliged to typologise. I chose the term "plutocracy" as applicable to American institutions. Weber's term for city elites in ancient Greece and Renaissance Italy was "patriciate," a concept that included inherited political status—membership in a Senate or a Council. In America even in pre-revolutionary days men of high status had no inherited rank or title to office. Hence it would have been inaccurate to speak of an American patriciate. There were economic limits on the suffrage and on rights to hold office. Prior to the democratization of the suffrage in the early decades of the nineteenth century it would be technically correct to characterize government in America as "plutocratic," in which only men of means were eligible to participate and compete. For the later period after the democratization of the suffrage one could use the term plutocracy to refer to the wealthy stratum of the population, which ceased to rule in the older sense but which continued to enjoy a substantially unequal share of political power. It is in these two senses that I used the term—as a type of polity, and as a social stratum enjoying privileged political access and power. Indeed, this is the dictionary definition.

Two other intellectual currents stirring at that time influenced my development even though they did not directly enter into the dissertation. The first of these was Freudianism and the "psycho-cultural" movement. This had come to me first through Lasswell's seminar in "Non-Rational Factors in Political Behavior," which I attended as an undergraduate the first time he gave it in 1930. The lectures he gave during that seminar were read from page proofs of *Psychopathology and Politics*,[5] which appeared later in that same year. I was both shocked and deeply impressed. Toilet training, incest, sodomy, and homosexuality were not then part of our everyday vocabulary. Lasswell's *World Politics and Personal Insecurity*,[6] developing these themes of politics and personality in relation to issues of war and peace, democracy and dictatorship, political culture and national character, appeared in 1935. Margaret Mead's *Coming of Age in Samoa* had appeared in 1928,[7] and Ruth Benedict's *Patterns of Culture* in 1934.[8] Margaret Mead visited the University of Chicago campus on a number of occasions during my early graduate years. Thus the makings of the psychocultural approach were very much present in those days at the University of Chicago. While I was laboriously uncovering the political sociology of the elite in the New York Public Library, I had a hunch that I would ultimately have to come to grips with the impact of wealth in politics from this personality and culture perspective.

Had it not been for my hubris this book would have been published more than half a century ago,[9] at a time when Charles Merriam was ready to recommend publication of the original dissertation. I insisted that the published book include a number of chapters dealing with psychological aspects of wealth in politics. These would have given me the claim of being a political psychologist as well as a political sociologist. Merriam judged me to be a bit "too big for my britches" and refused to recommend publication of the book in its expanded form. I defied Merriam with the result that the only published product of my New York City research period prior to the present publication was "The Political Attitudes of Wealth."[10] In that article I argued that one could not automatically infer the political attitudes and behavior of an individual from his or her "class" status. Thus while the majority of the economically powerful would vote for conservative candidates for public office and favor public policies of a conservative sort, the relationship was relatively loose and probabilistic, and there were many cases of deviation in both the liberal and the "reactionary" direction. In the case histories of wealthy New York political activists reported in my 1945 article I contrasted the life histories of such New York conservatives as Chauncey Depew, Elihi Root, and Charles Evans Hughes, with such reactionaries as Jay Gould, John D. Rockefeller, and William Randolph Hearst, and such liberals as Abram Hewitt and Andrew Carnegie. From their memoirs, and from their biographies I presented hypotheses mainly drawn from Karen Horney's innovations in psychoanalytic theory, explaining why the economically powerful typically supported conservative causes, why some of them were reactionary, and why some of them supported liberal causes.

A second influence that was only partially reflected in my doctoral dissertation was the "process" approach to politics. Merriam and Gosnell were part of a larger movement that included younger contemporaries such as Peter Odegard, Pendleton Herring, and ultimately V. O. Key Jr., David Truman, Robert Dahl, and Avery Leiserson, who converted such political typologies as democracy and dictatorship into continua rather than dichotomies and turned Marxist absolutism into a set of more complex and subtle hypotheses. The emerging trade union movement in the 1930s was bringing the working classes into the family of power, which had previously been dominated by industrial and agricultural interests. The political process was defined as "pluralist" by most of the leading political scientists, even though the industrial and banking interests were recognized as the most powerful members. Studies of pressure groups, political parties, and the media of communication—the "infrastructure" of democracy—was beginning to make the political science reputations in the 1930s.

My later research on American foreign policy,[11] on recruitment to and defection from the Communist Party, and on political development reflected these two latter intellectual currents. My doctoral dissertation had to settle for a political sociological method, and one that was doable in a limited period of time.

Clarence Stone generously attributes to this dissertation the accomplishment of having established a baseline in the evaluation of American democracy, of having traced empirically the emergence of the contemporary American political regime from its oligarchic politico-economic structure in the eighteenth and early nineteenth centuries to its inconclusive neither oligarchy nor democracy character of the present day. The democratization of the suffrage in the nineteenth century produced a professional politician class drawn from lawyers and small entrepreneurs primarily interested in office and the benefits office could give, and left the economically powerful elements in society relatively insecure vis-à-vis the public domain with its crucial controls over public order, land and its uses, taxation, public franchises, the creation and maintenance of infrastructure, and the like. The dissertation describes the set of arrangements of an indirect sort and the historical patterns that had emerged by the mid-1930s to cope with this loss of direct political control by the economically powerful. These included the financing of political campaigns, the formation and support of economic interest groups, the maintenance of lobbyists at the various levels of government, ownership and control of the mass media, and the like. It also describes the intermittent activization of the economically powerful classes in periods of large-scale corruption and scandal, in the crises of wartime, and in economic breakdowns such as the Great Depression, when the very survival of this mixed politico-economic regime seemed to be in question. In crises such as these this bifurcation of economic and political power could not be tolerated, and bankers, industrialists, and great merchants again made direct appearances on the political stage, bringing political and economic power together.

In order to make his larger point about the persistence of this divided political economy regime, Clarence Stone may have understated the changes that have occurred in the sixty years since this dissertation was written. The "welfare state," with its "social safety net," was then just a gleam in the eyes of Franklin Roosevelt and Harry Hopkins. Social democracy on the European continent suffered from a deep ambivalence about "bourgeois parliamentarism" and had already played its tragic part in the rise of Fascism and Nazism. It was not at all clear that democracy and capitalism could survive together, or separately. This was not only the view on the left. Frank Knight expressed anxious doubts on these questions in his University of Chicago lectures in the early 1930s. Harvard economist Joseph Schumpeter delivered a lecture on the "Survival of Capitalism" at the U.S. Department of Agriculture in January of 1936 anticipating the pessimistic arguments of his book of the early World War II years.[12]

Thus at the time this dissertation was being researched and written there was widespread doubt that democracy could survive the onslaught from the right and the left and the cowardice, self-deception, and doctrinal rigidity of the beleaguered democratic elites. This doubt was also expressed in the concluding chapter of the dissertation. The threat to democracy stemmed from the unwillingness of the economically powerful classes to accept modifications in the market system that might mitigate the social costs of the business cycle and provide a welfare net for the poor and economically vulnerable. Today, the survival of democracy is not in question, but rather its efficiency and equity. What was an uneasy and uncertain accommodation in 1935 has become the success story of the 1990s—the regime of market economy and liberal democracy now widely emulated throughout the world. Wherever this regime has been successful in the long run it has been accompanied by some kind and degree of redistributive welfare net.

The system of indirect controls that I described in the 1930s has been much elaborated and professionalized. The lobby now represents a much more complex set of interests, including an array of influential civic and public interest organizations. In the sixty years since the submission of my dissertation organized labor has gone from weak to strong and in recent decades has declined in size and influence. Frank Kingdon's "iron triangles" of Congressional committees, subcommittees and their staffs, bureaucratic specialists, and special interest professionals from the private sector have established separate "sub-governments" in particular economic sectors and other areas of public policy.[13] The media have become more powerful and more autonomous. Investigative post-Watergate journalism seems to know no friends and to take no prisoners. Politics and economics operate in its unforgiving illumination.

The state of our knowledge regarding the interaction of economic and political inequality has been greatly increased and improved in the last decades, as reflected in the recent work of Sidney Verba[14] and Robert Dahl,[15] among others. By comparison with the finer discriminations made in these contemporary studies, the picture I drew of politico-economic power in New York City in the 1930s was a tentative and uncertain sketch from a special urban setting. It may serve in a limited way as a baseline to contrast with an earlier plutocratic oligarchy and the contemporary more complex and more balanced system, but no more.

Nothing brings out more clearly the costs and consequences of this American political-economic regime than the crisis of the American city. All the efforts to deal with the problems of the inner city—the breakdown of the family, the deterioration of the educational system, the decay of the housing stock, the collapse of public order—founder on the resistance of the economically advantaged strata to maintain, to say nothing of increasing, the level of social expenditure. The savaging of welfare democracy that has been taking place in the last decades has served to discredit most forms of public expenditure and governmental regulation other than those for national security, public safety, and the construction and manning of prisons. The tragic irony of this fiscal ideology is that it condemns us to efforts to cope with the consequences of inner city breakdown rather than with its causes. The inner city holds the public safety and order of American society in hostage, and government can only respond by putting more policemen on the streets and building more prisons. Respectable society has turned its back on the collapsing society of the inner cities, only to find that it has ended up with governments that cannot provide the first function of the state—that of maintaining the public order and safety.

Notes

1. Almond, Gabriel A., with Harold D. Lasswell, "Aggressive Behavior by Clients on Public Relief," *American Political Science Review,* August, 1934.

2. Gosnell, Harold F., *Boss Platt and His New York Machine* (Chicago: University of Chicago Press, 1924).

3. Weber, Max, *Wirtschaft und Gesellschaft,* translated as *Economy and Society,* Two Vols. Editors Gunther Roth and Klaus Wittich (Berkeley: University of California Press, 1978).

4. Weber, Max (Editors Gerth, Hans, and Mills, C. Wright) *From Max Weber* (New York: Oxford University Press, 1958), Chapters 4 and 5.

5. Lasswell, Harold, D., *Psychopathology and Politics* (Chicago: University of Chicago Press, 1930).

6. Lasswell, Harold D., *World Politics and Personal Insecurity* (New York: McGraw Hill, 1935).

7. Mead, Margaret, *Coming of Age in Samoa* (New York: W. Morrow, 1928).

8. Benedict, Ruth, *Patterns of Culture* (Boston: Houghton Mifflin, 1934).

9. Almond, Gabriel A., *A Discipline Divided* (Newbury Park: Sage Publications, 1990), pp. 321–22.

10. Almond, Gabriel A., "The Political Attitudes of Wealth," *Journal of Politics*, August, 1945.

11. Almond, Gabriel A., *The American People and Foreign Policy* (New York: Harcourt Brace, 1950); *The Appeals of Communism* (Princeton, N.J.: Princeton University Press, 1954); Almond and Coleman, James, *The Politics of the Developing Areas* (Princeton, N.J.: Princeton University Press, 1960).

12. Schumpeter, Joseph, *Capitalism, Socialism, and Democracy* (New York: Harper, 1942).

13. Kingdon, Frank, *Agendas, Alternatives, and Public Policies* (Boston: Little Brown, 1984).

14. Verba, Sidney, Kay Lehman Schlozman, and Henry E. Brady, *Voice and Equality: Civic Voluntarism in American Politics* (Cambridge, Mass.: Harvard University Press, 1995).

15. Dahl, Robert A., *Democracy and Its Critics* (New Haven, Conn.: Yale University Press, 1989).

Introduction

THIS STUDY OF THE PLUTOCRACY and politics in New York City poses as its central problems the following: (1) What have been the consequences of the relatively rapid democratization in America for the activities and attitudes of the wealthier classes? (2) What transformations have occurred in the political and social attitudes of the wealthier classes as a result of the increasing lower class pressure of the last decades?

Seen against the background of European democratic development, America is unique in having won at so early a time so wide a spread of the franchise.

In Europe the extension of the franchise in the constitutional monarchies and democracies was a gradual process. In England the exclusive political privileges of the aristocracy and the plutocracy were restricted, stage by stage, by the gradual admission of larger and larger portions of the population. The Reform Act of 1832, which is generally viewed as having begun the process of the breakdown of the exclusive hold of the privileged classes upon political power, increased the electorate only by 200,000. The Reform Act of 1867 granted voting rights to an additional million; the Act of 1884 added another 2 million; that of 1918 brought the total electorate up to 16 million, substantial universal suffrage, although women under thirty years of age were excluded. This gradual extension of the suffrage permitted the assimilation of political democracy to the institutions of social, economic, and political inequality.[1]

The British aristocracy and wealthier classes have maintained until the present day a tradition of active and personal political participation. This is primarily due to the fact that political democratization has been gradual and peaceful, and has by no means destroyed the superior political position of the plutocracy and aristocracy but rather has grown up alongside of the older institutions. Despite gradual political democratization the general population continues to acquiesce in the superior social status of the "upper classes." Along with this continued acquiescence in the superior social

1

status of the court, the nobility, and the plutocracy even under democratic conditions went a natural acquiescence in the greater political initiative of these classes. Individuals who in their private life defer to wealth and status are likely to adopt the same attitude in their public life.

The political and social attitudes of Americans were significantly conditioned by the economic equality and independence of the frontier, and the extremely high rate of mobility, territorial and interclass, which resulted from the rapid expansion of the country and the development of its economy. On the one hand the greater measure of economic independence and equality in America, and the absence of traditional and repressive aristocratic institutions tended to develop in these classes a demand for an equal share in political power. On the other hand, the constant accession of new fortunes to the wealthier classes made the American plutocracy an unstable group, incapable of maintaining the superior political initiative and privileges which they enjoyed before and temporarily after the Revolution. Of considerable importance also in the early destruction of the political privileges of the wealthy classes in America was the fact that the American Revolution was fought and won in the name of the democratic values and principles of the eighteenth century. The spread of this ideology particularly in the frontier agrarian regions ultimately resulted in an effective challenge to the post-revolutionary conservatism of the advantaged classes on the Eastern seaboard.

The gradualness of the democratization of the suffrage in England and the continued maintenance of aristocratic institutions account for the fact that the upper classes in England to the present day are personally politically active on a scale far exceeding that of the American plutocracy. The consequences of this large measure of political participation on the part of the advantaged and esteemed classes for politics in England has been the relative absence of political corruption in England compared to that of the United States, and the high level of esteem in which public office is generally held. At the same time the political functions and responsibilities of the aristocracy and plutocracy in England have been responsible to some extent for the relatively "sober" character of upper class social life.

In contrast politics and government in America have been conducted in an atmosphere of widespread graft and corruption. Having lost its direct political controls, the plutocracy set about to establish indirect controls which have taken the form of bribery and other financial pressures, "behind the scenes" manipulation, and controls over propaganda. Political office tended to attract individuals from the middle and the lower classes who enjoyed little power in their own right, and whose offices gave them few controls over the economic order. Economic power tended to be concentrated in the upper levels of the plutocracy which on the whole were able to control public policy without engaging personally in political life. One of the consequences of this indirect and concealed control over political life on the part of the plutocracy was the bringing into disesteem of public office.

In America in contrast with England the plutocracy has tended to follow an "irresponsible" way of life. In considerable measure this irresponsibility has resulted from the fact that the American plutocracy has not enjoyed the political prerogatives which it enjoyed in the seventeenth and eighteenth centuries, or which are enjoyed by the English aristocracy and plutocracy of the present time. Had the American plutocracy continued to enjoy political privileges suited to their prominence in the economic sphere, a "gilded age" would not have been possible. To be sure, the great increase in their wealth in the nineteenth century would have resulted in greater expenditures for personal adornment, housing, and the like, and a greater expenditure on and elaboration of social life. But if as a class they had continued to enjoy a dominant share in the actual shaping of public policy, had they themselves occupied the seats of political power, they could not have developed, as so many of them did, an elaborate and extravagant social life as the central value of their existence. The extreme self-indulgence of the plutocracy especially in the post–Civil War era was the consequence of the dissociation of considerable elements of the plutocracy both from political and economic realities. The great bearers of this naive and immature social tradition were *rentier* "socialites," men and women who made a world for themselves away from the problems of political, economic, and social adjustment, a child's world, animated mainly by the pursuit of diversion.

It was concern over these general problems of the role of the American plutocracy in our political and general social life which led to this investigation. More particularly, it was concern over the future role of the plutocracy in America, its political alternatives and likely choices in the era of crisis in which we exist at present which led to the choice of this problem. In this last connection the writer has little to offer, save the hope that these historical studies will prepare him for a sounder grappling with the present problem than would otherwise have been possible.

Several reasons determined the choice of New York City as the best place to investigate on a limited scale the changing attitudes and activities of the American plutocracy. Among these was the age of New York City. This made possible a clear contrast between the plutocracy of the pre-democratic period with the plutocracy of the present. Another reason was its size and prominence in the economic, cultural, and social spheres. Many developments more or less common to the wealthier classes throughout the nation reached a clearer and more readily discernible stage in New York City than elsewhere.

Before proceeding to a description of the specific problems which have been considered and the methods employed, a definition of the concept of plutocracy is necessary. When the term plutocracy is used to designate a form of political order it denotes a political structure in which the wealthier classes have a formally exclusive control in the political sphere. The wealthy classes in plutocratic political structures are ordinarily based upon non-agricultural sources of wealth, although plutocracy does not exclude situations in which the holders of political power are a wealthy farmer class. The early American political order was one in which the wealthy farmer class played an influential role; and the pre–Civil War South was a plutocracy based upon land ownership. Typically, however, plutocracies have more generally developed in urban commercial and industrial economies such as those of ancient Greece, medieval and modern Italy, and the independent and autonomous cities of northern Europe and England.

More recently the term plutocracy has come to be applied to a wealthy class regardless of its formal political position. From a strictly literal point of view this is an incorrect usage, since the term denotes a form of political order, and not a special social class. However, the term used in the latter sense is not entirely incorrect, for it is on the whole clear that where there are great inequalities of wealth, and in the absence of a special hereditary political class—a feudality or a nobility—the wealthier elements of the population tend to control public policy, whether its control be legally exclusive as in plutocracy properly speaking, or whether its control be informal and indirect. The existence of a plutocracy in the loose usage of that term tends to make for a plutocratic political structure in the stricter meaning.

There are two main types of plutocratic order, the "closed" and the "open." A closed plutocracy is an order in which political rights are the monopoly of a wealthy class, and in which the admission of new elements into the politically privileged class takes the form of cooptation by the ruling group, or by intermarriage. Thus in many of the English cities of the Middle Ages access to political rights—the Freedom—was secured mainly through inheritance, and occasionally by the cooptation of apprentices after a period of service or by marriage with a freeman's daughter. In Venice by the beginning of the fourteenth century the wealthy merchant class established a system of strict hereditary succession of the political class, an hereditary plutocratic oligarchy. Even here, however, the practice was followed of enriching the treasury by the occasional admission of wealthy merchant plebians upon the payment of large sums. The story is told that there are even Venetian families today who retain as part of their name the designation of "head of the list" conveying the meaning that had the Venetian oligarchy maintained its independence for a longer period of time, the "head of the list" families would have been admitted to the Great Council, that is, to political rights.

The actual principle of the closed plutocracy was not so much the entirely fixed character of the political class—such was never achieved—as the fact that the possession of political rights and privileges was not immediately accorded upon reaching a certain level of wealth, but that it was within the power of the already constituted political oligarchy to grant or withhold these privileges, or that it was automatically accorded only by marriage into the oligarchy. Thus in closed plutocracy political power was the exclusive possession of an element among the wealthier classes, which formally controlled admission to political rights.

Open plutocracy is characterized by the establishment of purely economic barriers to entrance into the politically privileged class. These took the form of property limitations, the payment of a minimum tax, the ability to outfit oneself for military activity; in some cases the requirement was so low as to admit all individuals who would prove the possession of a residence. However, even where the property limitation was so low as to admit the majority of a city's population, as was the case in many of the European towns of the Middle Ages and early modern times, political power gravitated to the wealthier class. The reason for this was the fact that public office was unpaid. Only the wealthy—the local gentry and the wealthy merchant—were sufficiently "free to leave" their economic activities.[2] Not only his economic independence but the fact that the wealthy notable frequently had in his employ, in his debt, or in his patronage, large numbers of the poorer franchised elements, tended in the open more democratic plutocracies to give the initiative and control over politics into the hands of the wealthier families. Open plutocracy lends itself more readily to political democratization, since it is marked by a higher rate of mobility than the closed plutocracy, has not developed as strongly in the ruling class the tradition of hereditary succession and its moral concomitants, and has not bred a reciprocal attitude of complete political dependence on the part of the lower classes because of general impossibility of entrance into the political circle.

The study first undertakes a description of the political activities and the social life of the plutocracy in the era of the limited franchise. The relation between the wealthy classes and politics is indicated quantitatively by an analysis of the social composition of political office-holders, and by an analysis of the political activities of the officers and members of plutocratic social, cultural, economic, and philanthropic organizations. In the era of the extension of the franchise the gradual withdrawal of the plutocracy from politics, and the influx of individuals from lower occupational groups is also shown in quantitative form, and the general background and consequences of this democratic revolution are discussed. The point is made that the peaceable—or non-violent—character of this revolution was due, among other causes, to the weak character of government in America, a heritage of English democratic and liberal theories. The plutocracy, though threatened by these demands for political equality, was not threatened in its economic powers and privileges. The growing prominence of the urban industrial and commercial plutocracy, as over against the landholders, was also an important factor in this development, since the full-time preoccupation with economic life of the merchants and industrialists made them amenable to the loss of formal political control. The social life of the plutocracy in the era of the limited franchise and the immediately succeeding decades is shown to have been on the whole of a sober character reflecting the close identification of the wealthy classes with economic and political life. It was a recreational social life, and not a "full-time" social life, as it was later to become.

Parts Two and Three follow the plutocracy and its relation to politics up to the present period. Part Two takes up the nature of the activities and the attitudes of the plutocracy under democracy. The transition from direct to indirect controls over politics is first discussed. It is shown that there has been a general tendency in the last seventy-five or more years toward a further decrease in the personal political office-holding of the plutocracy. The development of indirect controls is then described as a compensation for the loss of personal control. The development of pressure groups, financial pressures, and controls over propaganda are discussed briefly. A special study is made of the qualities, characteristics, and activities of that specially esteemed group of the plutocracy—"society." The expansion and elaboration of the social activities of the plutocracy is related to its loss of political power, its extreme mobility, and its tremendously increased wealth. "Self-indulgence" in social life is shown to have been a consequence of the distance of the plutocracy from political and economic realities.

Part Three describes the social composition of the political leadership under democracy. The problem of the prestige of public office is first discussed. The low prestige of public office is attributed to the existence of a powerful plutocracy indirectly influencing and controlling a group of professional politicians mainly recruited from the economically less influential lawyers and entrepreneurs. A comparison is made of federal, state, municipal and party office-holders in terms of their social composition. It is shown that the plutocracy tended to hold only the most prominent political offices, the bulk of the more numerous offices going to the less esteemed and influential elements. As a consequence, the more prominent political offices continued under democracy to enjoy a relatively high level of prestige, the demand for them on the part of the wealthier classes continuing to be great. On the other hand, the prestige of the more numerous offices, especially in the state and municipal governments, was low, that is, they did not attract and were not held by the individuals enjoying the greatest social esteem in the community. The point was made on the basis of this analysis that as the powers of the government over economic life increased, as the government, in other words, became strong in the control over economic and social life, the prestige of public office would increase

Part Four takes up the general problem of the responses and reactions of the plutocracy to various types of challenge and threat to its powers and privileges. An analysis is made of the effect of the growing protest on the part of labor, agrarian, and humanitarian groups since the closing of the frontier upon the social life of the plutocracy. Three types of crisis are shown to have resulted in increased plutocratic political activity—political corruption, war, and lower class unrest. The reactions of the wealthy to these types of crisis are taken up historically. Special attention is given to the development of vigilantist pressure groups in the crisis of the last years. A concluding chapter recapitulates the phases of the general history of the plutocracy in New York dealt with in this study, and points to certain possible future developments.

For its approach, methods, and interpretations this investigation owes much to those political scientists and sociologists of this and previous generations who have taken a naturalistic view of the political process, and more especially to those who have contributed to the theory and historical analysis of leadership. Among the European writers and scholars who have approached the problems of politics from this point of view were Gaetano Mosca[3] who criticized Aristotle's classification of types of governments and saw all government as government by minorities, by the "political class." In Pareto[4] this conception was reformulated as the theory of the "circulation of the elite." In the sociological investigations of Max Weber[5] the problem of political control and domination has been treated from a broad and systematic historical and sociological point of view. The studies of Roberto Michels[6] have been of special value in pointing to the oligarchic nature of party control in democracies. More particularly for America, the works of Charles Beard,[7] Carl Becker,[8] and Dixon Ryan Fox[9] may be mentioned as having been of importance for the historical analysis of the American "ruling class." Of more immediate theoretical and practical influence upon the method, interpretations, and structure of the present study have been the works and personal direction and stimulation of Professor Charles E. Merriam[10] and Harold D. Lasswell[11] of the University of Chicago.

The execution of the present study was made possible by the grant of a pre-doctoral field fellowship from the Social Science Research Council for 1935–36. Through this award I was able to reside in New York City and make the necessary field and research contacts.

Notes

1. Charles Seymour and Donald P. Frary, *How the World Votes* (Springfield, Mass.: C. A. Nichols Co., 1918), Vol. I, chaps. iv–vii.

2. Max Weber, "Politik als Beruf," *Gesammelte Politische Schriften* (Munich: Drei Masken Verlag, 1921), p. 404.

3. See article by Renzo Sereno, "The Anti-Aristotelianism of Gaetano Mosca and Its Fate," *International Journal of Ethics,* July, 1938.

4. Vilfredo Pareto, *Les Systemes Socialistes* (Paris: V. Giard and E. Sriere, 1902); Pareto, *Mind and Society,* trans. by Andrew Bongiorno and Arthur Livingston (New York: Harcourt, Brace and Co., 1935).

5. Max Weber, *Wirtschaft und Gesellschaft: Grundriss der Sozialökonomik* (Tübingen, J. C. S. Mohr, 1925), Vol. III; "Politik als Beruf," in *Gesammelte Politische Schriften* (Munich, 1921).

6. Roberto Michels, *Political Parties* (New York: Hearst's International Library Co., 1915); Michels, *Umschichtungen in den Herrschenden Klassen nach dem Kriege* (Berlin: W. Kohlhammer, 1934).

7. Charles A. Beard, *An Economic Interpretation of the Constitution* (New York: The Macmillan Co., 1913); Beard, *The Economic Basis of Politics* (New York: A. A. Knopf, 1922).

8. Carl Becker, *The History of Political Parties in the Province of New York* ("Bulletin of the University of Wisconsin," No. 286, History Series, Vol. II, No. 1 [Madison, 1909]).

9. Dixon Ryan Fox, *The Decline of the Aristocracy in the Politics of New York* (New York: Longmans, Green and Co., 1919).

10. Charles E. Merriam, *New Aspects of Politics* (Chicago: University of Chicago Press, 1931); Merriam, *Four American Party Leaders* (New York: The Macmillan Co., 1926); and Merriam and Harold F. Gosnell, *The American Party System* (New York: The Macmillan Co., 1928).

11. Harold D. Lasswell, *World Politics and Personal Insecurity* (New York: McGraw-Hill Book Co., 1935); Lasswell, *Politics* (New York: McGraw-Hill Book Co., 1936).

Part One

From Oligarchy to Democracy

1

Plutocracy in Politics Under the Limited Franchise

UNTIL THE FIRST DECADES of the nineteenth century the economically influential classes of New York exercised a personal control of the politics of the province and state. There was, to be sure, a movement dating back to the revolutionary era demanding a share of political power for the less advantaged elements of the population. But until the Constitutional Convention of 1821 the older ruling elements were able to check efforts directed toward destroying their legal and traditional privileges.

The dominant political elements in the population were the merchants, landholders, and lawyers. The lawyers, frequently related by blood or marriage, or allied economically to the large landowners and merchants, already during the eighteenth century supplied the bulk of the more important statesmen. These three elements in the early New York leadership held between them the greater part of the landed and mobile wealth of the province. The relatively exclusive position of this class in the control over politics rested upon a franchise restricted by wealth, and upon the general economic, cultural, and moral dependence of the lower classes, both in the country and in the city, upon these privileged groups.

Economic Stratification

Before the nineteenth century by far the largest proportion of the wealth of the province was in the form of land, and a large part of the most valuable land was held by a few families. By the close of the administration of Lord Cornbury (1708) Long Island, Manhattan, Westchester, Kings, Dutchess, and Albany counties were carved by the great estates of the landed notables.

11

On Long Island the estates of Remsen, Rapalje, Nicoll, and Smith embraced some 200 square miles of the most valuable land in Kings, Queens, and Suffolk counties. Livingston and Van Cortlandt whose property was chiefly in Albany and Westchester counties, also had small possessions in Kings County. On Manhattan Island the most valuable estates were those of Stuyvesant, Bay ard, Heathcote, Delancey, De Peyster. . . . The County of Westchester contained six manors, which together covered more than half of the entire county; Morrisania, Fordham, and Pelham, in the South, were comparatively small, but Scarsdale, belonging to Caleb Heathcote, Cortlandt Manor, and Phillipsburgh covered approximately four hundred square miles of the choicest land in the province. In Dutchess County the Phillipses had a second estate, larger than the manor, which made that family second only to the Van Rensselaer in landed possessions. Beekman and Schuyler had possessions in Dutchess County, which also contained the Great or Lower Nine Partners patent. In Albany County lay the Livingston Manor, and the princely estate of Van Rensselaer, together covering nearly a million acres on both sides of the Hudson.[1]

New York City had its merchant "aristocracy." In the beginning of the eighteenth century there were already ninety-four burghers whose estates were valued at more than a thousand guilders; and twenty-two of these estates represented between five and ten thousand guilders. Hendrick Philipson was worth eighty thousand guilders, Cornelius Steenwick, fifty thousand, Nicholas de Meyer, fifty thousand, Olaf Van Cortlandt, forty-five thousand, John Lawrence, forty thousand, Jeronimus Ebbing, thirty thousand, Cornelius Van Ruyven, eighteen thousand, Johannes de Peyster, fifteen thousand. John Spratt was worth almost four thousand pounds, and Colonel Lewis Morris, five thousand. These merchants had accumulated their wealth primarily from fur and timber, and from general trade.[2] Needless to say by the close of the eighteenth century both the number of the wealthy merchants and their wealth had greatly increased.

The lawyers constituted a third element in this ruling class. Their rise into power had come later, but certainly by the time of the Revolution they constituted a considerable element of the political office-holders. In the period before the Revolution the lawyers were generally closely allied by blood, marriage, or economic ties to the merchants and landholders. A study of almost any one of the great merchant and landholding families during the latter part of the eighteenth century reveals this close relationship between the rising legal profession and the families of wealth and power. In the sixth generation (1790–1840) of the wealthy de Peyster family, Frederick de Peyster became a prominent lawyer in New York City, and in the seventh generation Frederick J. de Peyster also engaged in the law. The fifth generation of the Van Cortlandt family, one of the most important of the old landholding families, also produced an attorney, Pierre Van Cortlandt (c. 1770–1840). Josiah Ogden Hoffman, a descendant of the powerful Hoffman family in the fifth generation was also a prominent attorney in the pre- and post-revolutionary days. In the sixth generation two of the descendants of the Hoffman family were lawyers. William Livingston, a descendant of the first Lord of the Manor in the third generation (b. 1723) devoted his life to the law; Walter, Brockholst, and Edward Livingston of the following generation also became lawyers. In the fourth generation (1718–1810) two of the Morrises, Richard and Gouverneur, practiced law. In the fifth generation (1775–1840) two of the merchant and landholding Lawrence family, Samuel and John L., were members of the legal profession.[3]

Limitations on the Franchise

This landed, commercial, and lawyer ruling class dominated a population of tenants and small landholders in the country, and mechanics, small tradesmen, handicraftsmen, indentured servants, and slaves in the cities. Only a small percentage of the population of the province had the franchise. "In 1790 the proportion of electors to the total population was approximately 12 percent which, applied to the Colonial Period, would give a voting population of 2,168 in 1598, and 20,256 in 1771."[4]

The enfranchised population on the countryside was made up of large landholders, small freeholders, and leaseholders. The enfranchised in the cities of New York and Albany were the freemen and electoral freeholders.

Freemen were those who had purchased the privilege of engaging in certain occupations within the corporations of Albany and New York, wholesalers, retailers, and independent handicraftsmen. The fee for "freedomes" was five pounds in New York.... the number of freemen was small; so late as 1790 there were only 45 in Albany and 93 in New York, an insignificant proportion of the total electorate of either county. The electoral freeholders were those who possessed, free of encumbrance, an estate in fee for life, or by courtesy, of the value of forty pounds.[5]

These limitations upon the franchise resulted in the disfranchisement of a considerable portion of the adult male population, how many is not exactly known, but certainly more than half.

The political position of the large landholders—and this group would include many of the merchants and lawyers—was further safeguarded by making the state senate a body composed entirely of relatively large landholders. The Constitution of 1777 provided that the Senate was to be composed of freeholders, and that only freeholders possessing one hundred pounds worth of land could vote for state senators and the governor. A lower property qualification limited the electors eligible for voting for the members of the House, admitting freemen of the incorporated towns, leaseholders with leaseholds having an annual value of forty shillings, and a few others, but kept out the lower levels of the population.[6]

The ability of the class of merchants, landholders, and lawyers to maintain their control of politics resulted not only from these limitations upon the franchise and the right to hold office, but from a number of further factors. A second condition was that despite the fact that the majority of the electors were not members of the "ruling class," but were rather small freeholders and leaseholders, a large number of them resided on the estates of the great landowners and were thus subject to their influence.

> It was said that in 1770 the freeholders in the manors of Livingston and Rensselaerwyck were sufficient to control the elections of Albany County; and in fact the Albany elections were largely determined by the Van Rensselaers, Schuylers, and Livingstons, for it was taken as a matter of course that tenant voters would follow their landlords. In Westchester County an even larger proportion of the electors were within the six manors, and elections were powerfully influenced if not determined by Phillipse, Cortlandt, and Morris. In other counties the economic and social relations of landlord and tenant were hardly so pronounced a feature of the situation, but the prestige of landed wealth and social position was everywhere sufficient to confer an excessive influence upon a few men.[7]

In New York City proper before the outbreak of the Revolution less than a tenth of the total white population voted in municipal elections. And it is likely that here too the wealthiest elements of the franchised groups by virtue of their influence, patronage, and prestige were able to dominate the lower levels of the franchised population.[8]

Occupations of Political Office-Holders

Table 1.1 describes the occupations of the various types of political office-holders in the years between 1789–1835. Most impressive of all are the figures showing the number of lawyers holding office. The lawyers dominated in practically every legislative, executive, and judicial agency, while merchants had direct representation only in the federal House of Representatives, the state senate and assembly, and the board of aldermen. In the last legislative body, the merchants had by far the largest representation. But in the bulk of the more prominent offices requiring much time for their performance the lawyers were the largest occupation represented.

The causes of the development of this lawyer-professional politician class are not far to seek. In a primarily agrarian economy the seasonal character of agriculture makes it possible for the large landholder to devote considerable time to the pursuit of politics. The life of the urban merchant is not as easily reconcilable with active political participation since his work occu-

TABLE 1.1 Occupations of Political Office-Holders from New York City, 1789–1835*

		Lawyers	Merchants	Landholders	Industry	Other Professions	Unknown	Total
Federal Executive and Cabinet Officials	1789–1830	7	—	—	—	—	—	7
Diplomats	1789–1830	9	—	—	—	1	1	11
Federal Judiciary	1789–1830	11	—	—	—	—	1	12
Federal Senators	1789–1830	7	—	—	—	—	—	7
Federal Representatives	1789–1830	20	7	5	—	1	3	36
Governors	1789–1830	8	—	—	—	—	—	8
State Judges	1789–1835	11	—	—	—	—	—	11
State Senators	1790	4	2	1	—	—	2	9
State Assemblymen	1790	2	4	—	1	—	1	8
Mayors	1794–1830	5	1	—	—	—	1	7
Aldermen	1789–1791	—	14	—	3	1	7	25
Total number		84	28	6	4	3	16	141
Total percent		60	20	4	3	2	11	100

*Lists of political office-holders were taken from the New York City Common Council, *Minutes, 1675–1776* (New York: Dodd Mead and Co., 1905), and *ibid.* for 1784–1831 (New York: M. B. Brown and Co., 1917); the *New York Red Book* (Albany: S. B. Lyon Co., 1892); *New York Civil List, 1855* (Albany: Secretary of State's Office, 1855); and Charles Lanman, *Biographical Annals of the Civil Government of the United States During Its First Century* (Washington: James Anglin, 1874). Biographical data were taken from New York City Directories for the years 1776–1835; *Dictionary of American Biography* (New York: Charles Scribner's Sons, 1936); the *National Cyclopedia of American Biography*, compiled by George Derby (New York: J. T. White and Co., 1906); and other miscellaneous sources. Occupations of state senators and assemblymen are given for only one term. No final conclusions are possible as to the occupational composition of those holding these offices during this period.

pies him all year long. Then too, the increasingly complex character of law-making and administration in a commercial economy tends to discriminate against those lacking both in the time and skill necessary for the political function, and to favor the lawyers. Under conditions of a limited franchise, however, it was still possible for merchants to engage in politics, especially local politics, since the struggle for political office was restricted to a relatively small class and had not become, as it was to become in later decades, a full-time job.

Economic Origins of Political Office-Holders

Aside from occupational information, biographical information for the wealthy politicans was not readily available. An estimate as to the class origin of this group of politicians was possible on the basis of data available concerning occupations and wealth of fathers, and access to educational opportunities. Eighty-six, or 61 percent, of the 141 politicians had come of wealthy or well-to-do origins. Nine percent were known to have come of poorer families; while information was not available for 30 percent. The rate of mobility in these early years was, compared to the period to follow, extremely low.

Education of Political Office-Holders

In the latter part of the eighteenth century college education was restricted largely to the sons of the wealthy classes, and those desiring and able to fit themselves for the ministry or law. The practice of attending college before practicing law was by no means universal; a common method was apprenticeship to a practicing lawyer. It was a common practice for the larger landholders and merchants to send their sons to college. Thus, college education, generally, was the mark of the cultured level of the wealthier classes.

A tabulation of educational data for this group of political office-holders may serve as an indication of the degree to which this cultured element of the ruling class participated actively in politics (cf. Table 1.2 and Table 1.3). We find that 64, or 46 percent, of the total number of politicians attended college. Nineteen percent served apprenticeship in law offices. Only 6 percent had no higher education whatsoever; and data for 29 percent were not available.

The New Yorkers holding offices in the newly constituted federal government more frequently had college educations than those holding state and municipal offices. If we exclude members of the House of Representatives we find that 24, or 65 percent, of the 37 federal executive, diplomatic, judicial, and senatorial officers had college educations, and 7, or 18 percent, had served apprenticeships in law offices. The proportion of federal offi-

TABLE 1.2   Education of Political Office-Holders from New York City Holding Office Between 1784–1835*

	College Education	Professional Training	No College Education	Unknown	Total
Federal Executive	5	1	—	1	7
Diplomatic	6	2	—	3	11
Federal Judicial	8	2	—	2	12
United States Senators	5	2	—	—	7
United States Representative	16	12	7	1	36
State Governors	2	—	—	6	8
State Judicial	8	2	—	1	11
State Senate	3	2	—	4	9
State Assembly	2	—	—	6	8
Mayors	3	3	1	—	7
Aldermen	6	1	1	17	25
Total number	64	27	9	41	141
Total percent	46	19	6	29	100

*Lists of political office-holders were taken from the New York City Common Council, *Minutes, 1675–1776* (New York: Dodd Mead and Co., 1905), and *ibid.* for 1784–1831 (New York: M. B. Brown and Co., 1917); the *New York Red Book* (Albany: S. B. Lyon Co., 1892); *New York Civil List, 1855* (Albany: Secretary of State's Office, 1855); and Charles Lanman, *Biographical Annals of the Civil Government of the United States During Its First Century* (Washington: City Directories for the years 1776–1835; *Dictionary of American Biography* (New York: Charles Scribner's Sons, 1936); the *National Cyclopedia of American Biography*, compiled by George Derby (New York: J. T. White and Co., 1906); and other miscellaneous sources. Education of state senators and assemblymen is given for only one term. No final conclusions are possible as to the occupational composition of those holding these offices during this period.

cers, exclusive of congressmen, having either college education or professional training was 84 percent. The more important federal offices were held in this period almost exclusively by this cultured "layer" of the wealthier classes. The group of 36 congressmen included 44 percent with college education, and 33 percent with professional training; while 19 percent had no higher education whatsoever. In contrast to the more important federal offices, the office of congressman was accessible to the less advantaged elements of the politically active levels of the population.

Only 15, or 42 percent, of the state officers had college educations. State office, thus, may be viewed as less attractive at that time to the cultured elements of the politically active population. State judges were in most cases college graduates in contrast to state governors, senators, and assembly-

TABLE 1.3   Colleges Attended by Political Office-Holders from New York City Holding Office Between 1784–1835*

	Princeton	Columbia	Yale	Harvard	Union College	Brown	Williams	University of Edinburgh
Federal Executive	2	1	1	—	—	1	—	—
Diplomatic	2	2	—	1	—	1	—	—
Federal Judicial	2	3	1	—	1	—	1	—
United States Senators	2	—	1	1	—	—	—	1
United States Representative	5	5	5	1	—	—	—	—
State Governors	1	—	—	1	—	—	—	—
State Judicial	4	2	1	—	1	—	—	—
State Senate	—	—	3	—	—	—	—	—
State Assembly	1	—	—	1	—	—	—	—
Mayors	2	1	—	—	—	—	—	—
Aldermen	2	2	1	1	—	—	—	—
Total	23	16	13	6	2	2	1	1

*Lists of political office-holders were taken from the New York City Common Council, *Minutes, 1675–1776* (New York: Dodd Mead and Co., 1905), and *ibid.* for 1784–1831 (New York: M. B. Brown and Co., 1917); the *New York Red Book* (Albany: S. B. Lyon Co., 1892); *New York Civil List, 1855* (Albany: Secretary of State's Office, 1855); and Charles Lanman, *Biographical Annals of the Civil Government of the United States During Its First Century* (Washington: James Anglin, 1874). Biographical data were taken from New York City Directories for the years 1776–1835; *Dictionary of American Biography* (New York: Charles Scribner's Sons, 1936); the *National Cyclopedia of American Biography*, compiled by George Derby (New York: J. T. White and Co., 1906); and other miscellaneous sources. Colleges of state senators and assemblymen are given for only one term. No final conclusions are possible as to the occupational composition of those holding these offices during this period.

men, Municipal office-holders as a group included the smallest number of college-educated individuals.

In summary then it may be concluded that the cultivated wealthy in these years before democratization tended to hold the national offices of greatest prominence, while the ordinary wealthy and well-to-do tended to hold the national offices of lesser prestige in the state and municipal governments.

In these early days, as well as in the present, Princeton, Columbia, Harvard, and Yale were the colleges most frequently attended by the wealthier elements in the population. Princeton, a Presbyterian college relatively close at hand in New Jersey, was the most popular institution in the group. Columbia was second, and Yale and Harvard, third and fourth. The greater popularity of Columbia and Princeton may be attributed to the difficult conditions of transportation of that period. As we shall see at a later point, with the improvement in transportation, Harvard College was to become the most popular college for the sons of wealthy New Yorkers.

Occupational Composition of the Business, Social, and Cultural Leadership

The degree to which the more established classes engaged in politics before the era of democracy has been indicated by an analysis of the occupational and class composition of political office-holders. Such an index of political participation is subject to the qualification that for some types of offices no data were offered and in some cases the selections were taken only for short periods of time. A supplementary study was made of the occupational composition and political office-holding of the officers and members of various business, cultural, and convivial associations of that time to substantiate the high degree of political participation for the wealthy and advantaged elements of the population, and in order to indicate in greater detail the political and cultural divisions in the wealthier classes.

Table 1.4 lists the occupations of various "upper class" groups: the officers of the Chamber of Commerce, the subscribers to the Tontine Association—a coffee house group—the officers of the New York Historical Society, and the officers of the Society of the New York Hospital. The officers of the Chamber of Commerce for this period were almost all merchants, the exceptions being two manufacturers and two mariners. The Tontine Association, a group which founded the Tontine Coffee House, were almost all merchants too, the exceptions being 9 lawyers, 12 landowners, 3 manufacturers and handicraftsmen, 2 mariners, and 1 physician, out of a total of 159 subscribers. The officers of the New York Historical Society, who may be viewed as a group of the cultural leaders of the community were, on the other hand, almost all lawyers and clergymen, which raises the presumption, although sufficient data are not given here to be conclusive, that the

20

TABLE 1.4 Occupations of Officers of Business, Cultural, Convivial, and Philanthropic Associations in New York City, 1776–1835*

	Total	Lawyers	Merchants	Landowners	Manufacturers and Handicraftsmen	Mariners	Physicians	Clergymen	Unknown
Officers, New York Chamber of Commerce	24	—	18	—	2	2	—	—	2
Subscribers Tontine Association	159	9	127	12	3	2	1	—	5
Officers New York Historical Society	16	10	1	—	—	—	1	4	—
Officers Society of New York Hospital	10	2	7	1	—	—	—	—	—
Total number	209	21	153	13	5	4	2	4	7
Total percent	100	10	73	6	2	2	1	2	4

*Lists of the officers and members of these organizations were found in *Catalogue of Portraits* (New York: Chamber of Commerce, 1924); *The Centennial History of the Protestant Episcopal Church in the Diocese of New York, 1785–1885*, edited by James Grant Wilson (New York: D. Appleton Co., 1886); Presbyterian Church in the United States, *Digest of Records* (Philadelphia: printed for the trustees, 1820); George Folsom, *Historical Sketch of the New York Historical Society* (New York: New York Historical Society, 1841); Robert Hendre Kelby, *The New York Historical Society, 1804–1904* (New York: New York Historical Society, 1905); Austin Baxter Keep, *History of the New York Society Library* (New York: The DeVinne Press, 1908); *The Scrap Book of the Tontine Coffee House* (New York: the Tontine Society, 1796); John Francis Richmond, *New York and Its Institutions, 1609–1872* (New York: E. B. Treat, 1872). For biographical data some of the same sources were used. Additional data were obtained from the *Minutes of the Common Council, Analytical Index*, compiled by David Maydole Matteson (New York: M. B. Brown Printing and Binding Co., 1930); the *New York Directory* (New York: Trow City Directory Co., 1786–1835); *The Dictionary of American Biography* (New York: Charles Scribner's Sons, 1928–1937); and the *National Cyclopedia of American Biography*, compiled by George Derby (New York: J. T. White and Co., 1906).

cultural "elite" at that time was largely made up of lawyers and clergymen, and, no doubt, the college-educated sons of wealthy merchants and landholders. The officers of the Society of the New York Hospital included 7 merchants, 2 lawyers, and 1 landowner.

Political Office-Holding of the Wealthy and Esteemed Classes

That it was the common thing for these wealthy and cultured elements to hold political office before the democratization of the franchise is clearly brought out in Table 1.5. Nineteen, or 79 percent, of the officers of the New York Chamber of Commerce had held some political office. The "average" Chamber of Commerce officer had held 2.5 political offices. Forty-eight, or 45 percent of the 106 lay officers of the Episcopalian Church had also held such office, the average number of political offices held being 1.2. An examination of the political offices held by the trustees, deacons, and elders of the three most important Presbyterian churches indicates a similar situation, although the percentage is lower than that of the Episcopalian denomination. This difference is to be explained by the fact that the Episcopalian denomination before the Revolution was an "established" church. It was the denomination of the British governing class, and thus a greater degree of political prominence for its influential members was to be expected.

There was considerable variation in political participation by the various groups of church officers. Nine out of the 11 wardens of "Old Trinity" Church (the church of the former provincial governors) had held political offices. All of the 7 trustees of the Church of St. Charles in The Bowery had held political office; 7 out of the 11 wardens of Christ Church, 6 out of the 10 wardens of St. James Church of Hyde Park, and 4 out of the 5 trustees of St. Michael's Church had held political office. The lay officials of the balance of the churches of the Episcopalian denomination were less influential politically; in a few they held no political offices at all.

Of the three largest Presbyterian churches of New York in this period, the lay officers of "Brick Church" were the most influential politically, 21 out of 29 holding or having held some political office. The Fifth Avenue and the New York Presbyterian Church officers were less influential politically.

If we take the officers of the New York Historical Society and the Subscribers to the Society Library, the first collective library of New York, as representative of the cultural leadership of New York City, we must conclude that the political participation of the cultural leadership was almost universal. Eleven of the 16, or 69 percent of the officers of the New York Historical Society, and 43 of the 50, or 86 percent of the Subscribers to the Society Library had held political office. The typical cultural leader of New York had held two or more political offices. The reason for this high degree of political participation on the part of the cultural leadership was the fact

TABLE 1.5 Political Office-Holding of the Officers of Economic, Religious, Cultural, Social, and Philanthropic Associations, 1776–1835*

	Total	No. Holding Political Office	Percent Holding Political Office	Total Number of Offices Held	Average No. of Offices per Individual
Officers New York Chamber of Commerce	24	19	79	61	2.5
Lay Officers Episcopalian Church	106	48	45	129	1.2
Lay Officers Presbyterian Church	87	34	40	86	1.
Officers New York Historical Society	16	11	69	44	2.7
Subscribers Society Library	50	43	86	103	2.
Subscribers Tontine Association	159	89	55	167	1.
Officers New York Hospital Society	10	9	90	25	2.5
Officers Institution for Deaf and Dumb	26	17	66	51	2.
Officers New York Eye and Ear Infirmary	22	12	55	27	1.2

*Lists of the officers and members of these organizations were found in *Catalogue of Portraits* (New York: Chamber of Commerce, 1924); *The Centennial History of the Protestant Episcopal Church in the Diocese of New York, 1785–1885*, edited by James Grant Wilson (New York: D. Appleton Co., 1886); Presbyterian Church in the United States, *Digest of Records* (Philadelphia: printed for the trustees, 1820); George Folsom, *Historical Sketch of the New York Historical Society* (New York: New York Historical Society, 1841); Robert Hendre Kelby, *The New York Historical Society, 1804–1904* (New York: New York Historical Society, 1905); Austin Baxter Keep, *History of the New York Society Library* (New York: The DeVinne Press, 1908); *The Scrap Book of the Tontine Coffee House* (New York: the Tontine Society, 1796); John Francis Richmond, *New York and Its Institutions, 1509–1872* (New York: E. B. Treat, 1872). For biographical data some of the same sources were used. Additional data were obtained from the *Minutes of the Common Council, Analytical Index*, compiled by David Maydole Matteson (New York: M. B. Brown Printing and Binding Co., 1930); the *New York Directory* (New York: Trow City Directory Co., 1786–1835); *The Dictionary of American Biography* (New York: Charles Scribner's Sons, 1928–1937); and the *National Cyclopedia of American Biography*, compiled by George Derby (New York: J. T. White and Co., 1906).

that there were many lawyers among them; and lawyers at this time constituted to a large extent the professional political stratum of the ruling classes.

A number of the old memoirists and diarists writing on the pre–Civil War Era viewed the old Tontine Association Coffee House group as a kind of board of censors, ruling finally in matters of conduct. The story is told that this group was responsible for the abolition of the custom of distributing silk scarfs to all the mourners at funerals, since it was too extravagant, placing too heavy a burden upon poorer families. We may view the Subscribers of the Tontine Association as a selection of the wealthier classes, which enjoyed certain moral powers, how broad and effective is open to question. Fifty-five percent of the Subscribers had held political offices. The predominance of merchants as over against lawyers accounts for this relatively low degree of political participation.

The officers of the New York Hospital Society, the Institution for the Deaf and Dumb, and the New York Eye and Ear Infirmary are taken as representative of the philanthropic leadership of "Knickerbocker" New York. Their political office-holding varied from 9 out of 10, or 90 percent, for the New York Hospital Society officers, to 55 percent for the officers of the New York Eye and Ear Infirmary.

Types of Political Offices Held by the Wealthy and Esteemed Classes

The types of political offices held by these groups of leaders will be seen to have varied with the occupation and interests of the various types of leaders (cf. Table 1.6). The officers of the New York Chamber of Commerce, being largely merchants in occupation, were too preoccupied with trade and commerce, and lacking in higher education, particularly in legal education, to become statesmen, that is to say, professional holders of the more important federal and state executive and judicial offices. Seventy-four percent of the offices held by the Chamber of Commerce leadership were municipal offices; and by far the largest proportion of these offices were of a minor or "occasional" administrative character—election inspectors, street and tax assessors, and similar offices. They were, however, fairly well represented in the United States House of Representatives, the New York State Assembly, and the Board of Aldermen. The wardens, trustees, and deacons of the Episcopalian churches had a similarly high percentage of municipal and administrative municipal offices. But their representation in national and state office was considerably higher than that of the officers of the New York Chamber of Commerce. This is to be accounted for by the fact that many lawyers were also prominent Episcopalian church leaders. The representation of the Presbyterian church leaders in politics is, again, largely municipal, and municipal-administrative in character, which may be accounted for

TABLE 1.6   Political Offices Held by Officers of Business, Religious, Cultural, Convivial, and Philanthropic Associations in New York City, 1776–1835*

	Officers New York Chamber of Commerce	Officers Episcopalian Church	Officers Presbyterian Church	Officers New York Historical Society
National offices:				
Number	4	23	14	9
Percent	7	18	17	20
Executive	—	5	11	1
Diplomatic	—	7	—	4
Judicial	—	4	1	—
Senate	—	2	1	1
Representative	4	4	1	3
Military	—	1	—	—
State offices:				
Number	11	28	10	17
Percent	19	22	12	40
Executive	3	9	4	3
Judicial	—	12	1	5
Senate	—	1	—	2
Assembly	8	6	4	7
Military	—	—	1	—
Municipal offices:				
Number	42	78	59	17
Percent	74	60	71	40
Mayors	1	3	—	1
Recorders	—	2	1	2
Aldermen	4	7	8	2
Administrative	37	66	50	12
Total number	57	129	83	43
Total percent	100	100	100	100

*Lists of the officers and members of these organizations were found in *Catalogue of Portraits* (New York: Chamber of Commerce, 1924); *The Centennial History of the Protestant Episcopal Church in the Diocese of New York, 1785–1885*, edited by James Grant Wilson (New York: D. Appleton Co., 1886); Presbyterian Church in the United States, *Digest of Records* (Philadelphia: printed for the trustees, 1820); George Folsom, *Historical Sketch of the New York Historical Society* (New York: New York Historical Society, 1841); Robert Hendre Kelby, *The New York Historical Society, 1804–1904* (New York: New York Historical Society, 1905); Austin Baxter Keep, *History of the New York Society Library* (New York: The DeVinne Press, 1908); *The Scrap Book of the Tontine Coffee House* (New York: The Tontine Society, 1796); John Francis Richmond,

(continues)

TABLE 1.6 (*continued*)

Subscribers New York Society Library	Subscribers Tontine Association	Officers New York Hospital Society	Institute for the Deaf and Dumb	New York Eye and Ear Infirmary	Total Number	Percent
11	18	3	11	1	94	—
11	11	13	21	4	—	14
1	5	1	2	1	27	4
1	1	—	1	—	14	2
1	2	—	1	—	9	1.3
—	2	—	2	—	8	1.2
8	8	2	2	—	32	5
—	—	—	3	—	4	.5
28	19	9	9	—	131	—
28	12	39	18	—	—	19
6	5	2	4	—	36	5.3
5	5	2	—	—	30	4.3
3	2	2	1	—	11	1.6
14	7	3	3	—	52	7.6
—	—	—	1	—	2	.2
62	127	11	31	26	453	—
61	77	48	61	96	—	67
3	2	—	3	—	13	1.9
3	5	2	1	—	16	2.5
9	20	—	3	6	59	8.7
47	100	9	24	20	365	53.9
101	164	23	51	27	678	—
100	100	100	100	100	100	100.0

New York and Its Institutions, 1609–1872 (New York: E. B. Treat, 1872). For biographical data some of the same sources were used. Additional data were obtained from the *Minutes of the Common Council, Analytical Index*, compiled by David Maydole Matteson (New York: M. B. Brown Printing and Binding Co., 1930); the *New York Directory* (New York: Trow City Directory Co., 1786–1835); *The Dictionary of American Biography* (New York: Charles Scribner's Sons, 1928–1937); and the *National Cyclopedia of American Biography*, compiled by George Derby (New York: J. T. White and Co., 1906).

by the fact that the Presbyterian denomination consisted in part of the newer merchants, less influential in state politics than the older and more established Episcopalian denomination.

The officers of the New York Historical Society and the Subscribers to the Society Library held a proportionately large number of state and federal offices. As was indicated above, there was a close relationship between the cultural and legal leaderships which accounts for the greater representation of full-time or professional statesmen among them.

The Subscribers to the Tontine Association were almost all merchants, which explains the fact that 77 percent of the offices held by them were municipal. The great majority of these municipal positions were minor administrative in character of the type of street inspector or tax assessor. The large number of state and federal offices held by the officers of the philanthropic institutions is also to be explained by the number of lawyer statesmen in their memberships.

In summary, in the years before political democratization the political control of the wealthier classes was marked by a division of labor in which the lawyers held the more important executive and judicial offices—in other words, were the professional statesmen; while the merchants served to a considerable extent in the various legislative bodies and held the minor administrative posts. Insofar as the lawyers of that time, to a considerable measure, constituted the cultural "elite," it may be said that in the decades before democratization, politics was not only the general concern of the wealthier classes, but it was the special concern of the most cultivated levels of these classes, a situation of the greatest contrast to the recruitment of politicians after the democratization of the franchise.

Notes

1. Carl Becker, *The History of Political Parties in the Province of New York, 1760–1776* ("Bulletin of the University of Wisconsin," No. 286, History Series, Vol. II, No. 1 [Madison, 1909]), pp. 8 ff.

2. Esther Singleton, *Social New York at the Time of the Georges* (New York: D. Appleton and Co., 1902), p. 53.

3. Margherita Aulina Hamm, *Famous Families of New York* (New York: G. P. Putnam's Sons, 1902).

4. Becker, *op. cit.*, p. 10.

5. *Ibid.*, p. 8.

6. Charles J. Lincoln, *Constitutional History of New York* (Rochester: Lawyers Cooperative Publishing Co., 1906), I, 514.

7. Becker, *op. cit.*, pp. 13–14.

8. George William Edwards, *New York City as an Eighteenth Century Municipality, 1731–1776* (New York: Columbia University Press, 1917), pp. 42 ff.

2

Plutocracy in Politics in the Era of Democratization

ALTHOUGH THE MERCHANTS and landholders of New York City in the latter part of the eighteenth and early part of the nineteenth centuries enjoyed substantial control of the economic and political life of the state and city, and further, because of their cultural, religious, and social prominence, influenced the lives of the lower classes in other spheres, nevertheless certain forces were already at work even in the Colonial Period which threatened their exclusive position and wrung from them concessions which could not later be withdrawn. In the struggle between the provincial assembly and the Royal Governors the demands of the colonial ruling class were necessarily fortified by current revolutionary ideas. Becker points out:

> A local and an aristocratic assembly could not consistently oppose monarchical and external authority by pleading the natural rights of a class or the general welfare of the few. The practical result of the Assembly's long contest with the Governors was thus to foster the theory of political equality; to give life to the notion that governments derived or ought to derive their authority from the consent of the governed. At a later time when these notions began to yield their proper fruit in the demands of the unfranchised for political recognition, the landowners began to draw back.[1]

Background of the Struggle for Democratization

The merchants and landholders, thus, in order to present a common front to the British Parliament and the Royal Governor, were forced to enlist the support of the mechanics and the farmers. This attempt to popularize and enlist support for their demands had the consequence of destroying the earlier idyllic conditions of political management. The politically privileged classes could no longer rely upon an obedient electorate. It was necessary to create the impression of unanimous unrest and dissent from the parliamentary decrees which threatened the interests of the provincial notables. This could not be done through the existing political instruments, the provincial assembly and the informal party organizations, because of their restricted bases of selection. They had to appeal to the interests and patriotism of the franchised but relatively powerless middle class and the unfranchised lower rural and urban classes. New political techniques designed to draw in larger elements of the population had to be devised.

The practice of informal nomination of candidates was supplanted by that of public meetings which attempted to reach a larger proportion of the population. The earlier political controls through the economic and social pressure of the large landholders and merchants gave way to "appeals to the voter's intelligence or interest, in the form of public letters or resolutions setting forth the principles for which the candidates stood. Candidacies began to be announced in the public prints."[2] And the public mass meeting began to replace the earlier informal political gatherings.

A further development during this period which had the consequence of drawing the middle and the lower classes into politics was the establishment of the many Revolutionary committees. Here too, the cause of this shift in power from the legal assembly to the extra-legal committee was the necessity of organizing the whole colony in resisting the Governor. "The establishment of this extra-legal machinery was the open door through which the common freeholders and the unfranchised mechanic and artisan pushed their way into the political arena."[3] The behavior of these newer political elements as evinced particularly in the "Stamp Act" riots revealed to the older political leadership the danger implicit in this democratic development. But they were unable to sacrifice their struggle against the British for their immediate class interests. This latent struggle between the older bearers of political power and the newer demanding elements was temporarily overshadowed during the Revolution by the immediate necessities of cooperation. After the Revolution this conflict between the older privileged classes and the rising middle and lower classes supplied the economic and social basis for political struggle.

The struggle for political democracy following upon the Revolution thus only continued a struggle that had already begun before the Revolution. The Republican Party, drawing much of its support from the northern small farmers and urban middle and lower classes necessarily first developed those political techniques which enabled the political leadership to reach the mass of the electorate. The aristocratic Society of the Cincinnati,[4] its membership limited to the officers and their descendants in the male line of the Continental Army, had its counterpart in the "Columbian Order" or the Tammany Society, which shortly after its establishment assumed a significant political role. The followers of Jefferson in New York adapted their political organizations to the needs of reaching the masses. "Societies were formed where mutual encouragement might circulate with pots of ale, and plots be laid against the enemy."[5] Charity was also used to bind the lower classes to the party.

The Federalists in their turn, seeing the success of the Jeffersonian methods, foresaw the necessity of imitating these popular convivial and charitable techniques as early as 1802, when Hamilton wrote to Bayard outlining a plan for a "Christian Constitutional Society," designed to appeal to the masses through the development of a "cult" of Washington, and benevolent activities.[6] Such an organization was not founded until 1808, after the injurious Jefferson Embargo, when a number of New York Federalists organized the Washington Benevolent Society. This successful imitation of the Jeffersonians by the Federalists resulted in their winning a number of elections: in 1804 they elected a majority to the New York City Common Council; and in 1809, following upon the Embargo, they won a majority of the Senate and the Assembly. But their good fortune held out for only a single term.

The Federalist Party fell largely because of the mass base of the Republican Party, and because of conflicts of the various economic groups under the Federalist standard. Consisting both of landholders and the merchants of the seaboard, it was difficult to compromise on the basis of taxation. The urban mercantile interests opposed too heavy a tax upon imports. And the landholding classes naturally resented any attempt to tax land too highly. Then too, the rise of a class of manufacturers favored a protective tariff which naturally was opposed by the importing merchants. The Federalist Party, with its pretension to exclusive rule on the part of those with wealth, was doomed to fall, given the ideological and economic environment of the time. It last sought to defend its fast waning privileges in the New York Constitutional Convention of 1820. The old landholders and merchants protested vigorously and at length against the destruction of authority, prophesying the direst consequences. But their eloquence could not stand against the consensus of the Convention.

The Constitutional Convention of 1820

One of the first tasks of the Convention was the democratization of the New York Militia. No longer were the great landholders to have almost prescriptive rights to military office. All officers of militia were to be elected by their men. Many former appointive positions were made elective. The municipalities were to have the right to elect all of their own officials. The office of governor was strengthened by granting him many important appointive powers previously held by the "Council of Appointment." The governor's power was further strengthened by granting him the veto power, and his term was limited to two years. "The franchise was extended to include all male citizens twenty years of age or more who had resided for six months within his district and paid taxes or an assessment, had performed some work upon the roads, or had been enrolled in the militia."[7]

Following upon the Convention the conservatives in their attempt to regain their power sought to outdo the Democrats in their claims to equalitarianism. For a while they assumed the name of the "People's Party." This in turn pushed the Democrats further to the "left," and in the spring of 1825 they presented and passed a constitutional amendment which provided for the popular election of justices of the peace, and established full manhood suffrage. Thus by 1825 all legal restrictions favoring the older New York ruling class were destroyed.

The Occupational Composition of Political Office-Holders After Democratization

The consequences of this democratic movement for political participation are partially summarized in Table 2.1. We still find lawyers constituting the largest proportion of political office-holders. Of the 140 political office-holders in the selection holding office between the years 1835–1860, 50, or 36 percent, were lawyers, while only 15, or 11 percent, were merchants. This compares with 60 percent lawyers and 20 percent merchants in the years between 1789–1835. The decrease in the proportion of lawyers, as we shall see later, was a temporary matter. The older lawyers had been to a considerable extent identified with the old merchant and landholding ruling class. The development of the middle and lower class lawyer-professional politician had its beginnings in this period, but it is not to be expected that this development would be clearly reflected in the figures of this Pre–Civil War Era. The decrease in the proportion of merchants is to be expected. In a situation of political democracy their interest in holding political office was bound to decrease; the general prestige level of politics having fallen, and the conditions of political competition having become more severe.

Fifteen percent of the politicians of the 1835–1860 sample were retailers or small shopkeepers, 9 percent were manufacturers, 7 percent were editors, publishers, and journalists, while the remaining were in other professions and other fields of business, banking and insurance, handicraft, etc. These general figures clearly record the influx of newer professional, middle, and lower middle class elements into politics under conditions of political democracy. Although there was a high percentage of lawyers and merchants in politics, what this table does not reveal is that these merchants

TABLE 2.1   Occupations of Political Office-Holders from New York City, 1835–1860*

Office-Holders	Dates for Selection	Lawyers	Physicians	Editors and Publishers	Journalists	Writers
Federal:		19	—	7	2	2
Executive	1835–1860	1	—	—	—	1
Diplomatic	1835–1860	6	—	4	2	1
Senate	1835–1860	1	—	—	—	—
Congress	1839–1849	11	—	3	—	—
State:		22	—	—	—	—
Governors	1835–1860	2	—	—	—	—
Senate	1840	2	—	—	—	—
Assembly	1840	6	—	—	—	—
Judicial	1840–1855	12	—	—	—	—
Municipal:		9	2	1	—	—
Mayors	1835–1860	2	—	1	—	—
Aldermen	1842–1845	7	2	—	—	—
Total						
Number		50	2	8	2	2
Percent		36	1	6	1	1

*For the lists of executive and cabinet officials of the federal government from New York City the following sources were used: *World Almanac* (New York: Press Publishing Co., 1892). For members of the Senate, House of Representatives, judiciary and diplomatic service, The *Tribune Almanac, 1838–1868* (New York: the New York Tribune, 1868). Biographical sketches of the officers of the federal government were found in Charles Lanman, *Biographical Annals of the Civil Government of the United States* (Washington: James Anglin, 1876); *The Dictionary of American Biography* (New York: Charles Scribner's Sons, 1928–1937); and *The National Cyclopedia of American Biography,* compiled by George Derby (New York: J. T. White and Co., 1906). For lists of governors and mayors of New York State and City: the *World Almanac.* For other state officers, *The New York Civil List* (Albany: J. B. Lyon Co., 1855). Biographical data were taken from general biographical sources listed above. Where biographical sketches were lacking data on occupations, they were taken from the *New York Directory* (New York: Trow City Directory Co., 1835–1860). For municipal officers, the *Manual of the Corporation of the City of New York,* compiled by D. T. Valentine (New York: published by the city, 1842–1870). For biographical data the sources listed above were used.

(*continues*)

TABLE 2.1 (*continued*)

Scholars	Merchants	Manu-facturers	Retail	Handi-craftsmen	Financial	Unknown	Total
1	3	1	4	—	2	7	48
—	—	—	—	—	—	- -	2
1	1	—	—	—	1	6	22
—	—	—	—	—	—	—	1
—	2	1	4	—	1	1	23
—	3	—	3	—	1	5	34
—	1	—	—	—	—	—	3
—	1	—	—	—	1	—	4
—	1	—	3	—	—	3	13
—	—	—	—	—	—	2	14
—	9	12	14	2	—	9	58
—	4	3	—	—	—	3	13
—	5	9	14	2	—	6	45
1	15	13	21	2	3	21	140
1	11	9	15	1	2	15	100

and lawyers were not, generally speaking, among the wealthier citizens of the city. This point will be made quantitatively in a later tabulation.

Taking this selection by political jurisdiction, certain other significant differentials emerge. The tabulation of federal political office-holders for this period indicated a high proportion of lawyers, almost 40 percent, while editors, publishers, journalists, writers, and scholars accounted for more than another 20 percent. Among state officials two-thirds were found to be lawyers. Both of these groups are to be contrasted with the municipal office-holders where we find relatively few lawyers and professional men and a high proportion of retailers, manufacturers, and merchants. Thus in the municipal jurisdiction the influx of non-professional middle and lower middle class elements has been highest.

Of the two federal executive officials from New York City during this period, the first, Benjamin Franklin Butler, Secretary of War, and Attorney General in the cabinets of President Jackson, was a lawyer. The second, James K. Paulding, Secretary of the Navy in the cabinet of Van Buren, was a member of the literary circle of Washington Irving, Henry Brevoort, and others. He was the son of a prosperous shipowner, while Butler was the son of a well-to-do merchant. Paulding devoted much of his life to political office-holding under presidents Madison, Monroe, Jackson, and Van Buren.

Six of the 22 diplomatic officers from New York City in these years were lawyers. With one exception, all of these 6 lawyers had held a considerable number of other political offices. Alfred Conkling had served as a City Prosecuting Attorney, congressman, United States District Judge, and United States Minister to Mexico. Murphy was attorney and mayor of Brooklyn, congressman, state senator, and assemblyman, and Minister to the Hague. George W. Lay was a New York assemblyman, congressman, and Chargé d'affaires to Sweden. Daniel D. Barnard served as district attorney, congressman, and Minister to Prussia. Enos T. Throop was a congressman, circuit judge, lieutenant governor, and governor of New York, and Chargé d'affaires to the Two Sicilies. These lawyer politicians generally received their diplomatic appointments at the close of long political careers, as rewards for party and political service.

Six of the diplomats of this period were editors and publishers, journalists, and writers. Some of these had received their appointments as a reward for their propagandistic services to the political parties. James Watson Webb, Minister to Brazil in 1850, was the proprietor of the *New York Courier* and *New York Enquirer*. Ephraim George Squier, Chargé d'affaires to Central America was associated with the *New York State Mechanic*, and later with the *Hartford Daily Journal*. Charles Eames, Minister to Venezuela under President Pierce, was the associate editor of the *Washington Union*. John L. O'Sullivan, Minister Resident to Portugal, was a journalist and contributor to magazines. Washington Irving, one of the most prominent literary men in America during these years, was Minister to Spain in 1842.

Among the remaining diplomatic officers were George Folsom, librarian of the New York Historical Society, August Belmont, representative of the Rothschild banking interests in America, and at one time chairman of the democratic national committee. He served as Minister to the Netherlands. Churchill C. Cambreleng, Minister to Russia in 1840, was a merchant associated with John Jacob Astor.

Thus, the diplomatic officers from New York City were old and honored party men, or important party contributors, wealthy business men and lawyers, editors, publishers, and journalists. Diplomatic office had become a reward for party service, or campaign contributions, a reward much desired particularly among the ambitious because of the contact with foreign and aristocratic courts to which diplomatic office accorded entry.

The only United States senator from New York City proper, in this period, was Hamilton Fish, descendant of the prominent Fish family. He was a lawyer by occupation, but spent much of his time managing his family estate. He was prominent in the Whig Party, and was elected in 1847 as lieutenant governor, and in 1849 as governor. He served in the Senate in the fifties and afterwards as federal Secretary of State. Of the congressmen of this period 11 were lawyers, 3 were editors and publishers, 2 were merchants, and 4 were retailers. Thus, less advantaged and esteemed individuals had access to a certain extent to the federal House.

Three residents of New York City during this period were governors of New York State. Two, Hamilton Fish and John A. King, were lawyers, and the third, Edwin D. Morgan, was a merchant. Both of the lawyer governors were descendants of prominent political families. John A. King, a banker himself, was the son of Rufus King, the Revolutionary statesman. Morgan came of relatively poor rural origins, but became a wealthy wholesale grocer. All three had held a number of other political offices. As the heads of party tickets in the state the governors were chosen not only because of their political power and prominence, but in many cases because of their social prestige and "respectability." Fish's career has already been reviewed. King was his father's secretary of legation in England, served as a member of the New York Assembly, served in Congress, and was prominent in Whig and Republican party congresses. Morgan was a state senator, a United States Senator, and prominent generally in Whig and Republican politics. Of the 17 members of the New York Senate and Assembly 8 were lawyers, 2 were merchants, and 3 were retailers. Here as in the House of Representatives less advantaged elements were enabled to rise.

Among the 10 mayors of New York City during 1835–1860 concerning whom data were available, there were 4 merchants, 3 manufacturers, 2 lawyers, and 1 publisher. The heads of municipal party tickets were frequently chosen for their "respectability" and social prestige; hence the merchants and manufacturers in their number. Among the 45 aldermen there were 14 small shopkeepers, 9 manufacturers, 5 merchants (in the shipping, commission, or auction business) and 7 lawyers. The office of alderman at this time seems to have been the office most accessible to the lower levels of the middle classes.

Attitudes of the Wealthy Classes Toward Politics After Democratization

Comments describing the attitudes of the wealthier classes toward politics and the influences conditioning these attitudes after the breakdown of their exclusive hold upon the franchise are to be found in the general literature of the early nineteenth century.

> "Heaven save me from politics!" a wealthy American is reported as having said in conversation with a European observer in the later 1830's.
> "It is certainly not a flourishing trade in this country," said I.
> "Not only that, sir; but it is not a respectable one."
> "And why not?"
> "Because every blackguard meddles in it."
> "But not every blackguard is successful in it."
> "Quite the reverse; it is only the blackguard who is successful."[8]

And later in the discussion;

"We have all more or less passed the age in which respectable Americans take an interest in politics; and are, thank God, not yet sufficiently old and decrepit to run to it once more because we are unfit for everything else. . . . A man never takes to politics in this country unless he is ruined in business!"[9]

De Tocqueville, also writing in the 1830s, remarked upon and interpreted this withdrawal of the wealthier elements from politics:

At the present day the more affluent classes of society are so entirely removed from the direction of political affairs in the United States, that wealth, far from conferring a right to the exercise of power, is rather an obstacle than a means of attaining to it. The wealthy members of the community abandon the lists, through unwillingness to contend, and frequently to contend in vain, against the poorest classes of their fellow citizens. They concentrate all their enjoyments in the privacy of their homes, where they occupy a rank which cannot be assumed in public; and they constitute a private society in the state which has its own tastes and pleasures. They submit to this state of things as an irremediable evil, but they are careful not to show that they are galled by its continuance; it is even not uncommon to hear them laud the delights of a Republic government, and the advantages of democratic institutions when they are in public.[10]

The wealthier classes not only retired generally from political struggle, but developed an attitude of contempt for politics. Thus a merchant eulogist writing in the 1850s declaimed:

There is no nobility in this country. There is a class of princes, and they are the highest in the city. These princes can be seen every day (except Sunday) at a daily congress in the Merchant's Exchange, between one and two o'clock. There can be seen Princes of Commerce, and such names as are good in Asia, Africa, Europe, or in any part of America. These are the Princes Goodhue, Aspinwall, Aymar, Perit, King, Grinnell, Minturn, Howland, Boorman, Griswold, and a pit full of other names.

What do such men as these care for the ephemeral four year names of Buchanan, Pierce, Polk, Cass, Cobb, Tyler, Fillmore, Everett, Floyd, and some five hundred others, equally notorious names that have figures in politics!

No, Sir! The merchant princes despise such names. They are not good in Wall Street, nor would the bearers be received in the social domestic circles of the self-satisfied merchant unless they could be regularly introduced by an equal, or by some regular correspondence of "the firm," in this or other cities.[11]

And again, writing of their influence, he exclaims:

Of how little consequence beyond their own sphere, or "off change," have any of them been!

How very few have wielded party influence, or obtained political power! The exceptions to this rule are so remarkable, that one can count upon his fingers the names of almost every prominent man, who in the last half century has been elected to the lower house of Congress, or even to either branch of our state legislature.[12]

The merchant congressmen of this period referred to by Scoville as exceptions were the banker James Gore King and the merchants Moses H. Grinnell, John I. Morgan, and Gideon Lee. Among the New York mayors he finds Fernando Wood, A. C. Kingsland, Gideon Lee, W. H. Havemeyer, Phillip Hone, and D. F. Tieman. Two merchants had also been governors of the state, Edwin D. Morgan and Oliver Walcott, Jr. Scoville goes on to point out that one of the primary reasons for the lack of political activity on the part of the merchants was the changed character of politics itself. A politician, in order to maintain himself in power, had to keep in constant touch with the masses, to subject himself to party organization and party discipline. A merchant was called upon for political work

> because a party or men wished to use him, either for money, respectability, or some other selfish purpose. . . . Many a merchant of both or all parties has waited in his counting room for a nomination to Congress. Such a man may wait until Doomsday, before he is nominated for that or any other position. Did such a man stoop to mix with the rank and file of the people, serve in ward committees, help elect them, get on general committees, know the masses, learn to pull the strings, he could eventually be elected anywhere if his party had power.[13]

The attitude of the wealthier classes toward the professional lawyer politicians is expressed again by our merchant eulogist, one of the first great celebrators of the triumphs of the self-made American business man:

> Take our lawyers who have turned their attention to politics—a class that the live merchant despises—but still men who have got a right to attach the doubtful meaning word "Honorable" to their names, say W. B. Maclay, John McKeon, Elisha Ward, Horace Clark, Judge James I. Roosevelt, and that class. As practicing lawyers they are dead. Having been in Congress, the administration gives an office to some of them, if asked for. I could name five hundred men—political lawyers—if I had a directory before me, who could not pay their office rents by their regular law business. No. In rank, the lawyer occupies a secondary position, for he lives, and thrives off the business created for him by the more planning, combining genius of the great merchants.[14]

Social Composition and Political Participation of the Wealthy Classes in the Pre–Civil War Era

To say that the withdrawal of the wealthier classes from politics was universal would be an exaggeration. We have already seen that they still frequently held the offices of greater prominence and prestige in the three levels of government. The question may be raised at this point as to whether or not the participation of the wealthier classes in politics was uniform, or whether it varied for different groups of the wealthy. The wealthier classes then as now were divided into the "arrived" or the older families and the "parvenu." The "arrived" were the inheritors of wealth for one or more generations. They were culturally and socially differentiated from the general mass of the plutocracy. Fortunately for this period there was available a directory and biographical compilation of the wealthy elements of New York City.

Moses Yale Beach, editor of the *New York Sun* during a part of this period, prepared and issued a biographical directory of the citizens of New York City worth $100,000 and over, for the decade 1844–55. Although, no doubt, there are many omissions and exaggerations, the great majority of the New York fortunes are reported in the work, and at least their approximate size indicated. In addition Beach furnished a varying amount of biographical material on these individuals. From this it was possible to estimate very approximately the social composition and the political participation of the wealthier classes of New York City during these years.[15]

Beach listed some 1,035 individuals in 1855 whose wealth was estimated as of this magnitude. Twenty-nine of these were millionaires, 118 were worth between $500,000 and $1,000,000; 347 between $200,000 and $500,000; and 541 between $100,000 and $200,000. Partial biographical information was available for 63 percent of this group. Hence the percentages given in Table 2.2 must be qualified by the fact that there was an unknown group of considerable size.

Fifteen percent of this group were listed as inheritors of wealth, and thus, no doubt, constituted the core of the "*bon ton*" of New York City of the Pre–Civil War Era. Five percent had married into wealthy families, and would thus constitute an eligible but not quite as esteemed group in "exclusive society." Forty-three percent were *parvenus*,[16] some of whom, no doubt, through economic, ethnic, religious ties, and ties of blood also had access to these older circles. This large percentage of *parvenus* among the wealthy class reflects the great social mobility in this prosperous and expanding era. The inundation of the older wealthy stock by the newer wealthy had important effects upon the political attitudes of the wealthy group as a whole. The older families were the bearers of the conservative "oligarchic" political tradition. The newer wealthy were largely of lower middle class farmer or urban origins, and, if anything, were the bearers of a narrowly economic and religious tradition. The newer wealthy were largely content with the conditions of political participation under democracy.

Fifty-two percent of the millionaires had their wealth or at least a substantial portion of it by inheritance or marriage, and 48 percent were self-made. Of the owners of $500,000 to $1,000,000, 39 percent inherited their wealth or got much of it by marriage; while the lowest wealth group in-

TABLE 2.2 Distribution of Men of Wealth by Source of Wealth in New York City in 1855*

Wealth Group	Inheritance		Marriage		"Self-Made"		Total for Whom Data Were Available	Percent Unknown
	Number	Percent	Number	Percent	Number	Percent		
$1,000,000 & over	9	39	3	13	11	48	23	21
$500,000 to $1,000,000	25	30	8	9	52	61	85	28
$200,000 to $500,000	69	25	14	6	153	69	236	32
$100,000 to $200,000	54	18	27	9	217	73	298	45
Total	157	24	52	9	433	67	642	37

*Moses Yale Beach, *The Wealth and Biography of the Wealthy Citizens of the City of New York* (New York: published by the *New York Sun*, 1855).

cluded only 27 percent who had inherited or married into wealth, and 73 percent who had accumulated it themselves. The largest number of *parvenus* were thus in the lower levels of Beach's wealthy citizens; and great wealth was found to be frequently inherited wealth.

Summarizing Table 2.3 it is possible to generalize that the most wealthy element—those having half a million or over—included a slightly larger number of rentiers[17] and real estate owners, while the lower wealth groups were more heterogeneous generally and included more individuals from the professions.

Table 2.4 makes the point that the wealthier groups of New Yorkers in this period engaged in politics hardly at all. Thus, of the 1,035 whose wealth is estimated at $100,000 or over, only 32, or 3 percent, were recorded by Beach as having held political office. None of the millionaires were listed as having held office. Only 1 of the 118 having wealth between $500,000 and $1,000,000 had held political office. Five percent of the $200,000 to $500,000 group had held such office; and 3 percent of the $100,000 to $200,000 group had seriously engaged in politics. Thus political activity was lowest among the higher wealth groups, which were to some extent the inherited wealth groups. Political activity, in other words, was lowest among those who had the most secure economic and social positions—the *"bon ton"* or "society" of that era.

The 32 wealthy political office-holders had held in all 49 political offices, of which 15 were federal, 13 state, and 21 municipal. The lowest wealth group had held the largest number of political offices, which indicates that some of these were in the professional politician group.

The wealthy professional politicians listed by Moses Beach were Fernando Wood, William Marcy Tweed, and Michael Ulshoeffer. Wood was a member of Congress and mayor of New York City. He was dominant in Tammany in the 1850s and later formed a rival democratic organization, Mozart Hall. Beach describes him as having made his start selling bad liquor at outrageous prices to the stevedores working in the North River. He was supposed to have made a tidy sum through having the wages of the stevedores paid through him after deducting charges for real or imaginary liquor consumed by them. Tweed in the Pre–Civil War Era was active in Tammany, and held office as alderman and member of Congress. Beach speaks of this corrupt politician par excellence as "one of the few men who managed to save something out of their salaries while holding office."[18] Michael Ulshoeffer was the son of a German immigrant musician, was a Sachem of Tammany and is said to have been one of the "charter dealers" at Albany, individuals who aided the granting of bank charters in exchange for offices in the banks and bribes.

Ten of the 32 wealthy political office-holders were self-made men. Horatio Mott, an alderman, began as a grocer, and later became a distiller and

TABLE 2.3 Occupations of Men of Wealth of New York City in 1855*

Occupational Group	$1,000,000 and over		$500,000 to $1,000,000		$200,000 to $500,000		$100,000 to $200,000		Total	
	Number	Percent	Number	Percent	Number	Percent	Number	Percent	Number	Percent
Merchants	8	36	28	36	70	34	108	38	214	37
Finance and insurance	2	9	8	12	24	12	23	8	57	10
Manufacturers	1	5	6	8	15	7	24	9	46	8
Real estate	4	18	8	12	10	5	10	4	32	6
Transport	1	5	—	—	4	2	2	0.7	7	1.5
Wholesalers	—	—	—	—	10	5	20	8	30	5
Lawyers	—	—	—	—	13	6	19	7	32	6
Clergymen	—	—	2	—	—	—	1	0.3	3	0.5
Physicians	—	—	1	—	1	0.05	10	4	12	2
Writers and publishers	—	—	—	—	3	1.5	5	2	8	1.5
Druggists	—	—	1	—	2	1	5	2	8	1.5
Rentiers	6	27	24	32	54	26	44	17	128	21
Total	22	100	78	100	206	100	271	100	577	100
Unknown	7	24	40	33	141	40	270	50	458	44

*Moses Yale Beach, The Wealth and Biography of the Wealthy Citizens of the City of New York (New York: published by the New York Sun, 1855).

TABLE 2.4 Political Offices Held by Wealthy Citizens of New York*

Political Office	$1,000,000 and over	$500,000 to $1,000,000	$200,000 to $500,000	$100,000 to $200,000	Total
Number in class	29	118	347	541	1,035
Holding office:					
Number	—	1	16	15	32
Percent	—	1	5	3	3
Federal offices held:					
Executive	—	—	—	2	2
Diplomatic	—	—	—	1	1
Legislative	—	—	3	6	9
Judicial	—	—	—	1	1
Administrative	—	—	—	2	2
Total	—	—	3	12	15
State offices held:					
Executive	—	—	—	1	1
Legislative	—	1	1	2	4
Judicial	—	—	2	3	5
Administrative	—	—	2	1	3
Total	—	1	5	7	13
Municipal offices held:					
Executive	—	—	4	2	6
Legislative	—	—	8	5	13
Judicial	—	—	1	—	1
Administrative	—	—	—	1	1
Total	—	—	13	8	21
Total	—	1	21	27	49

*Moses Yale Beach, *The Wealth and Biography of the Wealthy Citizens of the City of New York* (New York: published by the *New York Sun*, 1855).

liquor wholesaler. After a change of heart he became a temperance man, and went into the ship chandlery business. Richard Compton, also an alderman, was a grocer and liquor seller, and later engaged in the ice business. Among the other *parvenu* wealthy political office-holders were John Pettigrew, a building contractor and alderman, William Mandeville, a cabinet maker and alderman, Richard Carman, a carpenter and builder and alderman, John A. Bunting, a mason and alderman, Alonzo A. Alvord, a hat maker and an alderman, Aaron Clark, a "lottery master" and Mayor of New York, and Zadoch Pratt, a tanner and congressman. William F. Havemeyer, a large sugar manufacturer, was mayor of New York for several terms.

The wealthy lawyer politicians were Francis R. Tilyon, a recorder of New York, Reuben Walworth, congressman, and circuit judge, Samuel R. Betts, a state and federal judge, Daniel S. Dickinson, a state senator, lieutenant-gov-

ernor, and United States senator, James R. Whiting, alderman and district attorney, James I. Roosevelt, alderman and judge of the State Supreme Court,
and William Samuel Johnson, a Whig politician and alderman.

The only wealthy politicians from the older established elements, from
"society" in other words, were James Gore King, George Bancroft, Cornelius Lawrence, Charles W. Lynde, James I. Roosevelt, Hamilton Fish, and
Gulian C. Verplanck. King was the head of one of the biggest banking firms
of the city, and a son of the Revolutionary statesman, Rufus King, and himself served in Congress and as a State Supreme Court Judge. George Bancroft, early American historian, a son of a Boston clergyman, served as collector of the Port of Boston, as Secretary of the Navy under Polk, and as
Minister to England. Cornelius Lawrence, of a "respectable" Long Island
family, became a wealthy auctioneer, and served as collector of the port of
New York and as mayor of New York. Charles Lynde, quoted as worth
$850,000 by Beach, was a New Englander, descended from two Massachu-
setts Supreme Court judges, and served as state senator from Brooklyn.
Hamilton Fish has been referred to above. Gulian C. Verplanck was a literary man with an assured income from inheritance, and served in the state
senate.

Of the wealthy political office-holders only a minority were from the
older "respectable" and well-to-do stock and none at all from the very
wealthiest group. The largest proportion of these wealthy office-holders
were *parvenu* lawyers or business men in the less esteemed trades, liquor
manufacturing and selling, and the retail and building trades, individuals
generally in the lower levels of the plutocracy.

The Consequences of Democratization

The shift in the class character of political participation had important consequences for the prestige of political office. In a situation where the franchise was restricted according to wealth the general level of prestige of politics is high, since only the "esteemed," that is the wealthier elements of the
population, have access to it. In a situation of formal political democracy in
which all elements of the population are enabled to compete for political
office, the general prestige level of politics declines. If the wealthier classes
are attracted to politics at all, they tend to seek the more prominent offices,
leaving the lower offices to the less advantaged classes. Hence in a situation
of political democracy the more prominent political offices—the federal executive, diplomatic and senatorial offices, the governorship and the mayoralty—continue to enjoy prestige, although less than in a situation of a restricted franchise, while the prestige of the federal Congress, state senate
and assembly, and board of alderman declines to the level of those who
compete for it, that is, the middle and lower middle classes.

The general causes of this movement for democratization were the increased size of the rural and urban middle classes and the spread of the equalitarian ideology of the eighteenth and nineteenth centuries. The revolution took place peacefully because the powers of government at that time were weak. The lower classes were animated mainly by a search for political equality. The dangers of indirect control over politics by the wealthier classes were not clearly foreseen by the general population, although some keen observers were not unaware of its possibility. Thus De Tocqueville remarked:

> I am of opinion, upon the whole, that the manufacturing aristocracy which is growing up under our eyes, is one of the harshest which ever existed in the world; but at the same time it is one of the most confined and least dangerous. Nevertheless the friends of democracy should keep their eyes anxiously fixed in this direction; for if ever a permanent inequality of conditions and aristocracy again penetrate into the world, it may be predicted that this is the channel by which they will enter.[19]

Not only could the wealthier classes cede their exclusive political power without great danger to their economic position because of the weak character of government in America, but also, the rising class of professional politicians in an expanding economy were animated mainly by motives of individual economic aggrandizement. Wealth and power were not to be got by genuinely championing the cause of the lowly, but rather by service for service arrangements with wealthy entrepreneurs.

Among the more important consequences of political democratization were the decline in the prestige level of political office, already discussed, the rationalization of political life, and the shift of the center of policy-making from the group of political office-holders to external pressure groups. By "rationalization of politics" is meant the setting up of permanent party organizations, with permanent headquarters and staffs, the regularization of meetings—in other words the partial elimination of the spontaneous and informal elements in politics. This party bureaucratization was necessary because of the size of the electorate. In the earlier situation of a restricted franchise the relatively small group of the politically privileged, allied by ties of blood and friendship, was able to frame political policy and decide upon candidacy in more informal intercourse. A political party, seeking political office under conditions of political democracy could not reach and hold the loyalty of the masses without a regular and permanent machinery. The professional politician, in contrast to the merchant and landholder "occasional" politician of the earlier period, generally had no political convictions save that of getting into and holding political office. The landholder, or merchant, or "upper class" lawyer politician, having no class "above" him, did not have his policies or convictions dictated to him. The professional politician came to serve as a "functionary," a tool of effectively organized groups, taking his policies from the demands and moods of the hour, balancing always the potential strengths of the articulate groups, with an eye to the policy which would get him the most votes and alienate the fewest. To a considerable measure, therefore, the center of policy initiation, and hence of control, in the political process, was no longer among the group of office-holders, but rather among the more powerful of the organized pressure groups.

As long as there was free land, and economic opportunities in the cities, there was only occasional political pressure from the lower classes. In a prosperous expanding economy lower class organization lagged. The center of control over the political process was generally among the groups of industrialists and financiers. The gradual closing of the frontier and the consequent tendency toward fixed and unequal classes resulted in the increase of lower class agrarian and proletarian organization, and thus increased their influence over politicians.

In the early and later nineteenth century political democratization was responsible for the relative equalization of educational and cultural opportunity. It was also responsible for the ultimate legalization of trade unionism. And by no means an unimportant consequence of democratization was the winning of access to political office and favors on the part of the lower classes. But the group which has enjoyed the most continuous and effective control over the shaping of public policy in America, under conditions of political democracy, were the well-organized industrial and financial groups. To be sure, their controls were challenged in situations of depression, but partial concessions in those periods were sufficient to maintain their power relatively unimpaired. In situations of prosperity their domination, in collaboration with the controllers of the electorate—the professional politicians and party bosses—was on the whole secure and ineffectively challenged.

Notes

1. Carl Becker, *The History of Political Parties in the Province of New York, 1760–1776* ("Bulletin of the University of Wisconsin," No. 286, History Series, Vol. II, No. 1 [Madison, 1909]).

2. *Ibid.*, p. 18.

3. *Ibid.*, p. 21.

4. See Bernard Fay, *The Revolutionary Spirit in France and America* (New York: Harcourt Brace and Co., 1929), pp. 204–05 for a discussion of the reaction of democratic elements in North America and France to the formation of the Society of the Cincinnati.

5. Dixon Ryan Fox, *The Decline of the Aristocracy in the Politics of New York* (New York: Longmans Green and Co., 1919), p. 87.

6. *Ibid.,*

7. *Ibid.,* p. 251.

8. Francis J. Grund, *Aristocracy in America: The Sketch Book of a German Nobleman,* ed. by F. J. Grund (London: R. Bentley, 1839), p. 26.

9. *Ibid.,* p. 27.

10. Alexis De Tocqueville, *Democracy in America,* trans. Henry Reeves (New York: A. S. Barnes Co., 1862), I, 192.

11. Joseph Scoville (pseudonym Walter Barret, Clerk), *Old Merchants of New York* (New York: Thomas R. Knox and Co., 1885), II, 94.

12. *Ibid.,* p. 1.

13. Ibid., p. 13.

14. *Ibid.,* p. 165.

15. Moses Yale Beach, *The Wealth and Biography of the Wealthy Citizens of the City of New York* (New York: published by the *New York Sun,* 1855).

16. The term *parvenu* is used here to refer to individuals who have arisen from lower class origins and who are therefore not immediately admitted to the more established wealthy circles. The term has both an economic and a "social" connotation.

17. The term *rentier* is used throughout this work to refer to individuals who live from wealth accumulated either earlier in life, or inherited from previous generations. In other words, it refers to economically inactive individuals. The term as used here includes individuals totally inactive in business life, and individuals only occasionally identified with economic life. The criterion used in the quantitative treatment of occupation throughout this study was either explicit evidence of economic inactivity, or the absence of any formal business connection or occupation. It was thought justifiable to assume in the latter case that an individual was either totally inactive in the business world, or was only occasionally active.

18. Beach, *op. cit.,* p. 74.

19. De Tocqueville, *op. cit.,* II, 172.

3

Self-Restraint in the Social Life of the Plutocracy

THE POLITICAL AND ECONOMIC circumstances of the wealthy classes have a natural influence upon their social or recreational life. Wealth brings leisure and the power to use this leisure to realize aspirations of various kinds. These aspirations are conditioned by the activities in which the wealthy engage, by the problems with which they come in contact, by the patterns which have been set by the wealthy and privileged groups in previous generations or in other areas. The hypothesis is proposed here that while the wealthier classes had an exclusive control of politics, their social life tended to be limited to recreational proportions. Under the limited franchise politics and political leadership were one of the most important spheres and objects of social competition among the wealthy. Honor and prestige were to be gained mainly by political prominence and recognition. Social affairs were in considerable measure politically oriented. Political activity made greater claims upon the time and energies of the wealthy. Their responsible political functions and the general security of their status made for a more mature attitude, an attitude which prevented a great elaboration of social life. To be sure their exclusive political position was not the only force restricting the development of an irresponsible social life. Wealth was not as easily attained during this period, and economic and religious norms were restrictive influences.

Social Life in the Pre-Democratic Period

The social life of the wealthier elements of the early Dutch settlers was conditioned by their political responsibilities as well as by the relative recency of the acquisition of their fortunes and their economic activities. The great patroon families, the Van Rensselaers, Schuylers, Van Cortlandts, and others came of recently arrived merchant fortunes.[1] The early Dutch were bearers of a middle class social tradition, a social life largely occasioned by natural events—birth, marriage, death, and religious holidays. A student of the early Dutch Era enumerated the types of social events in that period. She noted that childbirth was an important social event, giving rise to "caudle" parties, so named after a special drink served on these occasions. Marriage was a festive event and death was the occasion for a more sober kind of conviviality. During the year there were occasional homely gatherings at private residences. A Dancing Assembly was supported by the "old Dutch" families of that day, among which were the Van Cortlandts, De Peysters, Kips, Lockermans, Lawrences, Stuyvesants, Bayards, Provoosts, Varlaths, Schencks, and a number of others. "As the young people grew up they were permitted to join these assemblies, which became a favorite place for courting and many matches were made at these hospitable gatherings."[2] Generally speaking the social life of the early Dutch wealthy was mainly of an instrumental character: that is, social events rarely had a justification of their own, but were legitimated by natural or religious events and by "normal" recreational needs. The early Dutch wealthy tended to be occupied full time with their commercial and political activities.

The seizure of the colony by the English occasioned at first a good deal of rivalry and snobbery between the newly arrived English settlers and the older Dutch. Gradually these barriers were overcome through intermarriage and commercial ties. The English domination brought in another complicating social factor. This was the Provincial Governor's "Court" and his aristocratic officers. These English aristocratic elements naturally assumed the leadership in the social sphere. The more fashionable of the landholding notables, both the older Dutch and the English were assimilated to this aristocratic court and came to follow its pattern of living.

The English element led by the provincial court introduced horse racing, drama, musical concerts and the formal ball. Under its influence a type of social life developed patterned after that of Georgian England. There was to be noted on a small scale the development of a "leisure class" led by the aristocratic officers, its life devoted to the cultivation of the social refinements.[3] The full development of such a culture was blocked by the bourgeois character of most of the aspirants to this life. With few exceptions the prosperous families of this era were bound to their business activities. Their exclusive political position tended to support their sense of social security and distance from the lower classes and make less necessary the drive for differentiation in the social sphere so characteristic of the later era. The combination on the part of this class of commercial and political functions tended to anchor them more securely in reality—social life performing the function of rest and recreation and not becoming the dominant value of the class.

During the first years of independence, New York served as the nation's capitol. During these years the social life of New York revolved around the social affairs of Washington and the members of the Cabinet and the diplomatic corps. Mrs. John Jay, the wife of the Secretary of State, was the acknowledged social leader by virtue of her husband's position, her family connections, and because it was her function to entertain the diplomatic corps. Mrs. Jay's "supper lists" of 1787–88 defined the exclusive social circles of that time.[4] Mrs. Jay's list included the outstanding state and national office-holders, members of the New York Bar, landholding and merchant families of New York. Despite the complaints against the frivolity of New York society during this era the general cast of social life was far more sober than that of the later periods, and primarily because its leadership was made up of men-of-affairs—commercial and political.[5]

Social Life in the First Half of the Nineteenth Century

During the decades before the Civil War the wealthier classes of the New York population underwent two great experiences from which these elements emerged greatly transformed. The first of these transformations was the loss of exclusive political privileges. The consequences of this development were the loss on the part of the wealthy of their secure political "distance" from the rest of the population. As Tocqueville observed in this era this development had the consequence of driving this class into private life exclusiveness.[6] In other words they sought to express their superior economic and, in some cases, cultural position by the elaboration of their social life. The second development arose from the fact of the tremendous economic expansion of this time which brought into prominence a large class of wealthy *parvenus*. An analysis of the wealthy classes of 1855 (see Chapter 2) has already shown that, of the thousand or more individuals possessing wealth of $100,000 or over, about half were shown to be *parvenus*. The exact total was probably even greater, since the origins of more than a third were unknown. These elements were mainly recruited from the middle and lower classes of the New England states and from the same classes newly arrived from Scotland, England, Ireland, and Germany. These *parvenus* brought with them only a sober religious tradition and an eagerness for wealth and economic power. Such was their number and wealth that the older more cultured elements were overwhelmed. The new merchants and manufacturers had no tradition of public service and secular culture. They were largely content to remain within their counting houses and their churches, and to leave politics to the lawyers and the smaller entrepreneurs.

The social life of the upper classes of New York City in the decades before the Civil War was comparatively speaking sober and restrained. The older wealthy stock surviving from the days of the Federalists had culture and education and a certain sobriety that dated from their earlier responsi ble roles. The newer wealthy elements were largely without education and culture, but their social life was restrained by their religious and economic ethics. While there was little development in the social and cultural sphere there was a great development in the sphere of charity and philanthropy, mainly of a religious nature. A large number of charitable institutions sponsored by the various religious denominations were founded with the financial support and sponsorship of the wealthy *parvenus* of the time.[7]

A contemporary commentator describes a typical old Knickerbocker Sunday:

> What a contrast presents itself between the short rollicking Sunday of today with its music and dance, its brilliantly lighted salons filled with an eager crowd of pleasure-seekers; its endless train of promenades; its open shops in the full tide of successful traffic, and the solemn long Knickerbocker Sabbath, when the Fourth Commandment was in full force. The old time Knickerbocker Sabbath was in very truth a day especially set apart for worship. The laws of society so decreed, and public opinion was a stern master then; so woe betide the man, woman or child who dared to disobey or disregard its stringent rules. From early dawn all secular affairs were religiously avoided, the family meals were but cold collations of Saturday baked meats—it was decreed that man-servant and maid-servant should rest.
>
> No sound save the tolling of the Church Bell broke the awful stillness. At stated hours, three times during the day, at 10 o'clock, at 3:00, and at 7:00, stereotype processions of solemn men and women, accompanied by subdued, silent children even of the most tender age slowly wended their way to church, as if they were assisting at the funeral of a dear departed friend. A bare cold nod of recognition was all that was vouchsafed to the most intimate passing acquaintance. The coy maiden looked as demure as her spectacled grandmother who led her protectingly by the hand; the youth clad in best Sunday roundabout appeared as stolid as the well-fed museum anaconda for the boy had been crammed that morning with catechism; pater and mater familias bore upon their countenances the consciousness of their awful responsibility; while Betty, the help, arrayed in her best calico, cleanest pinafore, and brightest bandanna turban, trudged along in the rear of the family circle, as an evidence that the family was doing its whole duty. When the bell ceased tolling, and the service was about to commence, heavy iron chains were drawn tightly across the streets adjacent to the different places of worship, that no possible noise might distract the congregation from serious meditation.[8]

New York life in the Pre–Civil War period was largely in keeping with the sobriety of its Sundays. "Industry" and "assured competency" were its goals. Speculation was frowned upon. Frugality and modesty were primary virtues. Fashions were stable and uniform.

> In this [states Dayton] at least our progenitors were happier than their successors; they were not rendered supremely wretched by insatiate longing, now so painfully apparent in cosmopolitan New York; for respectable comfort, at-

tained by patient striving, fully satisfied their highest aspirations. Whether their limited views of the pleasures and happiness which this life should afford were correct might be a difficult question to argue with those of our day, whose lives have been and are one continuous round of giddy excitement, who look upon labor in any form as degrading, who have adopted as their motto "Dum Vivimus Vivamus" and who now are reaping the abundant harvest which their prudent ancestors so carefully planted, and are scattering it broadcast in wasteful extravagance and riotous living.[9]

But the moralizing commentator was not unaware of tendencies in this early period toward a more extravagant and fashionable way of life. He speaks of the fact that dancing was indulged in, though discountenanced by most of the churches. These dances consisted "at the best only of a humdrum cotillion, with occasional indulgence in the excitement of the Spanish dance, which would now be considered about as exhilarating as would be a glass of insipid 'orgeat' to an inveterate toper."[10] He noted the series of dances at the City Hotel called "Publicks," which were attended by the pupils, male and female, of the French dancing master John Channand, and their parents. The City Hotel dining room also was the scene of the famous Bachelor's Balls which originated in this period and were the central events of the social season, taking place on St. Valentine's day.

Of the economic life of the time Dayton remarks upon the slow and cautious character of transactions, of the fact that credit was more important even than capital; and that credit rested upon sobriety and regularity. The banker was the most honored member of the community.

> The presidents of these useful banks held their heads deservedly high among their fellow citizens, for the honor was conferred upon men who by their success in business had proven themselves worthy to be the trusted custodians of the property and interests of others. So they were excusable for any little vanity they might display by rapping the pavement rather hard with their gold-headed canes, as they walked with dignified tread through Broadway after their responsibilities had ceased for the day.[11]

The bearer of the greatest social honor at this period was the "man-of-affairs" as over against the "man-about-town" of post–Civil War and present epochs. The "man-of-affairs" was involved in politics, was a deacon of his church, and a reputable merchant or banker. The man-about-town, the clubman, and the socialite of the later period had none of these serious concerns. Aside from a possible connection in Wall Street, his interests were mainly in racing, yachting, party life, clothes, food, travel, and the like.

The *Diary of Philip Hone* reflects the tempo and content of the social life in this period. A *parvenu* himself, Hone made a fortune in auctioneering at an early age, after which he retired to devote himself to improving his mind and engaging in public service. He was a strong leader among the Whig merchants, a friend of Chancellor Kent, Webster and other leaders of the Whig Party. In 1821 he was elected to the mayoralty, serving one term. He traveled a great deal, read much, and attended the theater. He was a staunch admirer of the old aristocrats of the pre-democratic period, and saw little but confusion and disaster for the United States under the Jacksonian Democrats. He served as trustee of many philanthropic institutions. He was also a great entertainer and diner-out. In his diary, scrupulously and rather self-consciously kept for some thirty years, is a record of the social and political events of New York City seen from the eye of a crusty, verbose critic of democracy. He was worldly but sober, and thus represented a distinct contrast to the later clubman, man-about-town, or millionaire socialite.

The attempts and failure to maintain an opera reflects the absence of a sufficiently stable and cultured plutocracy. The high prices charged for admission and the extreme contrasts between the sections reserved for the aristocracy and the "Demos" aroused considerable comment in the press. The rules required smooth-shaven faces, evening dress, and white waistcoats, and kid gloves. What particularly outraged the press was a proposed cancellation of the free list for the press by the board of managers of the opera company. Although the opera house was the scene of a number of brilliant assemblages of the "elite," there was insufficient interest among them to support it. After a few weeks the performances were stopped, and the building thereafter was used as a theater.[12]

There were few clubs in New York City in this period. The merchants met in coffee houses and taverns or in private homes. The old Tontine Society, founded by some two hundred merchants for the purpose of building a coffee house, constituted itself as:

> a committee of general supervision; in matters of serious import their decisions were received as law, and public opinion was to a great extent based upon their approval. . . . When really great public interests were at stake, a voice has gone forth from the old Coffee House which was listened to throughout the length and breadth of the land.[13]

The clubs of this era were in many cases devoted to some cultural or intellectual end. The Black Friars, a club founded in 1784, had a membership mainly of lawyers and physicians. They held their meetings at the Merchants Coffee House. The Drone Club was a literary circle organized around 1792. "Its aim was intellectual advancement rather than social or festive enjoyment. Its members were recognized by people of authority and in its ranks was the best talent of the city."[14] The Belvidere Club was primarily a convivial association. Its members were of the riding, driving, and racing set; they held balls at their club. This seems to have been one of the few purely convivial clubs of the time, founded before the Union Club. The

Kent Club commemorating the chancellor was a lawyer's organization at which serious topics, primarily political, were discussed over well-prepared meals. The Hone Club, founded by friends of the diarist Philip Hone, was a dining club devoted to singing and good fellowship. The Book Club formed in the 1830s was a group of the more cultured elements which combined good fellowship with literary discussion.

Three other clubs were founded before the Civil War. In 1836 the Union Club, still the aristocrat of New York Social Clubs, was founded. Its organizers included some of the older stock and a large number of *parvenus*. The intention was to found a club like the London Clubs:

> To promote social intercourse among its members, and afford them the conveniences and advantages of a well-kept hotel, in conjunction with a reading room, library, and baths, in some proper house or apartments to be procured for the purpose; and in a manner combining elegance and comfort with order and economy.[15]
>
> From its inception [writes a commentator] it was the representative organization of the old families; Livingstons, Clasons, Dunhams, Griswolds, Van Cortlandts, Paines, Centers, Vandervoorts, Van Rensselaers, Irelands, Stuyvesants, Suydams, and other names of Knickerbocker fame, filled its list of memberships with a sort of aristocratic monotony of that Knickerbockerism which has since in solemn and silent Second Avenue (The Faubourg St. Germain of the city) earned the epithet of the Bourbons of New York. Hence sprang up that contest of the old magnates of New York Society with the new Napoleons of Wealth by trade, which for years agitated the club, and had occasionally threatened to rend it asunder; for these Vans of whatever final syllables, have always made a sort of grand fetish of Pedigree, insisting that a man, like a horse, ought always to be blooded.[16]

The Union Club was the first modern social club in New York. As we shall see later it was to start a vogue of similar clubs. The New York Club, similar in purpose to the Union Club, but not as exclusive, was founded in 1845. The Century Club founded in 1847 was composed of artists and amateurs in New York City and vicinity. Its early membership included judges, artists, men of letters and amateurs and commercial men of the pre–Civil War period. As time went on the Century was to include more and more men of business and professional achievement and fewer artists. This development was common to practically all of the artist clubs in New York City. The proportion of amateurs, business and professional, was limited to a minority; but after a time the financial condition of the club forced the artist into the background.

The New York Yacht Club was also organized in pre–Civil War days. In 1844 it was organized for the ostensible purpose of studying naval science. It had not as yet become general for wealthy individuals to own yachts; a few owned smaller craft. By the time of the Civil War the ownership of yachts had become more general and the yacht club had increased considerably in social importance.

The values for which clubs were organized in this era reflect a more serious social standard than was later typical of the New York wealthy circles, although some clubs existed for purely convivial purposes. This development, however, was only in its beginnings. The proliferation of upper class social and sporting clubs and associations had to await the tremendous increase in the number of wealthy families in the latter part of the nineteenth century and their emancipation from restricting religious and moral standards.

Although there were dancing classes and dancing parties in the early decades of the nineteenth century, these were relatively few. The crush of newly arrived elements offended the sensibilities of the older families, and a group of young men-about-town decided to hold an annual Bachelor's Ball to which would be invited only the more refined elements. Sometime in the second decade of the nineteenth century an effort of this kind was defeated by the old ladies and the clergymen. Later this effort was renewed and was successful. One of these exclusive Bachelor's Balls was given in 1831.

> The town was, it appears, filled with Parvenus and pretenders to fashion, low persons who had sprung up within the century, and who persisted in thrusting their unwelcome presence upon the "beau monde," not to mention the Bon Ton, of New York Society, so that finally it had become imperative to set in motion a new movement in fashionable life, and in fact a "reorganization of the old noblesse" no less.[17]

One hundred and fifty young men "representing the choicest and best blood of the city" decided to invite their female acquaintances and the survivors of the older Knickerbocker aristocracy to a ball. The first ball to be given was a spectacular affair,

> an apotheosis of artificial illumination. . . . Wherever one ventures one is met by the glare of a hundred lights, reflected by a thousand crystal pendants. In the ball room, two thousand candles shone in the Duchess of Broadway's gold sprig velvet.[18]

About eight hundred attended this social affair.

Aside from these organized attempts at establishing an exclusive "society" there were a number of individual families that sought social leadership by elaborate parties and affairs.

> They gave tremendous parties in the forties [writes Minnigerode] at which apparently the thing to do was to install a quantity of enormous mirrors, touch off several thousand candles, provide a sufficiency of potted plants, gilded settees, and wines at $10.00 a bottle, cover one's self with pink satin and diamonds, and gyrate with great dignity for several hours in a brilliant pother of grandiloquent banality.[19]

Mrs. Robert Ray's party in 1834 was an outstanding social event. According to Philip Hone:

> The fashionable world rushed with excited expectation to the gay scene and none were disappointed. Mrs. Ray has the finest house in New York, and it is furnished and fitted up in a style of the utmost magnificence—painted ceilings, gilded mouldings, rich satin ottomans, curtains in the last Parisian taste, and splendid mirrors which reflect and multiply all the *rays,* great and small ... unlike other entertainments of the kind, the spirit of jealousy and emulation cannot be excited to an inconvenient degree, for as no person possesses such a house, and very few the means to show it off in the same style, it will not be considered incumbent upon others to attempt to rival this splendid fete, and it will be no disgrace to play second fiddle to such a leader.[20]

The opening of Mrs. Brevort's home occasioned a large party in 1838; and in 1840 she gave her famous "Costume a la Riguer" which was the outstanding event of the period. Everyone was required to come in costume.

> The great affair which has occupied the minds of the people of all stations, ranks and employments, from the fashionable belle who prepared for conquest, to the humble artiste who made honestly a few welcome dollars in providing the weapons; from the liberal-minded gentleman who could discover no crime in an innocent and refined amusement of this kind to the newspaper reformer, striving to sow the seeds of discontentment in an unruly population— this long anticipated affair came off last evening, and I believe the expectations of all were realized.[21]

Hone also remarked upon the Young Men's City Ball of 1841, the Mott Ball of 1841, the Robert Ray Ball of 1842, the Dickens Ball of 1842, the Schermerhorn Costume a la Riguer of 1843, the Ray Ball of 1847, and the Woodbury Langdon affair of 1849. Although there were, no doubt, other large-scale affairs, compared to the later era they were remarkably few, attesting to the slower and more sober tempo of social life in these years.

Other adumbrations of the later society of the "Gilded Age" were increasing European travel which resulted in a refinement of taste and manners and fashions in entertainment. Although the organization of clubs and the increasing tempo of social life were anticipations of the later "Gilded Age" the social life of the time was marked by restraining influences of a religious and moral character and was conditioned by the relatively modest size of fortunes and the continuing influence of the older Knickerbocker stock. The loss of public service as a function of the upper classes, and the great rise of *parvenus* combined on the one hand to threaten the earlier more sober upper class tradition in which conviviality was incidental to more serious concerns, and to encourage on the other hand, once the religious, ethical and traditional barriers were overcome, the development of the naive and extravagant tradition of the latter half of the nineteenth century.

Notes

1. Dixon Wector, *The Saga of American Society* (New York: Scribner's Sons, 1937), p. 52.
2. May King Van Rensselaer, *Goede Vrouw Mana-ha-ta* (New York: Scribner's Sons, 1898), p. 145.
3. Esther Singleton, *Social New York under the Georges* (New York: Appleton Co., 1902), Part VI.
4. James Grant Wilson, *The Memorial History of New York* (New York: New York History Co., 1892), III, 87.
5. Wecter, *op. cit.,* p. 61. See Wecter for evidence of the reaction of a Boston newspaper to New York frivolity.
6. Alexis De Tocqueville, *Democracy in America,* trans. Henry Reeves (New York: A. S. Barnes and Co., 1862), I, 192.
7. J. F. Richmond, *New York and Its Institutions* (New York: E. B. Treat, 1872), chaps. v–x.
8. Abram Dayton, *The Last Lays of Knickerbocker Life in New York* (New York: G. W. Harlan, 1882), p. 6.
9. *Ibid.,* p. 13.
10. *Ibid.,* p. 60.
11. *Ibid.,* p. 78.
12. Meade Minnigerode, *The Fabulous 40's* (New York and London: G. P. Putnam's Sons, 1924), p. 179.
13. Dayton, *op. cit.,* p. 95.
14. *Yearbook of the Union Club: 1853* (New York, 1853).
15. W. Harrison Bayles, "Old Taverns of New York," *Journal of American History,* XXVII (1933), 188 ff.
16. Frances G. Fairfield, *The Clubs of New York, 1873* (New York: H. L. Hinton, 1873), p. 60.
17. Minnigerode, *op. cit.,* p. 250.
18. *Ibid.,* p. 254.
19. *Ibid.,* p. 245.
20. Bayard Tuckerman (ed.), *The Diary of Philip Hone* (New York: Dodd Mead and Co., 1889), I, 29.
21. *Ibid.,* p. 11.

Part Two

Plutocracy and Society Under Democratic Conditions

4

From Direct
to Indirect
Political Control

THE TRIUMPH OF DEMOCRACY in the first half of the nineteenth century was of the utmost importance for the political and social position, and the consequent values and attitudes, of the wealthy classes of the population in New York City as well as elsewhere. From the politically preponderant and secure element of the population it was reduced to a position of formal equality, forced to compete with the poor and the foreign-born in the shaping of public policy. Although considerable elements turned away from politics, for the class as a whole such a complete withdrawal was impossible. Large interests were at stake. On the positive side there were material returns to be gained from the governments; on the negative side it was essential that some control or check be exercised over democratic institutions. Without such control their material interests might have been endangered by the anti-"aristocratic" feelings and movements of the urban lower classes and the small farmers. If exclusive direct control of politics was impossible, there were indirect means of checking democratic "extravagances" and of using democratic institutions profitably. It is this shift from the direct to the indirect means that constitutes the theme of the present chapter.

In this first chapter of Part Two we take up the problem of the further trend in the political participation of the wealthy classes. The questions proposed are: (1) What was the general trend in personal political office-holding from the decade following the Civil War until the present? (2) What differences were there in the office-holding of business and "society" leaders? (3) To what general circumstances may we attribute the withdrawal of the wealthy from political life? (4) What substitutive political controls did the plutocracy develop in a situation of declining direct control?

The conclusions of the present and succeeding chapters are based upon biographical material concerning the officers and executive committees of the New York Chamber of Commerce, the New York Clearing House Association, and the Merchants Association of New York. These are among the most important associations of business leaders. The Chamber of Commerce included in its membership a large proportion of the most influential bankers, industrialists, merchants, and utility owners and controllers in New York City, and hence in the country. The Clearing House Association includes most of the prominent commercial bankers in the city, and the Merchants Association includes in its membership the most influential importers, exporters, and the larger department store owners.

As officers of a selected group of business associations this group of business leaders must be viewed as "weighted" in favor of the more honored and more powerful business leaders. Holding office in the New York Chamber of Commerce is a recognition of great economic power, or of long-standing business reputation, as is the case similarly for officers of the other two associations.

This selection of business leaders, therefore, includes a larger proportion of the more established business men of older families, and to the extent that it discriminates against *parvenus* of equal economic power is unrepresentative of the business leadership as a whole. A selection of business leaders made on the basis of wealth, or number of directorships in corporations of a minimum size would have included a larger element of *parvenus* than the selection used here. The data adduced below, therefore, may be viewed as characteristic of the more established elements of the plutocracy.

In all there were 202 officers of these three associations, 110 of whom held office between the years 1870–1906, and 92 between the years 1931–1935.

Analyses have also been made for these chapters of the officers and governing committees of a number of exclusive men's clubs. Agreement is fairly general that the Union and Knickerbocker clubs are the most exclusive clubs of New York City. The Metropolitan Club, the so-called Millionaire club, has declined considerably in exclusiveness in the last thirty years. It was included primarily for purposes of comparison. Although only three sets of club officers were included in the tabulations, ten groups of club officers were examined before this selection was made. It was found that these three groups of club officers were representative of the officers of the other exclusive clubs. The clubs included in this preliminary analysis were the Meadow Brook Hunt Club, the Racquet and Tennis Club, the Turf and Field Club, the New York Yacht Club, the Tuxedo Club, and the Coaching Club, in addition to the Union, the Knickerbocker, and Metropolitan clubs. A separate examination of the University and Century clubs indicated that these clubs differed from the clubs listed above by admitting individuals more on the basis of "merit," that is, achievement in various fields, than on the basis of birth and "fashion." Thus there were prominent professional men, judges and "statesmen," artists, and philanthropists, regardless of birth, included among the officers of the Century and University clubs.

The selections of "society" leaders included 170 individuals. Of these, 101 were officers of the Union, Knickerbocker, and Metropolitan clubs of the period 1870–1900. Sixty-nine were officers of the Union, Knickerbocker, and Metropolitan clubs of 1930–1935.

For the 1870 period data were available for three groups of officers, those of the Chamber of Commerce, the Union Club, and the Knickerbocker Club (cf. Table 4.1). Five of the Chamber of Commerce officers for this year, or a third of the total number, held political office, as compared with 5, or a little more than a quarter, for the Union Club and 3, or a quarter, for the Knickerbocker Club. The one-third proportion of political office-holders for the Chamber of Commerce officers in 1870 compares with 79 percent for the officers of 1789–1835. Of the three groups of officers in 1870, the Chamber of Commerce officers were more active politically, the average officer having held 1.2 offices as compared with .7 for the Union Club and .3 for the Knickerbocker Club. The business leaders were more active politically than the "society" leaders, a situation in direct contrast to the pre-democratic period, when the educated and more established plutocratic elements were the most active group politically.

The mere tabulation of the number of political office-holders in these groups does not give us an adequate index of the political activity of these elements of the population. Political offices vary greatly in power and in the amount of time required for their performance. In order to get at these differentials the offices were classified in terms of power and time required. The political offices were broken down into (1) policy-making offices, (2) administrative and lesser party offices, (3) honorific administrative offices, (4) honorific and "occasional" offices. This classification is based upon differences in power in terms of proximity to or distance from the centers of formal policy-shaping. Thus the first classification includes elected executive officials, legislators, the judiciary, and the higher party officials. The second includes the appointive administrators and lesser party officials. The third includes administrative officials in agencies, boards, and commissions somewhat more distant, at least theoretically, from the formal centers of policy-shaping, the rewards for which are frequently of a more honorific rather than a power character. This group includes officers in public charitable and cultural institutions and agencies, such as boards of charities and corrections, art commissions, and boards of education. This type of office is also marked by its "occasional" character, thus being compatible with business, cultural, and social activity. The fourth classification—honorific and occasional offices—includes only "occasional" offices carrying very little, if any, power. Included in this group, for example, are the office of commis-

TABLE 4.1   Political Office-Holders Among New York Business and Society
Leaders in 1870*

Degree of Political Activity	New York Chamber of Commerce Officers	Union Club Officers	Knickerbocker Club Officers
Number of officers	20	28	21
Number for whom data were available	15	18	12
Number of political officer-holders	5	5	3
Number of offices held	17	12	4
Average number of offices held	1.2	.7	.3

*Lists of officers were taken from the yearbooks and annual reports of the various associations and clubs. [Where the publisher is not given, it is assumed that it is the organization cited.] New York Chamber of Commerce, *Annual Report, 1870, ibid.*, 1900, *ibid.*, 1935; New York Clearing House Association, *Annual Report, 1894; ibid.*, 1935; New York Merchants Association, *Annual Report, 1906, ibid.*, 1931; Union Club, *Yearbook, 1870, ibid.*, 1900, *ibid.*, 1935; Knickerbocker Club, *Yearbook, 1872, ibid.*, 1932; Metropolitan Club, *Yearbook, 1892, ibid.*, 1935. For biographical data the following sources were used: *Appleton's Cyclopedia of American Biography*, edited by James Grant Wilson and John Fiske (New York: D. Appleton Co., 1888); Moses Yale Beach, *The Wealth and Biography of the Wealthy Citizens of New York* (New York: the *New York Sun*, 1842–1855); *Dictionary of American Biography*, edited by Dumas Malone (New York: Charles Scribner's Sons, 1928); Henry Hall, *America's Successful Men of Affairs* (New York: the *New York Tribune*, 1895–1896); Marguerita Aulina Hamm, *Famous Families of New York* (2 vols.; New York: G. P. Putnam's Sons, 1902); Moses King, *Notable New Yorkers of 1896–1899* (New York: M. King, 1899); *The National Cyclopedia of American Biography* (New York: J. T. White and Co., 1897); Lyman Horace Weeks, *Prominent Families of New York* (New York: The Historical Co., 1897); *Who's Who in America* (Chicago: A. N. Marquis Co., 1899); *Who's Who in Commerce and Industry, 1936* (New York: Institute for Research in Biography, Inc., 1936); *Who's Who in Finance and Banking* (New York: Who's Who in Finance, Inc., 1911); *Who's Who in New York City* (New York: Who's Who Publications, Inc., 1904–1929); *Who's Who in the East* (Washington: Mayflower Publishing Co., 1930).

sioner to foreign expositions, and the office of party convention delegate. The delegate is generally instructed as to his vote in the party primary, or in the event of a deadlock during a convention the general tendency is to follow the lead of the more important "bosses."

Table 4.2 indicates clearly the greater political activity of the Chamber of Commerce officers. One-third of the officers held policy-making offices, and 12 out of 15 offices held by them fell into this policy-making category. Among the Chamber of Commerce officers holding these policy-making offices were the banker and dry goods importer George Opdyke, who served

TABLE 4.2 Types of Political Offices Held by Officers of Selected Business Associations and Selected Social Clubs During the Period 1870–1872*

Types of Offices	Chamber of Commerce Officers	Number of Offices	Union Club Officers	Number of Offices
Policy-making office-holders	5	12	3	5
Administrative and lesser party office-holders	3	3	4	4
Honorific administrative office-holders	—	—	2	3
Honorific and occasional office-holders	2	2	—	—

*Lists of officers were taken from the yearbooks and annual reports of the various associations and clubs. [Where the publisher is not given, it is assumed that it is the organization cited.] New York Chamber of Commerce, *Annual Report, 1870, ibid.,* 1900, *ibid.,* 1935; New York Clearing House Association, *Annual Report, 1894, ibid.,* 1935; New York Merchants Association, *Annual Report, 1906, ibid.,* 1931; Union Club, *Yearbook, 1870, ibid.,* 1900, *ibid.,* 1935; Knickerbocker Club, *Yearbook, 1872, ibid.,* 1932; Metropolitan Club, *Yearbook, 1892, ibid.,* 1935. For biographical data the following sources were used: *Appleton's Cyclopedia of American Biography,* edited by James Grant Wilson and John Fiske (New York: D. Appleton Co., 1888); Moses Yale Beach, *The Wealth and Biography of the Wealthy Citizens of New York* (New York: the *New York Sun,* 1842–1855); *Dictionary of American Biography,* edited by Dumas Malone (New York: Charles Scribner's Sons, 1928); Henry Hall, *America's Successful Men of Affairs* (New York: the *New York Tribune,* 1895–1896); Marguerita Aulina Hamm, *Famous Families of New York* (2 vols.; New York: G. P. Putnam's Sons, 1902); Moses King, *Notable New Yorkers of 1896–1899* (New York: M. King, 1899); *The National Cyclopedia of American Biography* (New York: J. T. White and Co., 1898); Lyman Horace Weeks, *Prominent Families of New York* (New York: The Historical Co., 1897); *Who's Who in America* (Chicago: A. N. Marquis Co., 1899); *Who's Who in Commerce and Industry, 1936* (New York: Institute for Research in Biography, Inc., 1936); *Who's Who in Finance and Banking* (New York: Who's Who in Finance, Inc., 1911); *Who's Who in New York City* (New York: Who's Who Publications, Inc., 1904–1929); *Who's Who in the East* (Washington: Mayflower Publishing Co., 1930).

as member of the New York Assembly in 1850 and as mayor of New York in 1862–1863. Samuel B. Ruggles, a lawyer and a founder of the Bank of Commerce, served as a member of the New York Assembly in 1838. Edwin D. Morgan, a wholesale grocer, banker, and director in many corporations and philanthropic enterprises, served as alderman in New York City in 1849, as state senator in 1850–1853, vice-president of the National Convention of the Republican Party in 1856. He later served as United States senator and governor of New York. Elliot C. Cowdin, a millinery merchant, served as member of the New York Assembly in 1876. William Earl Dodge, inheritor of a large cotton business and a holder of many corporate offices, served as congressman in 1864.

In contrast only 3 out of 28 of the Union Club officers held policy-making offices, and of their total number of offices only 5 out of 12 fell into this policy-making class. The policy-making Union Club office-holders included Moses Grinnell, a congressman; Isaac Bell, a member of the New York Board of Supervisors; August Belmont, Chairman of the Democratic National Committee, and Minister to the Netherlands.

The larger proportion of political offices held by Union Club officers fell into the administrative categories. Thus Philip Schuyler was a Civil War general; Moses Grinnell was a collector of the port of New York; Isaac Bell, Federal Commissioner of Immigration; and William Cutting was a state civil service commissioner. For the honorific administrative offices held by the Union Club officers we find Moses Grinnell serving as commissioner of Charities and Corrections, and Isaac Bell as member of the Board of Education and president of the Board of Charities and Corrections. In terms of their closeness to the actual centers of political policy-shaping, the Chamber of Commerce officers were considerably more active politically than the Union Club officers.

For the period 1890–1910 we note little change in the proportion of business and "society" leaders holding political office (cf. Table 4.3). The proportion of Chamber of Commerce officers holding political office has increased from one-third to two-fifths, and the proportion of Union Club officers has decreased slightly. For the three groups of business association officers a total of slightly more than one-third is to be noted, and for the officers of the Union and Metropolitan clubs a total of one-fifth held political office, pointing again to the fact of the lesser political activity of "society." The computation of the average number of offices held for these two groups again shows the greater political activity of the business associations officers. This group held on the average .6 political offices to an average of .2 for the social club officers.

A breakdown of the office-holding of these two groups according to their policy-making, administrative, or honorific character (cf. Table 4.4) shows a general decrease in the importance of the offices held by these selections of the plutocracy, even though the percentage of individuals holding office has remained roughly the same. In the 1870 period one-third and less than one-fifth of the officers of the Chamber of Commerce and the Union Club respectively held policy-making offices, while in the 1890–1910 period only one-fifth of the business leader group and one-tenth of the social leader group held these types of offices. On the other hand, a little more than one-fifth of the social leader group held administrative, lower party and commission offices, to one-twentieth for the business leader selection. In the last

TABLE 4.3 Political Office-Holders Among Selected Business and Society Leaders in the 1890–1910 Period*

	Officers Chamber of Commerce (1900)	Officers Clearing House Association (1894)	Officers Merchants Association (1906)	Total	Officers Union Club (1900)	Officers Metropolitan Club (1892)	Total
Number for whom data were available	39	16	10	65	19	22	41
Number of political office-holders	16	5	1	22	5	3	8
Number of offices held	35	8	2	45	6	4	10
Average number of offices held	.9	.5	.2	.6	.3	.2	.2

*Lists of officers were taken from the yearbooks and annual reports of the various associations and clubs. [Where the publisher is not given, it is assumed that it is the organization cited.] New York Chamber of Commerce, *Annual Report*, 1870, *ibid.*, 1900, *ibid.*, 1935; New York Clearing House Association, *Annual Report*, 1894, *ibid.*, 1935; New York Merchants Association, *Annual Report*, 1906, *ibid.*, 1931; Union Club, *Yearbook*, 1870, 1900, *ibid.*, 1935; Knickerbocker Club, *Yearbook*, 1872, *ibid.*, 1932; Metropolitan Club, *Yearbook*, 1892, *ibid.*, 1935. For biographical data the following sources were used: *Appleton's Cyclopedia of American Biography*, edited by James Grant Wilson and John Fiske (New York: D. Appleton Co., 1888); Moses Yale Beach, *The Wealth and Biography of the Wealthy Citizens of New York* (New York: the *New York Sun*, 1842–1855); *Dictionary of American Biography*, edited by Dumas Malone (New York: Charles Scribner's Sons, 1928); Henry Hall, *America's Successful Men of Affairs* (New York: the *New York Tribune*, 1895–1896); Marguerita Aulina Hamm, *Famous Families of New York* (2 vols.; New York: G. P. Putnam's Sons, 1902); Moses King, *Notable New Yorkers of 1896–1899* (New York: M. King, 1899); *The National Cyclopedia of American Biography* (New York: J. T. White and Co., 1898); *Who's Who in America* (Chicago: A. N. Marquis Co., 1899); *Who's Who in New York* (New York: The Historical Co., 1897); Lyman Horace Weeks, *Prominent Families of New York* (New York: Institute for Research in Biography, Inc., 1936); *Who's Who in Finance and Banking* (New York: Who's Who in Finance, Inc., 1911); *Who's Who in New York City* (New York: Who's Who Publications, Inc., 1904–1929); *Who's Who in the East* (Washington: Mayflower Publishing Co., 1930).

TABLE 4.4   Types of Political Offices Held by Officers of Selected Business Associations and Selected Social Clubs During the Period 1890–1910*

Types of Offices	Business Association Officers	Number of Offices Held	Social Club Officers	Number of Offices Held
Major policy-making office-holders	13	23	4	6
Administrative or commission office-holders	4	9	5	5
Honorific administrative office-holders	9	12	1	1
Honorific and occasional office-holders	2	3	—	—

*Lists of officers were taken from the yearbooks and annual reports of the various associations and clubs. [Where the publisher is not given, it is assumed that it is the organization cited.] New York Chamber of Commerce, *Annual Report, 1870, ibid.,* 1900, *ibid.,* 1935; New York Clearing House Association, *Annual Report, 1894, ibid.,* 1935; New York Merchants Association, *Annual Report, 1906, ibid.,* 1931; Union Club, *Yearbook, 1870, ibid.,* 1900, *ibid.,* 1935; Knickerbocker Club, *Yearbook, 1872, ibid.,* 1932; Metropolitan Club, *Yearbook, 1892, ibid.,* 1935. For biographical data the following sources were used: *Appleton's Cyclopedia of American Biography,* edited by James Grant Wilson and John Fiske (New York: D. Appleton Co., 1888); Moses Yale Beach, *The Wealth and Biography of the Wealthy Citizens of New York* (New York: the *New York Sun,* 1842–1855); *Dictionary of American Biography,* edited by Dumas Malone (New York: C. Scribner's Sons, 1928); Henry Hall, *America's Successful Men of Affairs* (New York: the *New York Tribune,* 1895–1896); Marguerita Aulina Hamm, *Famous Families of New York* (2 vols.; New York: G. P. Putnam's Sons, 1902); Moses King, *Notable New Yorkers of 1896–1899* (New York: M. King, 1899); *The National Cyclopedia of American Biography* (New York: J. T. White and Co., 1898); Lyman Horace Weeks, *Prominent Families of New York* (New York: The Historical Co., 1897); *Who's Who in America* (Chicago: A. N. Marquis Co., 1899); *Who's Who in Commerce and Industry, 1936* (New York: Institute for Research in Biography, Inc., 1936); *Who's Who in Finance and Banking* (New York: Who's Who in Finance, Inc., 1911); *Who's Who in New York City* (New York: Who's Who Publications, Inc., 1904–1929); *Who's Who in the East* (Washington: Mayflower Publishing Co., 1930).

two classifications of offices—honorific administrative and honorific offices—the business leadership selection was more active.

The political office-holding of these groups of the plutocracy in the 1930–1936 period (cf. Table 4.5) shows little change in the number of office-holders. In the 1890–1910 period one-third of the business leader group held political offices as compared with approximately the same proportion in the

TABLE 4.5 Political Office-Holders Among Business and Society Leaders in the 1930–1936 Period*

	Officers of New York				Officers of			
	Chamber of Commerce (1935)	Clearing House Association (1935)	Merchants Association (1931)	Total	Union Club (1935)	Knickerbocker Club (1932)	Metropolitan Club (1935)	Total
Number for whom data were available	27	19	20	66	22	17	19	58
Number of political office-holders	12	3	6	21	3	—	10	13
Number of offices held	13	4	17	34	4	—	22	26
Average number of offices held	.5	.2	.9	.6	.2	—	1.2	.4

*Lists of officers were taken from the yearbooks and annual reports of the various associations and clubs. [Where the publisher is not given, it is assumed that it is the organization cited.] New York Chamber of Commerce, *Annual Report, 1870, ibid., 1900, ibid.,* 1935; New York Clearing House Association, *Annual Report, 1894, ibid.,* 1935; New York Merchants Association, *Annual Report, 1906, ibid.,* 1931; Union Club, *Yearbook, 1870, ibid., 1900, ibid.,* 1935; Knickerbocker Club, *Yearbook, 1872, ibid., 1932;* Metropolitan Club, *Yearbook, 1892, ibid.,* 1935. For biographical data the following sources were used: *Appleton's Cyclopedia of American Biography,* edited by James Grant Wilson and John Fiske (New York: D. Appleton Co., 1888); Moses Yale Beach, *The Wealth and Biography of the Wealthy Citizens of New York* (New York: the *New York Sun,* 1842–1855); *Dictionary of American Biography,* edited by Dumas Malone (New York: Charles Scribner's Sons, 1928); Henry Hall, *America's Successful Men of Affairs* (New York: the *New York Tribune,* 1895–1896); Marguerita Aulina Hamm, *Famous Families of New York* (2 vols.; New York: G. P. Putnam's Sons, 1902); Moses King, *Notable New Yorkers of 1896–1899* (New York: M. King, 1899); *The National Cyclopedia of American Biography* (New York: J. T. White and Co., 1898); Lyman Horace Weeks, *Prominent Families of New York* (New York: The Historical Co., 1897); *Who's Who in America* (Chicago: A. N. Marquis Co., 1899); *Who's Who in Commerce and Industry, 1936* (New York: Institute for Research in Biography, Inc., 1936); *Who's Who in Finance and Banking* (New York: Who's Who in Finance, Inc., 1911); *Who's Who in New York City* (New York: Who's Who Publications, Inc., 1904–1929); *Who's Who in the East* (Washington: Mayflower Publishing Co., 1930).

1930–1936 period. In 1890–1910 one-fifth of the social club officers held political office, as compared with a slightly larger proportion in 1930–1936. The average number of offices held has remained at .6 for the officers of business associations and has increased to .4 for the social leader group.

As a glance at the table indicates, the relatively high degree of political participation for the officers of exclusive social clubs is almost entirely attributable to the officers of the Metropolitan Club who show an extremely large measure of political activity. Fifty-three percent of their officers held political office, and on the average they held 1.2 offices. This comparatively great political activity for the Metropolitan Club officers is to be accounted for by the fact that it was a considerably less exclusive club than either of the others, tending to admit almost entirely on the basis of wealth.

A comparison of the offices held by these two groups according to their policy-making, administrative, or honorific character for the periods 1870, 1890–1910, and 1930–1936 points to a continued decrease in the proportion of policy-making office-holders among these groups of the plutocracy.

The proportion of business leader policy-making office holders has decreased from one-fifth in 1890–1910 to a little more than a tenth in 1931–1935; that of social leaders from one-tenth to slightly less (cf. Table 4.6). On the other hand, the proportion of administrative, party and commission office-holders has increased from a little more than one-twentieth to one-quarter in 1931–1935. For society leaders there has been an increase in this category of office-holding from a little more than one-tenth in the earlier period to a little less than one-fifth in the later period. There have also been slight decreases for both groups in the proportion of individuals holding honorific administrative and purely honorific offices.

Although the general proportion of individuals holding political office has remained roughly constant since 1870, the proportions holding various types of offices have fluctuated considerably. The most important development has been the general decrease in the proportion of wealthy and socially esteemed individuals holding policy-making offices. The percentage of those elements holding administrative, lower party, and commission offices shows a decrease from 1870 to 1890–1910 and an increase over the period 1890–1910 to 1930–1936. This increase in the number of individuals holding this type of office is almost entirely due to the World War and the depression of 1929–1932, when many wealthy business men were called to administrative commissions and boards. If we were to exclude these war and depression emergency office-holders, the percentage in this category in the 1930–1936 period would drop to a little more than one-tenth, making only a very slight increase in the number of this type of office-holder among the wealthy and esteemed elements.

The general conclusions which may be drawn from these data on office-holding are: (1) there has been a continued decrease since the Civil War in

TABLE 4.6 Types of Political Offices Held by Officers of Selected Business Associations and Selected Social Clubs During the Period 1931–1935*

Type of Offices	Business Association Officers	Number of Offices Held	Social Club Officers	Number of Offices Held
Policy-making office-holders	8	13	4	8
Administrative, party or commission office-holders	16	21	10	10
Honorific administrative office-holders	4	4	2	3
Honorific and occasional office-holders	1	1	2	2

*Lists of officers were taken from the yearbooks and annual reports of the various associations and clubs. [Where the publisher is not given, it is assumed that it is the organization cited.] New York Chamber of Commerce, *Annual Report, 1870, ibid.,* 1900, *ibid.,* 1935; New York Clearing House Association, *Annual Report, 1894, ibid.,* 1935; New York Merchants Association, *Annual Report, 1906, ibid.,* 1931; Union Club, *Yearbook, 1870, ibid.,* 1900, *ibid.,* 1935; Knickerbocker Club, *Yearbook, 1872, ibid.,* 1932; Metropolitan Club, *Yearbook, 1892, ibid.,* 1935. For biographical data the following sources were used: *Appleton's Cyclopedia of American Biography,* edited by James Grant Wilson and John Fiske (New York: D. Appleton Co., 1888); Moses Yale Beach, *The Wealth and Biography of the Wealthy Citizens of New York* (New York: the *New York Sun,* 1842–1855); *Dictionary of American Biography,* edited by Dumas Malone (New York: Charles Scribner's Sons, 1928); Henry Hall, *America's Successful Men of Affairs* (New York: the *New York Tribune,* 1895–1896); Marguerita Aulina Hamm, *Famous Families of New York* (2 vols.; New York: G. P. Putnam's Sons, 1902); Moses King, *Notable New Yorkers of 1896–1899* (New York: M. King, 1899); *The National Cyclopedia of American Biography* (New York: J. T. White and Co., 1898); Lyman Horace Weeks, *Prominent Families of New York* (New York: The Historical Co., 1897); *Who's Who in America* (Chicago: A. N. Marquis Co., 1899); *Who's Who in Commerce and Industry, 1936* (New York: Institute for Research in Biography, Inc., 1936); *Who's Who in Finance and Banking* (New York: Who's Who in Finance, Inc., 1911); *Who's Who in New York City* (New York: Who's Who Publications, Inc., 1904–1929); *Who's Who in the East* (Washington: Mayflower Publishing Co., 1930).

the proportion of policy-making office-holders among the plutocracy; (2) the more esteemed elements of the plutocracy, that group called "society," has been specially marked by inactivity in politics. In other words, in the post-democratic period the relation of the more and less esteemed levels of the plutocracy to formal political power has been entirely reversed. The specially esteemed levels of the wealthy classes have been less active in politics than those marked primarily by positions of honor and power in the economic sphere.

Why the Wealthy Withdrew from Politics

In interpreting this lack of political participation of the "better" elements of the community Lord Bryce referred to seven factors. He referred to the fact that Washington was not the social and commercial capital of the country. The wealthier and more cultivated elements of the American population, especially those of New York City, were not disposed to give up their social and cultural life for life in Washington. Second, he refers to the fact that there are scarcely any traditional political families in America. This, however, is an effect of the lack of political participation of the wealthy classes and not a cause. Third, he lists the instability of political life in America, which renders it less tempting to individuals who have some substantial place in the community. Fourth, he considers that politics are less interesting than in Europe. There were at the time of Bryce's writing no great questions of foreign policy or domestic constitutional change which would have tempted the wealthier classes to take a more personal share in the shaping of these policies. In other words, with a few exceptions there have been proportionately fewer great political problems in America, problems involving great shifts in the relative powers of classes within a nation, or a nation among nations, than in Europe. As an example he refers to the rise of the masses in European countries which, threatening the position of the wealthier classes, has given them "a strong motive for keeping tight hold of the helm of state."[1] In Bryce's time the class issue in America had not as yet risen in its present urgency, although he predicted it. A fifth cause given by Bryce is the tremendous opportunities and rewards open in other spheres of life. Thus business tends to attract talent that might otherwise have gone into politics. Bryce gives as a sixth cause the lower class origin of the politician, which eliminated the incentive of social ambition so marked in English politics. A seventh reason is the vulgarity of politics and the "exposure to invectiveness and ribaldry by hostile speakers, and a reckless press."[2]

Although Bryce lists the main deterrents, from a more systematic point of view the withdrawal of the wealthy classes from politics may be interpreted as (1) attributable to the objective difficulty of political struggle in American democracy, (2) attributable to the absence of adequate incentives.

To take up the problem of the objective difficulties first, it may be noted that under democratic conditions engaging in politics involved the devotion of considerable amounts of time to political manipulation and activity. A second objective deterrent lay in the types of contacts necessary for political success. A third objective difficulty lay in the types of skills necessary for political success, which the wealthy did not generally develop. A fourth difficulty was a fairly widespread attitude of hostility to wealth, which would have made their political participation on a great scale impossible. The amount of time necessary, the nature of the contacts in politics, the skills required of politicians, and anti-plutocratic attitudes were objective characteristics of American democracy which tended to make extremely difficult the political participation of the wealthy classes.

From the subjective point of view, that is, from the point of view of the incentives of the wealthy for engaging in political activity, we may classify these as (1) the incentive of self- or class-protection, and (2) desire for greater power and prestige. Even though the conditions of political participation had become extremely difficult, had the wealthier classes been seriously endangered, or had there been adequate incentives of power and prestige, they would have made serious efforts to exercise a more personal control over politics. First, as to danger, we have already pointed out that democratic government in America has not enjoyed important controls over economic life. Thus the wealthier classes were not forced to engage in politics on a great scale to defend their privileges. Again, there has not been in the past a great and continuous international threat, a situation which would have forced increased political action upon the wealthy classes.

In the absence of continuous danger of these types, another motivation for engaging in politics on the part of the plutocracy would have been that of acquiring added prestige or power or both. But the great size of the United States and its tremendous natural resources made business the activity yielding the greatest rewards. More power and prestige was to be won in economic life than in politics. A democratic situation made political life unstable, required wide and undiscriminating contacts, resulted in widespread publicity and inquiry into the personal life of candidates and officeholders. Individuals with a great and relatively stable position in the community, enjoying great power and prestige by virtue of their private powers and activities, had little incentive to endanger their stability and security in political life.

Indirect Political Controls

The shift from a limited franchise to political democracy had, as we have seen, the consequence of decreasing the personal political participation of the wealthy classes. Insofar as their relations to politics have been concerned, the shift from the early form of political domination to mass democracy had meant a shift from a situation in which the wealthy enjoyed a practically exclusive and personal control over politics to a situation in which the political participation of the wealthy classes took mainly an indirect form.

What general framework of interpretation can be laid down in which the nature of upper class political participation under democracy may be understood? We may first ask the question: What special motivating factors lie behind the political activities of the wealthy classes and condition their nature? The general answer to this question is that since the wealthy classes have a greater material stake in the established order, they have a greater interest in maintaining those conditions which make possible the continuance or increase of their privileges. The greater stake must be defended by greater political power. In other words, the plutocracy strives to achieve in political life, through indirect means, a power proportionate to their power in economic, cultural, and social life.

The need for political control on the part of the wealthy classes may be understood in terms of the powers of government over economic life. Although liberal democratic government rests in part upon the theory that the function of government is merely that of maintaining order, this function, as well as additional functions assumed by government, has an important bearing and influence upon economic life. Even the "liberal police" government has an important regulatory function in economic life in the administration of commercial law, the control and regulation of the monetary system, and the controls over commerce. From the common law the American government has acquired the power of regulating certain types of enterprise defined as having a public interest. And in America a great additional economic power of government has been the ownership of the public domain. The government thus touched the economic activities and ambitions of its citizens at many critical points.

The tremendous growth of the American population and the American economy rendered those spheres of the economy controlled by government of the greatest value. The rising plutocracy in America had at many points to turn to the government to have courts rule between litigants; to gain privileges in the form of franchises, leases, and contracts of various kinds; to gain tracts of land, and other favors; and to prevent the passage of legislation interfering with its interests.

The development on the part of the plutocracy of indirect types of control over politics was the natural consequence of the loss of personal political control. If the plutocracy were not to be personally represented in the seats of political power, it was essential for its security that it have in a measure beyond its numerical proportion influence in the choice of office-holders and in the shaping of policy, and general controls over democracy. They could not be passive in a situation of democracy, since popular movements designed to ameliorate conditions for the lower classes, unless checked, threatened their power. Therefore they sought by various means to develop instruments of control capable of keeping within bounds popular movements which directly or indirectly attacked them. We may classify these instruments and techniques of control according to the immediacy of their impact upon the political process. Two sets of control are thus to be distinguished, first those directed toward the control of party and governmental agencies, and second, those activities of less immediate effect upon formal politics, but tending to produce an attitude of acquiescence on the part of the general population. In the first type of political instruments and controls are (1) plutocratic political clubs, (2) general pressure groups, (3) vigilantist pressure groups, (4) special political agents and plutocratic politicians, (5) financial support to favorable political groups and machines, and (6) propaganda control.

A type of political institution which arose in the democratic period to give the wealthier classes contact with politics and politicians was the special upper class political club. Political clubs such as the Union League, the Manhattan (Democratic), the National Democratic, and National Republican clubs were convenient and necessary points of contact between the upper levels of politicians and the politically interested industrialists, merchants, and financiers. These upper class political clubs were among the important points at which upper class pressure for legislative issues and the selection of candidates was exercised. These clubs served the politician by giving him access to "money bags" for the financing of his "machine."

An analysis of the political club memberships of the business and social leader groups discussed in Chapter 4 shows a high proportion of membership for both groups in the 1890–1910 period, the business leader group having the higher proportion of memberships. The Republican Union League Club had the largest representation of business and social leaders, while the Democratic Manhattan Club had approximately only a fourth as many members. Twenty-four percent of the business leader group belonged to the City Club, and 20 percent to the Reform Club, showing a fairly high degree of interest in political reform on the part of these classes in this period (cf. Table 4.7). With the exception of the Manhattan and Democratic clubs the business leader groups show a higher membership in the political clubs listed here. The proportion of Democrats in the exclusive social groups seems to have been higher than that in the business leader group.

Political club memberships for these groups in the 1930–1936 period show a decrease which is especially marked for the society leaders. These latter have only a 2 percent membership in the Union League Club. The percentage of members of the Union League Club for the business leader groups has decreased only slightly, while there has been a great decrease in the Democratic Club memberships. The tabulations in Table 4.7 and Table 4.8 reflect a decreasing political activity for exclusive social groups and a general decrease for both groups in Democratic Club memberships. The Republican Party, particularly in contemporary years, has become the party par excellence of the wealthier classes.

74

TABLE 4.7 Percent Political Club Memberships of Officers of Business Associations and Social Clubs in Selected Years of the Period 1890–1910*

Political Clubs	New York Chamber of Commerce (1901)	New York Clearing House (1894)	Merchants Association (1906)	Total	Union Club (1900)	Metropolitan Club (1892)	Total
Number for whom data are available	39	16	10	65	19	22	41
Union League Club	44	63	20	45	16	27	22
National Republican Club	15	19	10	15	—	—	—
Manhattan Club	21	—	—	12	21	27	24
National Democratic Club	3	—	—	2	16	—	7
Reform Club	26	—	40	22	16	—	7
City Club	36	6	10	25	42	—	20

*Lists of officers were taken from the yearbooks and annual reports of the various associations and clubs. [Where the publisher is not given, it is assumed that it is the organization cited.] New York Chamber of Commerce, *Annual Report, 1870, ibid., 1900, ibid., 1935;* New York Clearing House Association, *Annual Report, 1894, ibid., 1935;* New York Merchants Association, *Annual Report, 1906, ibid., 1931;* Union Club, *Yearbook, 1870, ibid., 1900, ibid., 1935;* Knickerbocker Club, *Yearbook, 1872, ibid., 1932;* Metropolitan Club, *Yearbook, 1892, ibid., 1935.* For biographical data the following sources were used: *Appleton's Cyclopedia of American Biography,* edited by James Grant Wilson and John Fiske (New York: D. Appleton Co., 1888); Moses Yale Beach, *The Wealth and Biography of the Wealthy Citizens of New York* (New York: the *New York Sun,* 1842–1844); *Dictionary of American Biography,* edited by Dumas Malone (New York: Charles Scribner's Sons, 1928); Henry Hall, *America's Successful Men of Affairs* (New York: the *New York Tribune,* 1895–1896); Marguerita Aulina Hamm, *Famous Families of New York* (2 vols.; New York: G. P. Putnam's Sons, 1902); Moses King, *Notable New Yorkers of 1896–1899* (New York: M. King, 1899); *The National Cyclopedia of American Biography* (New York: J. T. White and Co., 1906); Lyman Horace Weeks, *Prominent Families of New York* (New York: The Historical Co., 1897); *Who's Who in America* (Chicago: A. N. Marquis Co., 1899); *Who's Who in Commerce and Industry, 1936* (New York: Institute for Research in Biography, Inc., 1936); *Who's Who in Finance and Banking* (New York: Who's Who in Finance, Inc., 1911); *Who's Who in New York City* (New York: Who's Who Publications, Inc., 1904–1929); *Who's Who in the East* (Washington: Mayflower Publishing Co., 1930).

TABLE 4.8 Political Club Memberships of Officers of Selected Business Associations and Social Clubs in Selected Years, 1930–1936*

Political Clubs	New York Chamber of Commerce (1935) Percent	New York Clearing House (1935) Percent	Merchants Association Percent	Total Percent	Union Club (1935) Percent	Knickerbocker Club (1932) Percent	Metropolitan Club (1935) Percent	Total Percent
Number for whom data were available	27	19	20	66	22	17	19	58
Union League	44	58	25	44	5	—	5	2
National Republican	15	—	10	9	—	—	—	—
Manhattan	11	—	10	8	—	—	—	—
National Democratic	—	—	—	—	—	—	—	—
Reform Club	4	—	15	6	—	—	—	—
City Club	18	5	5	11	—	—	—	—

*Lists of officers were taken from the yearbooks and annual reports of the various associations and clubs. [Where the publisher is not given, it is assumed that it is the organization cited.] New York: Chamber of Commerce, *Annual Report, 1870, ibid., 1900, ibid., 1935*; New York Clearing House Association, *Annual Report, 1894, ibid., 1935*; New York Merchants Association, *Annual Report, 1906, ibid., 1931*; Union Club, *Yearbook, 1870, ibid., 1900, ibid., 1935*; Knickerbocker Club, *Yearbook, 1872, ibid., 1932*; Metropolitan Club, *Yearbook, 1892, ibid., 1935*. For biographical data the following sources were used: *Appleton's Cyclopedia of American Biography*, edited by James Grant Wilson and John Fiske (New York: D. Appleton Co., 1888); Moses Yale Beach, *The Wealth and Biography of the Wealthy Citizens of New York* (New York: the *New York Sun*, 1842–1855); *Dictionary of American Biography*, edited by Dumas Malone (New York: Charles Scribner's Sons, 1928); Henry Hall, *America's Successful Men of Affairs* (New York: the *New York Tribune*, 1895–1896); Marguerita Aulina Hamm, *Famous Families of New York* (2 vols.; New York: G. P. Putnam's Sons, 1902); Moses King, *Notable New Yorkers of 1896–1899* (New York: M. King, 1899); *The National Cyclopedia of American Biography* (New York: J. T. White and Co., 1898); Lyman Horace Weeks, *Prominent Families of New York* (New York: The Historical Co., 1897); *Who's Who in America* (Chicago: A. N. Marquis Co., 1899); *Who's Who in Commerce and Industry, 1936* (New York: Institute for Research in Biography, Inc., 1936); *Who's Who in Finance and Banking* (New York: Who's Who in Finance, Inc., 1911); *Who's Who in New York City* (New York: Who's Who Publications, Inc., 1904–1929); *Who's Who in the East* (Washington: Mayflower Publishing Co., 1930).

Pressure Groups

By pressure groups we understand associations the objective of which is to formulate and represent the demands of groups or classes in the population before public opinion and public agencies. The special type of pressure groups of relevance here are those expressing the demands of the bigger industrial, financial, or commercial groups, such as the Iron and Steel Institute, or those expressing the demands of the wealthier groups as a whole, such as the United States Chamber of Commerce.

In addition to these permanent national bodies many state and local pressure groups have arisen to defend the interests of the wealthier classes before special bodies of public opinion and special governmental agencies. Among these are the state and local chambers of commerce, merchants associations, real estate boards, and other bodies similarly representing propertied interests. The various pressure groups for special industries and groups of industries and other types of economic enterprises in normal times are far indeed from pursuing a common policy. Special economic interests are frequently in conflict and attempt to mobilize public opinion and influence legislative and administrative policy for and against various industrial groups. Times of economic crisis and increased lower class pressure are marked by a tendency toward the unification of the wealthy classes, the diversion of competing industrial groups from their normal conflict to a common front to defend the "property order." We may term these pressure groups "vigilantist" pressure groups, since they play the role of raising the hue and cry against the attackers of the established order, who are identified in this vigilantistic propaganda as the enemies of America.

The development of formal vigilantist pressure groups has been most marked since the turn of the century. Following upon the crisis of 1884 there was, for example, a considerable increase in propaganda and organization challenging the wealthy classes. In New York City this development culminated in the campaign of the "single taxer" Henry George. No *ad hoc* organization was formed to meet this crisis, but the speeches of Abram Hewitt strike a familiar ring to readers of contemporary anti–New Deal propaganda. Crises since the turn of the century, however, have been of increasing seriousness and were marked by resort on the part of the plutocracy to these special defensive organizations.

Wealthy Political Manipulators

The controls of the plutocracy over politics are naturally all related to their financial power and derivative social prestige. To the political entrepreneur politics constitutes a means of self-aggrandizement. His success is dependent upon the goodwill of the political and financial powers of the area within which he seeks political prominence. Without the aid of these powers he is helpless, lacking in access to public opinion and lacking in the sinews of war—campaign funds.

In this indirect relationship between politics and wealth a type of plutocratic political agent has arisen—a semi-financial, semi-political manipulator. Sometimes these political types have been corporation lawyers, at other times large newspaper publishers, and at others purely financial manipulators. Some have themselves gone into politics; other have remained outside, content to manipulate, but unwilling to take a public office. Among these prominent upper class or closely allied political manipulators from New York City have been Chauncey Depew, Elihu Root, William Collins Whitney, August Belmont, Thomas Fortune Ryan, Frank Munsey, Thomas W. Lamont, Ogden Mills, and a large number of others. Their functions have been the gathering of campaign funds, the mobilization of opinion in wealthy circles and of the population generally through newspapers, magazines, through the building up of candidacies behind the scenes, and party manipulation.

Financial Contributions and Propaganda Control

Among the most important sources of income for the financing of primary and election campaigns are the large contributions of men of wealth. As the size of campaign funds increased in the 1880s and afterwards, the parties turned more and more to interested business men and corporations who, by virtue of their interests in legislation, were found to be specially amenable to *quid pro quo* arrangements with the party bosses. Pollock speaks of the practice of "levying assessments" upon business interests developed by Mark Hanna.[3] Tremendous sums of money were forthcoming from these sources. And the motives for these contributions were by no means disinterested. In many cases, especially for the earlier period, the contributions of wealthy men were given in return for coveted offices such as ambassadorships, or in return for political protection.[4]

Although Pollock maintains that the federal law of 1907, forbidding the contribution of corporations to political party funds, "forced" the parties "to turn to other sources of revenue,"[5] other sources seem to indicate that large contributions from private (not formally corporate) origins continued to play a significant role in the financing of campaigns. Thus, according to Overacker, in 1904 a little over 73 percent of the Republican National Committee fund was contributed in sums of $5,000 or over. Thirty-eight and eight-tenths percent of the total came in sums of $50,000 or over. In 1908, after the passage of the law forbidding corporate contributions, amounts of $5,000 and over accounted for 31 percent of the total. In 1912 they accounted for 44.8 percent, and in 1916 for 41.4 percent. In 1920 the

Republican Party resolved to accept only contributions of $1,000 or less. There are records of violation of this pledge, however.[6] In 1924 the proportion of the total Republican campaign fund made up of contributions of $5,000 or over accounted for 25.2 percent of the total, and in 1928 this again increased to 45.8 percent. For the Democratic campaign funds contributions of this size have been of less importance, with the exception of 1924 and 1928, when they accounted for 45.2 percent and 52.7 percent of the total. It is apparent, therefore, that the wealthier classes even after the passage of the 1907 legislation continued to furnish a considerable proportion of the party campaign funds.

Even more impressive are Overacker's figures for the proportion of national campaign funds coming in contributions of between $100 and $4,999. Contributions of this size may be assumed to come also from the upper middle classes. Thus at no time since 1908 have contributions of this size accounted for less than 60 percent of the total campaign fund. In 1928 contributions of this size made up 86 percent of the Democratic and 90.3 percent of the Republican Party funds.

The role played by the New York wealthy classes in the financing of national campaigns was of the greatest importance. Pollock refers to the great contributions made by Cleveland Dodge, Bernard Baruch, and James W. Gerard to the Democratic Party, and the contributions of the Rockefellers, Henry Clay Frick, Payne Whitney, Clarence Mackay, T. Coleman Du Pont, and J. P. Morgan to the Republican Party.[7] To these names Overacker adds large Republican contributors such as Chauncey Depew, George J. Gould, E. H. Harriman, C. S. Mellen, Frank A. Munsey, Douglas and W. C. Roosevelt, and H. H. Rogers; and Democratic contributors such as August Belmont, Thomas Fortune Ryan, Thomas I. Chadbourne, William F. Kenney, Norman H. Davis, Herbert H. Lehman, Joseph M. Hatfield, and Ralph Pulitzer.[8]

Contributions to election funds both national, state, and local are not the only financial aid the wealthier classes give to the political parties. In the primary campaigns for the various elections money plays a great role, and although there are exceptions, an ambitious politician without adequate contacts with a machine which supplies the contacts for him or direct contacts with the financial world, without an "angel" or "choir of angels" in other words, finds almost insuperable obstacles in the way of his candidacy and election.

There is naturally a direct relationship between the degree to which the position of the wealthy classes is threatened and the volume of campaign contributions coming from wealthy sources. Thus, in the campaign of 1896 $16 million is said to have been contributed to the war chest of the Republican Party in order to defeat Bryan.[9] Cornelius Bliss, Republican Treasurer, is quoted as having said that every bank and trust company but one and many of the insurance companies in New York City contributed to the fund.[10] Again in 1936 the Republican campaign fund amounted to almost $9 million.[11] New Yorkers contributed heavily to this total.[12]

The figures for campaign expenditures for the 1936 presidential campaign are of special interest, since the New Deal had been fairly clearly defined by the wealthier classes during that campaign as a serious threat to their position. Overacker found that both campaign funds, but especially the Republican, had increased greatly over the 1932 period, reflecting the intensified struggle between the conservative classes and the supporters of the New Deal. The Republican campaign expenditures amounted to a little less than $9 million; those of the Democratic party amounted to a little more than $5 million. The Republican National Committee drew more of its support from large contributors than the Democratic Committee.[13] Thirty percent of the contributors of $5,000 or over to the Republican fund were New Yorkers. Among these New York contributors were George F. Baker, W. Nelson Cromwell, Robert W. Goelet, Frederick A. Juilliard, Ogden Mills, J. P. Morgan, six members of the Rockefeller family, Mr. and Mrs. Alfred P. Sloan, Jr., Felix Warburg, and others.

The reaction of the wealthy classes to the Roosevelt threat was reflected in the shift of normally democratic wealthy supporters to the Republican camp. A few of the New Yorkers who shifted their support were Edward S. Harkness, William K. Vanderbilt, and Gertrude Vanderbilt Whitney.[14] At the same time only one-third of the large contributors to the Democratic campaign fund in 1932 were to be found among the 1936 contributors.[15]

The liberal and progressive program of Roosevelt thus resulted in (1) the greatly increased volume of the Republican campaign expenditures, (2) the desertion of the Democratic Party by two-thirds of its wealthy supporters, and the slight repairing of this loss by the help of labor organizations, and (3) the secession of a number of formerly democratic supporters to the Republican camp.

The propaganda instruments of the plutocracy are newspapers and magazines, advertising, and specialized public relations counsellors, and consultants. As the most influential wealthy group of the nation it may naturally be assumed that the New York plutocracy is powerful in newspaper and magazine ownership, in advertising pressure, and in the power to hire the talents of specialists in the manipulation of public opinion.[16] The owners of the larger newspapers and magazines are themselves large entrepreneurs and may be assumed in most cases to be identified with the interests of and to propagandize for the maintenance of a situation safe for the wealthy elements.

Formally Non-Political Activities Having Political Consequences

In addition to the agencies and forms of control deliberately intended to influence political policy there are types of activity the objectives of which are overtly non-political, but the effects of which are political in the sense of serving to defend and justify the superior advantages of the plutocracy. Among these activities and controls are (1) affiliation with patriotic and ancestral groups, (2) recreational and social activities, (3) cultural activity, (4) controls over institutions of higher education, and (5) controls over private charitable institutions.

Some of the ancestral associations, such as the Daughters of the American Revolution and the Society of the War of 1812, act openly as propagandist and pressure agencies in opposition to progressive and radical policies and groups. Although all of these ancestral associations do not engage in widespread propaganda and pressure designed to maintain the established order, they may be viewed as agencies whose net effect is to supply subjective legitimation or justification of the position of their members. These ancestral associations commemorate the long identification of the older and wealthier families with American history, some even perpetuating the identification of elements of the plutocracy with the feudal era. By means of these associations the social and political attitudes of their membership are fortified by a superior sense of belonging to American history and institutions. Their attitudes become the legitimate American attitudes, and the attitudes of the newer elements of the population un-American and unpatriotic. These ancestral associations are not so much important as pressure and propaganda agencies for the general population, but as internal psychological props and cohesive influences supporting the political position of the plutocracy.

The ancestral associations are but one of the many social psychological influences which support the morale of the plutocracy in the struggle to maintain their superior advantages. Among the other supporting influences are their identification with social refinement and cultural activity. The wealthier classes follow a more elaborate routine of living than the rest of the population and have developed, at least in the more established portion, more elaborate standards of conduct. These elaborate rituals, applicable, of course, primarily between the members of the plutocracy, function as means of distancing the plutocracy from the rest of the population and justify the treatment of the rest of the population as on a lower level of human sophistication and development. These rituals of conduct also serve to dull the consciences of the plutocracy to injustice and oppression in the world outside, for they not only view their group as of superior birth and refinement, but the rituals of gift-giving and general refinement narcotize them from too uncomfortable a realization of the needs and plight of other elements. The elaborate private life of the plutocracy serves in considerable measure to separate them out in their own consciousness as a superior, more refined element. On the other hand, the superior refinement and way of life of the plutocracy has a certain legitimating effect upon considerable elements in the general population. The lower classes, following the doings of the plutocracy in the society pages, in many cases view the rituals and conduct of the upper classes with awe. The imagined brilliance of their social affairs, their self-assurance, their dress, food, and pastimes become a vision lifting the readers of society pages out of their humdrum. Thus even the elaborate way of life of the plutocracy serves as a kind of safety valve.

More directly defensive in their intent and effects are the philanthropic and cultural activities of the plutocracy. Their own reasoning takes the following form: cultural values, the appreciation of music, literature and art are good in and of themselves. The search for these values rests upon taste, leisure, and money. They provide a service to the population by seeking these values and by making them accessible to themselves and others. This type of activity serves to fortify their sense of following a moral and just way of life as well as serving as good propaganda. The same may be said of charitable activity. In this sphere they fulfill their social obligations by taking care of the less fortunate and the less able. In crisis situations private charitable institutions have played a significant political role, preventing riotousness and bridging a period of unrest until the crisis has been overcome.

The educational and religious activities of the plutocracy also serve an effective defensive purpose. By religious activities and philanthropies they fortify their own sense of self-esteem and moral rightness. Through this means they gain the strategic services of clergymen who tend to divert the impulses toward political action into the spiritual and supernatural causes and remedies. The educational activities of plutocracy are of critical value in their defense. Through their control of the great private institutions of higher learning they exercise an influence over the teaching profession which tends to restrict the development of an intellectual opposition leadership.

These activities, influences and controls, while not immediately political, are frequently political in their intent and consequences. Social, cultural, and philanthropic activities serve to legitimate the superior advantages of the plutocracy, to defend them from adverse criticism, and to divert the attention of the lower classes.[17]

Notes

1. James Bryce, *American Commonwealth* (New York: The Macmillan Co., 1891), II, 71.

2. *Ibid.*, p. 73.

3. James K. Pollock, Jr., *Party Campaign Funds* (New York: Alfred Knopf, 1926), p. 112.

4. *Ibid.*, p. 128.

5. *Ibid.*, p. 112.

6. Louise Overacker, *Money in Elections* (New York: The Macmillan Co., 1932), pp. 138–142.

7. Pollock, *op. cit.,* pp. 127–28.

8. Overacker, *op. cit.,* pp. 141 ff.

9. Figure estimated by the *New York World* (cf. Ferdinand Lundberg, *America's 60 Families* [New York: The Vanguard Press, 1937], p. 60).

10. *Ibid.*

11. *New York Times,* referred to in Lundberg, *op. cit.,* p. 55.

12. Lundberg, *op. cit.,* pp. 484–86.

13. Louise Overacker, "Campaign Funds in the Presidential Election of 1936," *Political Science Review,* June, 1937, p. 483.

14. *Ibid.,* p. 494.

15. *Ibid.,* p. 491.

16. See Lundberg, *op. cit.,* pp. 257 ff. for an analysis of the newspaper and publication ownership of the wealthier classes. See also George Seldes, *Lords of the Press* (New York: Julian Messner, 1938).

17. Tabulations of the social and philanthropic activities and affiliations of the officers of business associations and exclusive social clubs are given in chaps. v, vi, and vii.

5

Origins, Status, and Economic Activities

Wᴀᴛ ᴀʀᴇ ᴛʜᴇ ᴛʏᴘɪᴄᴀʟ ǫᴜᴀʟɪᴛɪᴇs and activities of the wealthy classes of New York City? By what qualities and activities is "society" distinguished from the "lower" levels of the plutocracy? The point has already been made that "society" in its special American form was a consequence of democratization. That is, the special forms and activities of "society" developed in a situation in which the wealthy classes enjoyed no formal legal, or traditional privileges. This peculiar structure "society," that is, a group in the wealthy class following a life of pleasure and recreation relatively unrelieved by more serious concerns, arose out of an effort to affirm the superiority of the wealthy to the democracy.[1]

The special points discussed in the present chapter are the social origins, the status, and economic activities of selections of the plutocracy and "society." In addition to the social club officers described in the previous chapter, data concerning two other "society" groups are introduced in this and the following chapter.

Most sources agree that the group around Mrs. Astor constituted the core of "fashionable" society in 1900. A commentator on society of that era, C. W. DeLyon Nicholls, conveniently listed the 150 members of this "set."[2] According to his word this list had the imprimatur of Mrs. Astor herself. When younger members of families were eliminated, it was found that the 150 had been reduced to 78. For the contemporary period the preparation of such a list of concentrated "fashion" was impossible, since no such integrated group exists. Nevertheless there continue to be exclusive groups among the New York plutocracy.

Among the more important of these exclusive groups are one or two of the periodic dancing groups. One of the most exclusive dancing circles in New York City is the Junior Assembly. The subscribers to this assembly are those acceptable elements among the wealthy classes of New York City who have debutante daughters. Its membership therefore changes from year to year, but the officers of this group are self-perpetuating and recruit subscribers on the primary basis of "birth," a certain level of wealth being assumed generally. The Subscribers to the Junior Assembly of any given year are representative of a much larger and more heterogeneous group than Nicholls' 150. The latter after all were the "*crème de la crème*," while the former are only a representative sample of the whole bottle. In making comparisons it will be necessary constantly to keep in mind these important differences.

Birthplace[3]

As a group the selection of business leaders of New York City are overwhelmingly native, the great majority having come from the eastern seaboard states—New York City and State, New Jersey, Pennsylvania, and the New England states. Ninety-one percent of these business leaders were native. Only 34 percent were native New Yorkers; 22 percent were born outside of New York City but in New York State; 16 percent were New Englanders; 9 percent came from the Middle Atlantic states—New Jersey and Pennsylvania; 6 percent from the East North Central states. Only 4 percent came from other areas of the United States. Of the 9 percent foreign born, 3 percent came from Germany, 1.5 percent each from Ireland, Canada, Scotland, and England.

A comparison of the birthplace of the business leaders of the 1870–1906 period with those of the 1930s reveals a number of interesting changes. Thus the number of foreign-born has decreased from 14 percent in the 1870–1906 period to 4 percent in 1931–1935. The proportion of native New Yorkers has increased from 30 percent to 38 percent, and the number from New York State has decreased from 22 percent to 17 percent. The number of New Englanders has halved during this period. The proportion from the Middle Atlantic states has increased only slightly, while the number from the East North Central states has increased from 2 percent to 10 percent. There has been an increase generally of New York "big businessmen" deriving from areas outside of the eastern seaboard. The decrease in the number of foreign-born in the upper levels of business leadership is largely due to the fact that for the later immigrations access to economic power was far more difficult, since the country was largely "owned" by the time of their arrival.

The proportion of the native born among the officers of the Union, Knickerbocker and Metropolitan clubs is even greater than that of the selection of officers of business associations, the percentages being 98 percent to 91 percent. Only 2 social club officers were born abroad: one in Scotland and one in England. Seventy percent of these officers of exclusive social clubs were born in New York City to 34 percent for our selection of business leaders. These figures permit the conclusion that the leaders of New York society were a far more homogeneous group, being recruited primarily from New York City families, in contrast to the officers of business associations who were recruited from various parts of the United States and from Europe. Of the three groups of club officers those of the Metropolitan Club were most heterogeneous in origin. Almost half of its officers were born outside of New York City, while the officers of the Union and Knickerbocker clubs were with few exceptions native New Yorkers. The Metropolitan Club officers of 1892 were mostly natives of New York City (17 to 5); those of 1935 came mostly from outside of New York City (3 to 13). In territorial origin the officers of the Metropolitan Club for 1935 were similar to the group of business leaders.

Nationality Origins[4]

Particularly in the United States, where wave after wave of foreigners from practically all parts of the world have immigrated, has nationality origin played a significant role in the formation of social classes and class prejudices. Those who immigrated earlier, with the exception of the Negroes, have generally become more established economically and socially, and tended thus to evaluate the succeeding groups negatively. Thus the English, Scotch, Dutch, and French early immigrants, greatly intermingled by the 1830s, viewed the incoming Irish of the 1840s and 1850s, who derived largely from lower class origins, as less cultivated, and therefore closed their "society" to them. The Irish and Germans in turn viewed the later immigrations of Slavic stocks and Southern Europeans negatively. The nationality stratification of the American population, to a great extent coincident with its economic and social stratification, thus tends to coincide with the time of arrival.

The great majority of New York business leaders in this group—81 percent—were of native parentage. In the majority of cases these business leaders were of English, Scotch, and Dutch stock, with a sprinkling of early Irish and French Huguenot. The balance—19 percent—were of foreign birth or parentage. The largest percentage of business leaders of the later immigrations was Jewish. In all cases these Jewish business leaders were of the earlier German Jewish immigration, which dated back to the 1840s and 1850s or earlier. The next largest were Germans—4 percent. The balance were Irish, Scotch, English, and Canadian in origin.

A comparison of the nationality origins of those business leaders holding office in the 1870–1906 period and those in the 1931–1935 period indicates a slight increase (2 percent) in the number of native born of native parents. There were 5 German Jews among the later business leaders to 3 in the earlier period. In the 1931–1935 period there were no foreign born or first generation native born Scotch and English.

The most important conclusion to be drawn from the tabulations is that the greatest economic power in New York is almost entirely in the hands of the older stock. Even the Jews are all of the pre–Civil War immigration. The post–Civil War immigrations—the Polish and Russian Jews, the Scandinavians, Slavs, and Italians—are for the most part limited economically to proletarian, lower middle class, and middle class destinies. The earlier immigrations—the English, Scotch, Dutch, some few Germans, French, Irish, and German Jews—constitute the "heavy capital" group.

The available information on nationality origin for society leaders and business leaders is unfortunately not quite comparable. For business leaders it was only possible to go back two generations, while for exclusive society leaders the genealogy has in many cases been carried back for many generations. To take the aristocratic Union Club as an example, we find that 46 of the 58 officers upon whom data were available came of families which had arrived in America before the Revolution. The families of 9 other officers had immigrated before 1840, and only 3 had arrived between the years 1841 and 1860. The officers of the Knickerbocker Club for 1872, and the officers of the Metropolitan Club of 1892, also came of "old" families. Unfortunately sufficient information on the contemporary officers of the Knickerbocker and Metropolitan clubs is not available. In spite of the lack of comparable data the generalization may be advanced that society leaders as a group come of older American families than the general run of the business leadership.

These society leaders are mainly descended from English families, 60 percent deriving from that stock. Ten percent are of Dutch origin, 9 percent of French origin, and 7 percent of Scotch derivation. Naturally there has been much intermingling of these nationality stocks. No Jews were in these exclusive groups, in contrast to the business leadership where we found 6 percent of this origin. Although both business leaders and society leaders came generally of the earlier immigrations, the latter derive almost entirely from the older English, Scotch, Dutch, and French stock, while in the former a number deriving from later immigrations were able to enter.

Economic Class Origin[5]

For the 138 New York business leaders in the present selection 66 percent were found to have come from wealthy or well-to-do families, and 34 percent were self-made men. The criteria used to determine the economic level of parents were occupation and wealth of father, where indicated, and access to expensive schooling. It was considered justifiable to assume that a young man sent away from home to expensive Eastern preparatory schools, or to Yale, Harvard, Princeton, Williams, and other colleges, came in the great majority of cases from the upper levels of the middle classes.

Thirty-two percent of the officers of these business men's associations holding office between the years 1870–1906 were self-made men. Thirty-seven percent of those holding office in the years 1931–1935 were of such origin. This slight difference is not to be interpreted as meaning that the number of self-made big business men in New York has been increasing. In the first place the earlier group was rising in the business world around the middle part of the nineteenth century, and the latter at the end of that century. In those periods the rate of mobility fluctuated from time to time, but was generally high. The business leaders in the present sample are of the older generation. Taussig and Joslyn in their study of *American Business Leaders* were able to separate out a sample of business men between the ages of 35 to 39 years. The class origin of these younger men gives the correct picture of the increasingly fixed character of the upper business classes in the United States generally.[6]

For society leaders the percentage coming of wealthy or well-to-do origins is even more impressive. Eighty-three percent of these had come of wealthy families. A special analysis of the officers of the Union Club indicates that 32 percent of its officers had come of families which had had wealth for four generations or more, and 74 percent had had wealth for at least three generations. All of the officers of the Knickerbocker Club regarding whom data were available had come of wealthy families. The data for the Metropolitan Club indicate a relatively large influx of *parvenus*. Thus 7 of the 15 officers of the Metropolitan Club in 1935 had acquired their wealth in their own generation. This large influx of *parvenus* into the leadership of the Metropolitan Club accounts for the loss of prestige it has suffered in the last forty years. Founded by J. P. Morgan, in its early years it rivaled the Union Club in wealth and prominence of membership, though not in exclusiveness. At the present time it tends to admit almost purely upon the basis of wealth. In contrast to the business leadership as a group, the tabulations indicate that the officers of exclusive social clubs are almost universally derived from the older families of wealth.

Social Status and Origin[7]

The "Social Register" (cf. Chapter 7) is regarded by many as including the most important people "socially" in those communities which possess them. The criteria of inclusion of the Social Register are secret, being the private property of the small secret committees which make the selection. For present purposes it is sufficient to point out that on the basis of examination of the Social Register of New York two major criteria are employed. These are wealth and birth. Good birth is conditioned upon wealth, especially in those areas of great industrial and financial development, where "good birth" is largely determined by the number of generations of wealthy ancestors an individual has had. Most wealthy people are of Protestant, older American origins; and thus it is that "good birth" means also descent from old American families; in some few cases descent from foreign nobilities. From the religious point of view the Social Register is overwhelmingly made up of Protestant families; and the largest denominations represented are the Episcopalian and the Presbyterian. Catholics and Jews are to be found in small numbers. Generally, Jews have been admitted when they have intermarried with "old stock," although there are a few cases when they have been admitted in their own right.

Naturally there are other qualities which go with wealth; and it is these other qualities, dependent for their development upon wealth, which the defenders of American aristocratic institutions emphasize. These other qualities are "cultivation," taste—in general the material and spiritual elaboration of the routines of living. This whole problem will be dealt with in a later discussion of social life. It is sufficient to say here that wealth, birth, and derivative qualities are the criteria of admission to the Social Register.

Although there is some controversy in the upper social circles over the validity of Social Register inclusion, it can hardly be doubted that inclusion constitutes a kind of social legitimation. The importance of the Social Register is witnessed to by the fact that it is a commercial success; and this commercial success is ensured by the patronage of these same social circles. Being included in the Social Register signifies admission into a selected group of plutocrats who have in addition to money a claim to good birth in a large number of cases, and at least pretenses to a certain way of life, convivial and cultural. Inclusion in the Social Register may be viewed as a recognition of high social status.

One hundred and sixteen of the 202, or 57 percent, of the business leaders in this selection were included in the Social Register. The recency of the "social legitimation" of these plutocrat families is borne out by the fact that only 14 percent of the business leaders of the 1931–1935 period were second generation Social Registerites. The officers of the Chamber of Commerce included proportionately more of the old stock than either of the others, the proportion being 19 percent, to 10 percent, to 12 percent, for the officers of the Chamber of Commerce, Clearing House, and Merchants Association respectively.

It is also of considerable interest to observe that the proportion of these big business leaders included in the Social Register has decreased from 62 percent in 1870–1906 to 52 percent in 1931–1935. This development is attributable to the fact that in the earlier period the Social Register, and the "aristocracy" as well, was relatively new, and hence the standards of admission were a little less exclusive than at the present time. The admission of *parvenus* to the Social Register in the late nineteenth century was more rapid than at the present time.

Ninety-five percent of the officers of exclusive social clubs, and 96 percent of the members of exclusive social sets were included in the Social Register, as compared with only 57 percent for the selection of business leaders. While the parents of only 14 percent of the contemporary officers of business associations had been included in the Social Register, 68 percent of the contemporary officers of exclusive social clubs, and 69 percent of the Subscribers to the New York Junior Assembly were second generation Social Registerites. For the officers of the Union Club the proportion of second generation Social Registerites was even higher—96 percent as compared with 74 percent for the Knickerbocker Club, and only 33 percent for the Metropolitan Club. These figures again support the conclusion as to the *parvenu* plutocratic character of the contemporary Metropolitan Club. The Union and Knickerbocker Clubs and the Subscribers to the New York Junior Assembly are largely recruited from the exclusive social circles of the last generations. It may be said, therefore, that the more exclusive circles of New York society are largely hereditary.

Occupational Composition[8]

Large owners of property in capitalist democracies by virtue of their economic and social controls may be said on the whole to enjoy the greatest power and social honor of any occupational group in the community. Following capitalist promoters and rentiers in power and in social esteem are those lawyers whose interests are in large corporations. This type of legal and organizational activity leads to the entrance of the lawyer into the active direction of corporations. There are innumerable examples of lawyers who have risen from law into capitalist promotional status. Chauncey Depew, William Collins Whitney, and Elihu Root of the last generation, Owen D. Young, Silas Strawn, Fred Wesley Sargent of the present are examples that immediately come to mind. There are also many cases of engineers who have risen from consultant and employee status to directorial capacity in railroad, utility, and mining enterprises.

Although differences in power and esteem between and within occupations vary from individual to individual, certain general comparisons may be made and agreed upon. Certainly large corporation executives and rentiers are more powerful and enjoy greater social esteem than small entrepreneurs; small entrepreneurs are more powerful than unskilled and, with exceptions, skilled labor; professionals are a more powerful element than small entrepreneurs, and so on. The classification of occupations in the present study distinguishes first between the employers, the self-employed, and employees. There are of course employees who enjoy greater power than small or even "middle size" entrepreneurs. Managers of large enterprises constitute such an exception. But in many cases such managers have some ownership interest in their enterprise, and hence would enjoy both an employer and employee status. Another important exception are the salaried employees and skilled laborers who receive higher incomes than many petty entrepreneurs. With these exceptions it may be said that the employer and the self-employed on the whole are more powerful occupational groups than the employees. Among the employers and self-employed there are, of course, great differences.

The fact that our sample of business leaders was selected from the officers of specific business associations naturally weights the selection in favor of the type of business associations which were chosen. Insofar as corporate rank is concerned the great majority (92 percent) were officers of large corporations or firms. Only 2 percent were rentiers and 6 percent were recruited from the professions, in all cases, save that of one engineer, lawyers. The officers of the New York Clearing House naturally were in practically all cases specially interested in banking. Only 2 were not formally associated with banking institutions, and these were in commercial businesses. Of the officers of the Chamber of Commerce 4 percent were *rentiers* and 5 percent were lawyers. The balance were officers of large corporations and firms. Of this total 39 percent were officers of banking, investment, and insurance institutions, 20 percent of manufacturing enterprises, 17 percent of commercial companies, 9 percent in utilities and transportation, 3 percent were publishers, and 3 percent in realty and holding corporations. The Chamber of Commerce includes a far more representative group of business leaders than the Clearing House, since the Clearing House is limited to individuals engaged in banking. The Merchants Association has a larger representation of lawyers than either of the others. The largest proportion of its officers is recruited from manufacturing and commercial enterprises, and a relatively small number are drawn from the field of banking, investment, and insurance.

The New York Chamber of Commerce is of special interest here since by virtue of its age and tradition (it was founded before the Revolution) admission to it is of some honor, and holding office in it carries even greater prestige. Holding office in the New York Chamber of Commerce may be viewed as a "business" legitimation of the individual and his line of economic activity. Of those business men holding office in the Chamber of Commerce from 1776–1835, 18 of the 24 upon whom data were available were merchants of various kinds, 2 were manufacturers, and 2 were mariners (see Chapter 1). Of the 15 officers of the Chamber of Commerce in 1870, 6 were in banking, investment, and insurance, 3 were manufacturers, and 5 were merchants. Noteworthy here is the evidence of the rise of the finance profession as such (the early merchants had banking connections but in most cases were not specialized bankers) into the ranks of honored business men.

In 1901 we already find represented in the ranks of Chamber of Commerce officers railroad and utility officials (8 percent). We also note a diminution in the number of merchants (from 33 percent in 1870 to 17 percent in 1901). In 1935 the proportion of railroad and utility officers has further increased from 8 percent to 14 percent. There has been an increase in the representation of manufacturers and a further decrease in the number of merchants. And for the first time we note the representation of individuals whose interests are primarily in the real estate and building corporation field.

The rapid admission of business men in relatively new lines of business into the Chamber of Commerce is of considerable interest. For it illustrates that the upper ranges of the plutocracy as such have only one criterion of admission, and that is business success. In other words, the Chamber of Commerce responds relatively rapidly to shifts in power in economic life. It will be of importance in later chapters to compare this responsiveness to shifts in power in the business world and the relatively successful insistence upon other criteria of admission in the sphere of upper class social life. There are, to be sure, banking houses and brokerage concerns whose list of partners reads like a Newport guest list of the heyday of the Astor regime. Such a recognized overall business association as the Chamber of Commerce does not seem, however, to look to any extent "beyond money into blood."

A general comparison of the business leaders of 1870–1906 with those of 1931–1935 gives results similar to the trends already discussed for the Chamber of Commerce. The proportion of individuals in financial life has remained roughly the same. The proportion of individuals in manufacturing has increased. The proportion of railroad and utility men has increased slightly. The increase in the latter is primarily due to the great development in utility enterprises in the last decades. The number of merchants, that is, importers, exporters, wholesalers, and retailers, has decreased greatly from 22 percent in 1870–1906 to 8 percent in 1931–1935. The number of individuals specially interested in real estate has increased, the number of lawyers has decreased. The large drop in the number of merchants among the officers of these institutions reflects the smaller capitalization of commercial and trading enterprises. Comparatively speaking, these enterprises are of smaller capitalization than railroads, utilities, heavy industry, and banking.

One of the first differences that emerge in a comparison of the occupations of society leaders with those of the business leadership group is the relatively large number of *rentiers* among the former. Only 2 percent of the business leaders were retired from active economic life as compared with 14 percent for exclusive club officers. Of the members of Nicholls' "150" and the Subscribers to the New York Junior Assembly, 16 percent were *rentiers*. A second major difference in the occupational composition of society leaders and business leaders is the relatively large representation of the professions in the former. Eighteen percent of the officers of exclusive social clubs and 18 percent of Nicholls' "150" and the Subscribers to the New York Junior Assembly were lawyers, engineers, physicians, and academicians, as compared with only 6 percent for officers of business associations. With one exception all of the professional men among the group of business leaders were lawyers. Professions other than the legal were relatively frequently represented among the Subscribers to the New York Junior Assembly. There were thus 8 physicians among the Subscribers, out of a group of 100. There were also fewer individuals engaged in wholesaling, retailing, and general commercial business among society leaders, the proportions being 16 percent for the officers of business associations to only 2 percent for officers of exclusive social clubs, and 2 percent for the members of Mrs. Astor's "set" and the Subscribers to the New York Junior Assembly. The number of individuals primarily engaged in banking, investment, and insurance was slightly higher for the officers of business associations, the ratio being 47 percent for these as compared with 38 percent for officers of exclusive social clubs, and 41 percent for members of exclusive social sets. There were more manufacturers in the sample of business leaders than among society leaders, the ratio being 19 percent to 13 percent, to 6 percent for business leaders, prominent clubmen, and members of exclusive social sets respectively.

A general comparison of occupations of business leaders and society leaders indicates first a higher representation of *rentiers* and the professions, and a smaller representation of manufacturers and merchants among society leaders. As a group the upper levels of the plutocracy include those actively engaged in the businesses of greatest capitalization, irrespective of the nature of the business. The same is largely true for society leaders with the important exception of a larger representation of economically inactive individuals or *rentiers,* and the professions, and a smaller representation of industrialists and merchants.

The proportion of *rentiers* among the officers of the Union, Knickerbocker, and Metropolitan clubs is approximately equal, although, as examination of the table reveals, the proportion of *rentiers* among the contemporary officers of exclusive clubs is far less than that of the earlier periods. Thus only one contemporary Union Club officer is a *rentier* as compared with two in 1900 and three in 1871. Two contemporary Knickerbocker Club officers were *rentiers* to three in 1872. There were no *rentiers* among contemporary Metropolitan Club officers to 6 in 1892. This development seems to indicate that men in society more generally engage in active economic life at the present time than they did in the latter part of the nineteenth century. The *rentiers* among the Subscribers to the New York Junior Assembly for 1935 were in almost every case widows of wealthy men.

The officers of the Union and Knickerbocker clubs show a decided increase in banking, investment, and insurance occupations, while the officers of the Metropolitan Club show a decided decrease in the representation of these groups. The officers of the Union and Knickerbocker clubs also show a large decrease in the number engaged in utilities and transportation and manufacturing, while the officers of the Metropolitan Club show an increase. The increase in the number of financiers among the officers of the Union and Knickerbocker clubs and the decrease in the number of those engaged in heavy industry indicates that exclusive society tends on the whole to be recruited primarily at the present time from individuals associated with the money and securities sets. The increase in the representation of "heavy" industrialists among the officers of the Metropolitan Club and the decrease in the number of financiers is another index to its change in composition, accounting for its loss in social prestige.

There is a natural tendency for inheritors of wealth to gravitate to the securities market. This is largely influenced by both economic and social forces. Possession of large amounts of negotiable capital makes possible the acquisition of sufficient profit through security transactions, and hence makes unnecessary the day to day activities at a special place involved in industrial and commercial management. Active industrial management particularly would take the manager away from New York City, while good money is to be made with a smaller expenditure of time and effort on the "Street." Then too, the education and tastes of the children of the wealthy urge them to acquire more leisure, and this is more possible in the sphere of financial manipulation, while it is not as possible in the case of industrial or commercial management. Financial speculation is an "occasional" enterprise, rendering those who engage in it relatively independent of continuous economic activity, making possible long weekends for fox hunting, frequent vacations for yachting, and the like. These factors largely account for the increase in the number of financiers among the officers of the Union and Knickerbocker clubs. In many cases, too, the financial activities of these society elements consist mainly in handling the security holdings and real property inherited from parents. Many New York investment concerns are made up of small groups of these inheritors of fortunes. Their function tends to be solely that of caring for their own interests, and not seeking for clients. The decrease in the number of financiers among the officers of the Metropolitan Club reflects the lowering of standards of admission in that association. This conclusion rests not only upon this tabulation but upon the earlier ones of territorial, nationality, and economic origins in which it was demonstrated that the contemporary officers of the Metropolitan Club were in many cases first generation wealthy.

Similar tendencies emerge from a comparison of the occupations of Nicholls' "150" of 1903 and the Subscribers to the New York Junior Assembly in 1935. We find first a decrease in the number of *rentiers,* and an increase in the number of professionals. The proportion of financiers has increased from 39 percent in the selection of 1903 to 45 percent in the selection of 1935. And there has been a proportionate decrease in the representation of heavy industrialists—those engaged in large manufacturing enterprises and utilities and transportation. These changes are partly to be accounted for by the differences in the bases of the selection of the two groups. However, since these same tendencies were found among the officers of the Union and the Knickerbocker clubs, the conclusion is justified that, in the last generation, society leadership has come increasingly to be identified with financial occupations, in a few cases *rentiership,* and the upper levels of the professions, primarily the legal and the medical.

Ramifications of Business Activities[9]

In addition to their major business positions these business leaders were extremely powerful in large economic enterprises. Seventy-eight percent held directorial or executive offices in firms outside their main connection. Between them they held 1,072 such outside positions, an average of 6.5 per business leader. Their interests and controls extended into practically every field of large-scale economic activity, the financial world, transportation and utilities, real estate and building corporations, and manufacturing and commercial enterprises. The fact that 46 percent of the business affiliations of these business leaders was in the fields of banking, investment, and insurance, coupled with the fact that 47 percent of these individuals were mainly occupied in these fields, justifies the characterization of the largest proportion of them as finance capitalists.

The business leaders were also frequently represented among the officers and boards of railroads, other transport companies, and utility corporations. Third in importance were manufacturing corporations which constituted 16 percent of the total; fourth were real estate and building corporations offices, constituting 7 percent of the total. Only 1 percent of these offices were in commercial institutions, which raises the presumption that this type of economic activity was generally on a relatively small scale, and hence was not an important enough field of investment and control for these "upper business" leaders. Financial and insurance institutions, transportation and utilities, and manufacturing corporations, in the order named, were the fields of economic activity in which this sample of business leaders were mainly interested. Although directorships and executive offices do not universally reflect stock ownership, such is no doubt the case for the majority of these business affiliations. Thus both from the point of view of ownership and control this selection of business leaders was found to be extremely powerful in the economic enterprises of heaviest capitalization.

The officers of the Chamber of Commerce were by far the most powerful of the three groups of officers. On the average they held 8 offices in corporations or firms other than their main interest, as compared with 5.9 for the banker officers of the New York Clearing House Association, and 3 for the New York Merchants Association. Ninety-one percent of the officers of the Chamber of Commerce held offices in addition to their main occupation as compared with 89 percent for the officers of the Clearing House Association and 74 percent for the officers of the Merchants Association. The other economic controls of the New York Chamber of Commerce officers were mainly in the field of banking, investment, and insurance, and transportation and utilities, the percentages being 41 percent and 36 percent respectively. Thirteen percent of their offices were in manufacturing enterprises, 7 percent in real estate and building corporations, and only 1 percent in commercial institutions. Most of the offices held by the officers of the Clearing House were in the field of banking, investment, and insurance corporations. Only 14 percent were in the field of transportation and utilities; 15 percent in the field of manufacturing, 5 percent in real estate and building corporations, and 2 percent in commercial institutions. The officers of the Merchants Association were mainly interested in the field of finance, manufacturing, and real estate and building corporations, the percentages being 42 percent, 15 percent, and 34 percent respectively.

In summary, then, it can be said that this group of prominent business leaders were in the fields of heaviest capitalization—in the fields of finance, utilities, and transportation, and manufacturing. Taking the association officials separately it can be said, first, that the officers of the Chamber of Commerce are the most powerful economically, in terms of number of offices and also in terms of the extent of their controls in the fields of greatest capitalization. The officers of the Clearing House were less powerful in terms of the average number of other business offices. They also were infrequently represented in the field of transportation and utilities. The officers of the New York Merchants Association were least powerful economically, in terms of the number of corporate directorships and executive offices and their distribution among enterprises of relatively high and low capitalization.

The trend in the economic controls of these business leaders reveals a slight increase in the number of individuals with business affiliations outside of their main position. We find also that the average number of offices has increased slightly, from 6.4 to 6.6. The nature of the controls exercised by these business leaders has also altered. Thus, in the period 1870–1906 the proportion of executive offices to directorships was 26 percent to 74 percent, as compared with 33 percent to 67 percent in the period 1931–1935.

There have also been important changes in the fields in which these economic controls are exercised. Thus, in the period 1870–1906, 51 percent of the business positions held by these business leaders were in the field of banking, investment, and insurance. At the present time this percentage is only 40 percent, and there has been a corresponding increase in the field of transportation and utilities, from 26 percent to 33 percent.

As a group the selection of prominent club men and social leaders were less powerful economically than the selection of business leaders. Eighty-seven percent of the officers of business associations held offices in corporations outside of their main business connection, as compared with 78 percent for officers of exclusive social clubs, and only 49 percent for Mrs. Astor's "set" and the Subscribers to the New York Junior Assembly of 1903. The smaller economic power and less active economic role of "society" as over against the upper levels of the plutocracy is again borne out by the average number of "other corporate affiliations." The average for officers of business associations was 6.5 as compared with 5.4 for officers of exclusive social clubs, and only 2.8 for the members of exclusive social sets. The less active economic role of society is further substantiated by the relative proportions of executive and directorial offices held by these groups. Only 14 percent of the corporate affiliations of officers of exclusive social clubs, and 12 percent of those of our selections of exclusive society were executive in character, as compared with 29 percent for the selection of business leaders.

Among the business leaders we observed a great concentration of corporate affiliations in the field of banking, investment, and insurance. Forty-six percent of all their corporate officers were in these fields. Only 27 percent of the affiliations of officers of exclusive social clubs, and only 31 percent of those of the exclusive social sets were in the fields of finance and insurance. At the same time these groups of society leaders were proportionately more heavily interested than the selection of business leaders in transportation and utilities. This difference is to be attributed to the fact that a large proportion of the great New York fortunes of the late nineteenth century were made or were considerably increased through investment in railroads. The descendants of these railroad families, now largely included in exclusive social circles, continue to hold stock and directorships in these enterprises.

Of the three sets of club leaders the officers of the Metropolitan Club were far more powerful economically than the officers of the "bourbon" Union and Knickerbocker clubs. Thus the average Metropolitan Club officer held 9.2 offices as compared with 5.2 for the leaders of the Union Club, and 3.8 for the leaders of the Knickerbocker Club. As has already been pointed out, the newer plutocracy is more closely and actively identified with business activity than the older more aristocratic elements. The lower standards of admission of the Metropolitan Club thus account for the greater economic activity of its officers.

The officers of the Union Club in 1900 were very heavily interested in railroads and utility enterprises. These and their banking and insurance interests practically made up the total of their corporate interests. The contemporary group of Union Club officers in contrast is interested in real estate and building corporations in the same measure as utilities and transportation, and finance and insurance. Over half of the officers of the Knickerbocker Club of 1872 were in the fields of finance and insurance, which seems to square with the observations of commentators on social life of that time that the Knickerbocker Club was founded and maintained by young Wall Street "prigs" impatient with the extreme conservatism and long waiting lists of the Union Club. The Knickerbocker Club, judging by the economic interests of its officers, seems to have maintained these principles of admission to the present day. The business affiliations of the officers of the Metropolitan Club indicate a considerable decrease in the proportion of utility and transportation, and financial interests, and a corresponding increase in the proportion of manufacturing corporate offices.

The general trend in corporate affiliations for officers of exclusive social clubs seems to be in the direction of a decrease in the proportion of transportation and utility offices, a considerable increase in the proportion of interests in manufacturing enterprises, and a smaller, but definite increase in the number of offices in the field of real estate and building corporations.

These trends are further substantiated by an analysis of the business affiliations of the two exclusive social sets. As has been pointed out previously, the Subscribers to the New York Junior Assembly for 1935 are a far less influential and highly selected group than Mrs. Astor's set of 1903. Thus only 44 percent of the Subscribers had any directorships or executive offices in corporations other than their main business position, as compared with 56 percent for Mrs. Astor's set, which held on the average 4 "other" corporate offices, as compared with 2.3 for the Subscribers. Fifty percent of the corporate affiliations of Mrs. Astor's set were in the fields of utilities and transportation; 34 percent in banking, investment, and insurance; and 15 percent in the manufacturing field. In contrast, the corporate affiliations of the Subscribers to the New York Junior Assembly of 1935 were more equally distributed in the various fields of economic enterprise. Twenty-nine percent were in banking, 22 percent in transportation and utilities, 30 percent in manufacturing, and 14 percent in real estate and building corporations. The general conclusion is possible, therefore, that the business interests of exclusive society of the present day in contrast with that of the previous generations are more equally distributed among the various spheres of economic enterprise. This development may be due to the fact that the later generation of society has had time and opportunity to distribute its investments more safely in the various fields of enterprise. But this relatively equal distribution is also to be accounted for partly by the wider basis of selection of the Assembly Subscribers.

In summary these selections of established business leaders and society leaders of New York City were generally recruited from the older stock, primarily the early English, Scotch, Dutch, and French. The social leaders as compared with the business leaders were more frequently recruited from these early immigrations, while among the group of business leaders there was a larger representation of individuals of foreign birth or parentage. These foreign-born and first-generation native-born business leaders were mainly of German-Jewish, German and Irish origin. The business leaders were more heterogeneous in their American territorial origin, while the social leaders were largely recruited from New York City families.

A very high proportion of both the business and social leaders had been recruited from wealthy families. This, however, was true of only two-thirds of the honored business leaders, whereas it was almost universally true for society leaders. In many cases the social leaders had been recruited from families which had had wealth over four or more generations.

America's "Almanach de Gotha" is the Social Register. Inclusion in it is a kind of social legitimation for a man of wealth or high professional status. The Social Register does not admit solely on the basis of wealth. Thus only 57 percent of the business leader group were Social Registerites as compared with almost all for the social leaders. Only 14 percent of the contemporary business leaders came of families which had been included in the Register of the previous generation. More than two-thirds of the society leaders were second generation Social Registerites.

These selections of the plutocracy were in the great majority from the class of large corporation executives. The most important sphere of enterprise was that of banking, brokerage, and insurance. Also represented were manufacturing, utility and transportation executives. There were smaller representations of department store owners, wholesalers, importers and exporters, and the professions. The society leaders as compared with the business leaders included a larger proportion of *rentiers* and individuals from the professions. There were also fewer manufacturers among the society leaders.

An analysis of the scope and degree of the business activities of the two groups indicated for both a considerable control in various spheres of economic enterprise. The business leaders were markedly powerful in the sphere of greatest capitalization, banking, investment and insurance, utilities, transportation and manufacturing enterprises. The society leaders held on the average fewer directorships and executive offices in corporations outside of their main connection, as well as proportionately fewer executive offices as compared with directorships. The general conclusion was possible that as a group the society leaders were less actively and powerfully identified with economic life than the business leaders.

Notes

1. For some of the studies of the American wealthy classes in more recent times see F. W. Taussig and C. S. Joslyn, *American Business Leaders* (New York: The Macmillan Co., 1932); Pitirim Sorokin, "American Millionaires and Multi-million-

aires," *Social Forces,* May, 1925; Adolph A. Berle, Jr. and Gardiner C. Means, *The Modern Corporation and Private Property* (New York: The Macmillan Co., 1933); Gustavus Myers, *History of the Great American Fortunes* (Chicago: C. H. Kerr and Co., 1909); Matthew Josephson, *Robber Barons* (New York: Harcourt Brace and Co., 1934); Ferdinand Lundberg, *America's "60" Families* (New York: The Vanguard Press, 1937); Anna Rochester, *Rulers of America* (New York: International Publishers, 1936). The many biographies of individual wealthy families and individuals are partly given in Josephson, *op. cit.,* pp. 457 ff. For more general treatment of social stratification see Hans Speier, "Democracy and Social Stratification," *Political and Economic Democracy,* edited by Max Ascoli and Fritz Lehman (New York: W. W. Norton and Co., 1937); Speier, "Honor and Social Structure," *Social Research,* February, 1935, p. 74; Sorokin, *Social Mobility* (New York: Harper Bros., 1927); Max Weber, *Wirtschaft und Gesellschaft* (Tübingen: J. C. B. Mohr, 1925), chap. iv, Part I, chap. iv, Part II, chap. iv, Part III.

2. *The 469 Ultra-Fashionables of America* (New York: Broadway Publishing Co., 1912).

3. Figures given in the text are taken from tabulations given in Appendix A in the typewritten thesis version. Sources of data for these tabulations are as follows: New York Chamber of Commerce, *Annual Report, 1870* (New York, 1870), *Annual Report, 1900* (New York, 1900), *Annual Report, 1935* (New York, 1935); New York Clearing House Association, *Annual Report, 1894* (New York, 1894), *Annual Report, 1935* (New York, 1935); New York Merchants Association, *Annual Report, 1906* (New York, 1906), *Annual Report, 1931* (New York, 1931); Union Club, *Yearbook, 1870* (New York, 1870), *Yearbook, 1900* (New York, 1900), *Yearbook, 1935* (New York, 1935); Knickerbocker Club, *Yearbook, 1872* (New York, 1872), *Yearbook, 1932* (New York, 1932); Metropolitan Club, *Yearbook, 1892* (New York 1892), *Yearbook, 1935* (New York, 1935). Mrs. Astor's set was taken from Charles W. DeLyon Nicholls, *The 469 Ultra-fashionables of America* (New York: Broadway Publishing Co., 1912); the list of Subscribers to the New York Junior Assembly was taken from the *New York Herald Tribune,* Dec. 8, 1935, Society Section. For biographical data the following sources were used: *Appleton's Cyclopedia of American Biography,* edited by James Grant Wilson and John Fiske (New York: D. Appleton Co., 1888); Moses Yale Beach, *The Wealth and Biography of the Wealthy Citizens of New York* (New York: published by the *New York Sun,* 1842–1855); *Dictionary of American Biography,* edited by Dumas Malone (New York: C. Scribner's Sons, 1928); Henry Hall, *America's Successful Men of Affairs* (New York: the *New York Tribune,* 1895–1896); Marguerita Aulina Hamm, *Famous Families of New York* (2 vols.; New York: G. P. Putnam's Sons, 1902); Moses King, *Notable New Yorkers of 1896–1899* (New York: M. King, 1899); *The National Cyclopedia of American Biography* (New York: J. T. White and Co., 1898); Lyman Horace Weeks, *Prominent Families of New York* (New York: The Historical Co., 1897); *Who's Who in America,* 1899–1936 (Chicago: A. N. Marquis Co.); *Who's Who in Commerce and Industry, 1936* (New York: Institute for Research in Biography, Inc., 1936); *Who's Who in Finance and Banking,* 1911–1925 (New York: Who's Who in Finance, Inc.); *Who's Who in New York City,* 1904–1929 (New York: Who's Who Publications, Inc.); *Who's Who in the East* (Washington: Mayflower Publishing Co., 1930); *Poor's Register of Directors of the United States,*

1928–1937 (Babson Park, Mass.: Poor's Printing Co.); *Directory of Directors in the City of New York*, 1898–1927 (New York: The Audit Company of New York); *Social Register New York*, 1889–1936 (New York: Social Register Association).

4. *Ibid.*
5. *Ibid.*
6. Taussig and Joslyn, *op. cit.*, chap. xi.
7. See n. 1, pp. 112–13.
8. *Ibid.*
9. *Ibid.*

6

Education, Social and Philanthropic Activities

BEFORE THE RISE of mass education in the United States the wealthy classes enjoyed what amounted to a practical monopoly of education. Gradually during the nineteenth and twentieth centuries all elements of the population have come to enjoy access to some higher education; but stratification in education still exists. The wealthier classes are able, first, to select their preparatory schools and colleges without respect to expense, proximity, or the length of time required for acquiring the education desired. They may choose their schools not only in terms of the kind of education, but in terms of the prestige and tradition of the school. Hence we find the wealthier elements sending their sons and daughters to eastern preparatory schools and universities which enjoy a special prestige because of their age and tradition. The middle and lower classes in those cities which support municipal colleges have access to higher education, but they are forced to select their schools close at hand. State or city institutions or parochial schools where tuition rates are lower, where the schools are closer to home, and where they are better able, if necessary, to find part-time work, are the typical institutions of higher education for the middle and lower classes.

Education[1]

Since the selection of business leaders has been found to be primarily recruited from the wealthy or well-to-do classes, it is to be expected, first, that most of them have attended colleges and universities, and second, that they have attended the older traditional institutions of greater prestige. We find this generally to be the case. Sixty-three percent of the officers of these business associations attended college, to 24 percent who finished only grade or preparatory school. Fourteen percent had taken professional degrees, in almost all cases the law degree. Five percent had taken higher academic degrees, and 2 percent had received honorary degrees.

An analysis of the trend in the level of education of these officers of business associations reveals a decided increase in the number of those having college or university training. Forty-eight percent of those holding office in these associations in the years 1870–1906 had only grammar or preparatory school education, to only 15 percent in 1931 1935. The number of college graduates jumped from 52 percent to 85 percent, indicating a decided trend toward higher education for business leaders. The number of those with higher academic degrees and honorary degrees has also increased.

The institutions of higher education most frequently attended by these big business men are Yale, Columbia, Harvard, New York University, Princeton, and Williams, in the order named. With the exception of New York University, these and a few others are the upper class private universities in the United States attracting not only the upper classes of the eastern seaboard but those of the whole United States.

Thirty-four percent of the officers of business associations had only grammar or high school education, as compared with 29 percent for the officers of exclusive social clubs. The exclusive social groups had also more frequently acquired professional education, the proportion being 21 percent to 14 percent. For both the upper business groups and the exclusive social groups the trend has been toward the acquisition of higher education. Thus 48 percent of the 1870–1906 group of business leaders had only grammar or preparatory school educations, as compared with only 15 percent in 1931–1935. The proportion of professionally educated among the business leader group was 14 percent for both periods. For the exclusive social groups this proportion has doubled from 14 percent in 1872–1900 to 28 percent in 1932–1935. University educations and especially professional educations are thus more common among the exclusive social elements than among the upper group of business leaders.

We have already seen that Yale, Columbia, Harvard, and Princeton were among the most frequently attended institutions for the business leader group. Fifty-two percent of the college-educated business leaders attended these four institutions. For exclusive society the concentration was even more impressive. Eighty-five percent of the club officers attended Columbia, Harvard, Yale, and Princeton, in the order of frequency named. For the exclusive social sets the proportion is even greater—89 percent.

An equal proportion—39 percent—of Nicholls' "150" had attended Harvard and Columbia. Yale was third in importance with 21 percent, while Princeton was of no prominence whatsoever. The Subscribers to the New York Junior Assembly for 1935 attended Columbia in 21 percent of the cases as compared with 39 percent for Harvard, 27 percent for Yale, and 8 percent for Princeton. The trend in educational institution preference in exclusive social circles is therefore increasingly in favor of Harvard, Yale, and Princeton, at the expense of Columbia. The general educational difference between business leaders and officers of exclusive clubs is that the latter are more frequently college-educated and far more frequently attend those fashionable educational institutions, Harvard, Yale, and Princeton.

Social Affiliations[2]

The nature of social affiliations in the various strata of American society differ considerably. The upper social circles belong to more social clubs quantitatively, and there are more possibilities for "pure" recreation, that is, their social clubs are both more varied in their objectives, and these objectives are rarely instrumental, rarely devoted to other than pleasurable or recreational goals. Further, the clubs to which they belong are commonly viewed as desirable within the group capable of bearing the expense, and these clubs are exclusive in their standards of admission. The clubs and fraternal orders of the middle and lower classes are on the other hand more democratic in their standards, with the exception, of course, of religious, nationality, or territorial restrictions. They are more democratic generally, however, insofar as wealth is concerned. Aside from other excluding techniques the associations of the upper classes automatically limit their memberships by their high initiation fees and dues. The possible list of eligibles is much smaller for the Union, the Knickerbocker, and other clubs than that of the Masons, the Knights of Columbus, the Elks, and the like. The upper classes have the potentiality to affiliate with any association (disregarding non-pecuniary restrictions), while the associations of the upper classes are generally exclusive to all save the upper classes.

Another significant difference between the associations of the upper and lower classes lies in the nature of the values or the objectives for which they are organized. The convivial associations of the lower classes are commonly legitimated by other values, religious, nationalistic, economic security, respectable burial, and the like; while the convivial associations of the upper classes are more frequently freed from these types of legitimation or justification, and are explicitly formed for the pursuit of various kinds of recreation. It might be maintained that the members of the Knights of Columbus are as interested in "pure" pleasure as the members of the New York Yacht Club, but the point of difference is that Knights of Columbus is integrated into the complex of the Catholic Church organizations, whereas the Yacht Club exists as a yacht club. This secularization and institutionalization of convivial life among the upper classes is largely attributable to their economic power, to the broadening effects of this power, and to their imitation of the club patterns of the English upper classes.

Hypothetically, then, we may expect to find the upper classes belonging to more associations, and to more associations the ends of which are purely convivial. And since the upper levels of the plutocracy and society are largely recruited from the earlier immigrations we are also more likely to find them in many cases affiliated with ancestral associations. Ancestral associations include such groups as the Sons of the American Revolution, admission to which is based entirely upon ancestry.

Eighty-eight percent of the officers of business associations belonged to social clubs of various kinds. The average business leader belonged to 4.2 clubs. Only 3 percent belonged to fraternal orders, which have been defined as middle and lower class types of organizations. Twenty-nine percent belonged to ancestral associations of the type of the Sons of the American Revolution, the Mayflower Descendants, and the like. The officers of the Chamber of Commerce seem to be the most active group socially of the three dealt with here. Although fewer of these officers of the Chamber of Commerce belonged to social clubs (82 percent, compared with 92 percent and 100 percent for the officers of the Clearing House and the Merchants Association respectively), nevertheless each officer of the Chamber of Commerce belonged on the average to 5 clubs, as compared with 4.4 for the officers of the Clearing House, and 4.7 for the officers of the Merchants Association.

It is naturally to be expected that members of exclusive social groups would belong to more social clubs than the business leadership. All of the officers of exclusive social clubs were, of course, members of at least one social club, as compared with 88 percent for the officers of business associations. Only 1 percent of the officers of social clubs belonged to fraternal orders (characteristic middle and lower middle class affiliations), as compared with 5 percent for the officers of business associations. The average exclusive club officer belonged to 6 social clubs as compared with 4.2 for the officers of business associations. Since we have already found the officers of exclusive social clubs recruited more frequently from the earlier American immigrations it follows that they would more frequently be affiliated with American ancestral associations, the proportion being 39 percent for club officers to 29 percent for business association officers.

A comparison of the social affiliations of Mrs. Astor's "set" and the Subscribers to the New York Junior Assembly reflects first the difference in the principles of selection of these two groups. The contemporary Subscribers are far less frequently affiliated with social clubs than Mrs. Astor's set. On the average Mrs. Astor's set belonged to 6.2 social clubs as compared with 3.3 for the Subscribers. Only 81 percent of this contemporary group were affiliated with at least one social club, as compared with 94 percent for Mrs. Astor's set. On the other hand the greater proportion of ancestral association affiliations for the Subscribers reveals not a greater interest in genealogy and the commemoration of ancestry on the part of this contemporary group but rather the increase in the number of those organizations and the development of a greater vogue for membership in them.

Club Membership[3]

Social differentiation is not only realized in the types of organizations with which individuals are affiliated. Within these larger categories further distinctions are made by the admission requirements of individual clubs. Some associations restrict their memberships purely on the basis of birth and wealth, others on the basis of what they consider more solid achievement, others on the basis of interest in or skill in some type of sport or recreation. Wealth, birth, skill, and interest restrictions tend to include the same general group of individuals, since individuals of "good" or wealthy birth acquire similar interests or skills through attendance at the same educational institutions, and through social pressures which legitimate certain types of pursuits for their class.

The classification of social clubs employed here was made on the basis of the objectives of the clubs. The first category is of General Social Clubs, which provide eating and indoor amusement and sleeping accommodations. The second category is of Achievement Social Clubs, which mainly add cultural and intellectual objectives to the ends of the general social club, and which admit on the basis of achievement and tend to disregard birth. The third are Luncheon Clubs, which emphasize the provision of midday eating accommodations, although they may also provide amusement and other accommodations. The fourth category is Special Art and Culture Clubs, which emphasize various cultural pursuits, painting, music, dramatics, rare book collection and the cultivation of fine printing, and similar activities. The fifth category is Sport and Athletic Clubs. The sixth classification includes Fraternal Orders the purposes of which in addition to recreation in some cases include insurance arrangements for various purposes and charitable and benevolent activities.

The difference in social affiliation between the plutocracy selection and the society selection is realized not only in terms of the number of social club and ancestral association affiliations, but in their quality. Taking the first category, General Social Clubs, we find, naturally, that a far greater proportion of the officers of exclusive social clubs were members of the Union, Knickerbocker, Metropolitan, and Tuxedo Clubs. In the Achievement Social Clubs the differences were less impressive, but even here a larger proportion of the exclusive social club officers were affiliated with the Century and the University clubs. The more frequent representation of the business leaders in the Luncheon Clubs may be accounted for by the fact that this type of social affiliation fits in better with the active business life of the business leader.

In the Art and Culture Club category a concentration of society leaders was noted in two clubs—the Players (drama) and Grolier (bibliophile), while among business leaders the affiliations in this type of club were distributed among a more varied group of organizations.

In the field of sport and athletic clubs it was found that the exclusive social group is far more frequently represented. It was also found that society
tended to be concentrated in certain sport and athletic organizations; while
among business leaders there was to be noted first a relative infrequency of
membership, and second, relatively little concentration. Those clubs with
the largest proportion of memberships of exclusive club officers may be
taken to be the more exclusive sporting clubs. These include the Riding,
Racquet and Tennis, New York Yacht, Piping Rock, Turf and Field,
Westchester Country, Meadow Brook Hunt, South Side, Brook, National
Golf Links, and Westminster Kennel clubs. While in most cases the business
leader group had a number of affiliations in these exclusive sporting clubs,
the proportion of memberships was far less than for the officers of exclusive social clubs.

We noted above that 29 percent of these business leaders belonged to Ancestral Associations, that is, organizations based entirely on birth. The organization with most memberships is the New England Society. The Sons of
the American Revolution, second on the list, as its title suggests, is limited
to the descendants of those who fought in the American Revolution. The
St. Nicholas Society, limiting its membership to the descendants of families
settled in New York before 1785, was third on the list.

We have already seen that the officers of exclusive social clubs were more
frequently affiliated with ancestral associations. With only three exceptions
the officers of exclusive social clubs were more frequently represented in
each one of these ancestral and patriotic groups. The trend in ancestral association affiliation for club officers indicates a rather large increase, pointing to the conclusion that the vogue for this type of commemoration of ancestry and patriotism is greater at the present time than earlier.

The general conclusions from these tabulations of club memberships are:
(1) that the exclusive social group belonged to more clubs; (2) belonged
more frequently to clubs of a specially exclusive character; while (3) the
business leadership belonged on the average to fewer social clubs; but (4)
their memberships were distributed among a far larger group of more or
less exclusive clubs. The business leader elements were thus from a social
point of view a far more heterogeneous group, including individuals affiliated with both very exclusive and relatively non-exclusive clubs.

Philanthropic Activities[4]

Economic power permits not only exclusive recreational activities but
makes possible moral and cultural actions of various kinds. These activities
involve the contribution of money and time to charitable, cultural, educational, religious, and civic betterment institutions. Although these actions
are commonly viewed as "moral" and the philanthropist a "solid and good

citizen," the actual underlying motivations are far more complex. It is an established technique of the public relations counsellor to urge his wealthy clients injured personally and possibly economically by the contumely of liberal and radical critics to indulge in some spectacular philanthropy. Such is said to have been the consequence of Ivy Lee's advice to the Rockefeller family.[5] It is undeniable that many wealthy individuals give money and time to charitable, cultural, educational, religious, and civic betterment groups out of some definite interest in a specific problem. It is also undeniable that many individuals of wealth contribute money to philanthropy because of social pressures. This attitude is quite characteristic of a great number of wealthy individuals; and the existence of paid specialists to recommend and investigate worth while institutions in New York may be viewed as a symptom of the strength of the philanthropic impulse as well as of the objective difficulty of determining proper objects of philanthropy. The motivation for philanthropy is complex, including the desire to purchase good will, the desire to win prestige within the upper wealth group, as well as frequent and genuine interests in the arts and the social services.

Sixty-three percent of the officers of the business associations held office in, or had made substantial contributions to, philanthropic institutions. Twenty-nine percent of these philanthropic offices were in charitable institutions of various kinds; 25 percent in cultural institutions of the type of the American Museum of Natural History, the Metropolitan Museum of Art, the Metropolitan Opera, the Philharmonic Symphony Society, and the like. Twenty-two percent of these offices were in institutions of learning, universities, colleges, academies, and educational foundations. There were many trustees and regents of Columbia, New York, Yale, Harvard, Williams, Amherst, and other universities in this group. Twenty-one percent of the philanthropic affiliations were in religious institutions and organizations.

The degree of philanthropic and civic activity of these elements is indicated by the fact that they held on the average 2.1 philanthropic offices. The officers of the Chamber of Commerce were the most active, with an average of 2.4 affiliations.

A study of the trend in philanthropic affiliations for these officers of business associations brings out a number of interesting points. The proportions having such affiliations in the 1870–1906 period as compared with the 1931–1935 period are roughly equal. In the 1931–1935 period we find that charitable and educational philanthropies are most frequently represented while in the earlier period charitable, cultural, and religious philanthropies were more frequently represented. Of greatest interest is the drop in the proportion of religious philanthropies, from 25 percent in 1870–1906 to 15 percent in the 1931–1935 period. At the same time the proportion of secular educational philanthropies has more than doubled.

A comparison of the philanthropic activities of the selection of exclusive society and of business leaders indicates that the social leaders are less active in philanthropy. Thus only 46 percent of the exclusive club officers held office in philanthropic institutions as compared with 63 percent for the business leader selection. The comparatively greater degree of philan thropic activity for business leaders is again substantiated by the fact that they held on the average 2.1 philanthropic offices as compared with only 1.2 for society leaders. These differences are partially attributable to the fact of the greater wealth and economic power of the business leader selection. But it is also of interest to observe that the most fashionable and socially esteemed elements of the plutocracy are less actively engaged in cultural and charitable philanthropy than the honored elements of the plutocracy. This again points to the greater triviality of the way of life of exclusive society.

In summary, the majority of the business and social leader groups had enjoyed college education, but the proportion of college-educated was higher among social leaders than among business leaders. The contemporary social and business leaders included a larger proportion of college-educated individuals than the earlier selections. The majority of both groups attended the traditional eastern universities, Harvard, Yale, Columbia, and Princeton. The proportion attending these older schools was much higher for social leaders than for business leaders.

Both selections of the plutocracy were highly active in social and recreational club life, the social leaders naturally more so than the business leaders. The business leaders belonged to a more heterogeneous group of clubs, while the social leaders were concentrated in clubs of a specially exclusive character. Both groups were frequently identified with ancestral associations, that is, organizations commemorating descent from various early American political, nationality, and military groups. The proportion of such affiliations was naturally much higher for the social leader selection.

Both groups were active in the support and control of charitable, educational, cultural, and religious organizations. The general trend in emphasis upon fields of philanthropy has been toward a decrease in religious philanthropy and an increase in other types of philanthropy, reflecting the general tendency toward secularization in American life. The social leader group was less active in philanthropy than the business leaders.

This enumeration of the differences between society and the plutocracy indicates that society is marked by (1) a higher degree of descent from old families of wealth and prestige, (2) a higher degree of inclusion in the Social Register, (3) a greater emphasis upon social activities as measured by club affiliations, and (4) a less active political, economic, and philanthropic role than the selection of established business leaders.

Notes

1. Figures given in the text are taken from tabulations given in Appendix A in the typewritten thesis version. Sources of data for these tabulations are as follows: [Where publication dates are not given it may be assumed they are for the years cited.] New York Chamber of Commerce, *Annual Report, 1870; ibid., 1900; ibid., 1935;* New York Clearing House Association, *Annual Report, 1894; ibid., 1935;* New York Merchants Association, *Annual Report, 1906; ibid.,* 1931; Union Club, *Yearbook, 1870; ibid., 1900; ibid., 1935;* Knickerbocker Club, *Yearbook, 1872; ibid.,* 1932; Metropolitan Club, *Yearbook, 1892; ibid.,* 1935. Mrs. Astor's set was taken from Charles W. DeLyon Nicholls, *The 469 Ultra-Fashionables of America* (New York: Broadway Publishing Co., 1912); the list of Subscribers to the New York Junior Assembly was taken from the *New York Herald Tribune,* Dec. 8, 1935, Society Section. For biographical data the following sources were used: *Appleton's Cyclopedia of American Biography,* edited by James Grant Wilson and John Fiske (New York: D. Appleton Co., 1888); Moses Yale Beach, *The Wealth and Biography of the Wealthy Citizens of New York,* 1842–1855 (New York: published by the *New York Sun*); *Dictionary of American Biography,* edited by Dumas Malone (New York: Charles Scribner's Sons, 1928); Henry Hall, *America's Successful Men of Affairs,* 1895–1896 (New York: the *New York Tribune*); Marguerita Aulina Hamm, *Famous Families of New York* (2 vols.; New York: G. P. Putnam's Sons, 1902); Moses King, *Notable New Yorkers of 1896–1899* (New York: M. King, 1899); *The National Cyclopedia of American Biography* (New York: J. T. White and Co., 1898); Lyman Horace Weeks, *Prominent Families of New York* (New York: The Historical Co., 1897); *Who's Who in America,* 1899–1936 (Chicago: A. N. Marquis Co.); *Who's Who in Commerce and Industry, 1936* (New York: Institute for Research in Biography, Inc., 1936); *Who's Who in Finance and Banking,* 1911–1925 (New York: Who's Who in Finance, Inc.); *Who's Who in New York City,* 1904–1929 (New York: Who's Who Publications, Inc.); *Who's Who in the East* (Washington: Mayflower Publishing Co., 1930); *Poor's Register of Directors of the United States,* 1928–1937 (Babson Park, Mass.: Poor's Printing Co.); *Directory of Directors in the City of New York,* 1898–1927 (New York: The Audit Company of New York); *Social Register New York,* 1889–1936 (New York: Social Register Association).

2. *Ibid.*

3. *Ibid.*

4. *Ibid.*

5. Dixon Wecter, *Saga of American Society* (New York: Charles Scribner's Sons, 1937), p. 473.

7

Self-Indulgence in Social Life

THE DECLINING POLITICAL PARTICIPATION of the wealthy classes in the latter part of the nineteenth century, the constant influx of *parvenus,* and the general increase in the wealth of the plutocracy resulted in an era of great irresponsibility and self-indulgence.

Writing of New York society shortly after the Civil War, a contemporary observer remarked:

> Fully a half million of our population are absorbed in a perpetual struggle to avoid physical suffering; while a hundred thousand, probably pass their lives either in being or trying to be fashionable. That hundred thousand are very gay, and seem positively happy. Yet their woes and throes are innumerable and their struggles with conventionality and gentility, though less severe, are as numerous as those of the half million in penury and want.[1]

The writer goes on to describe three sets in New York society. Among these were the Knickerbockers, who "display conspicuously in their private galleries their plebeian ancestors in patrician wigs and ruffles, that the thrifty old Dutchmen never dreamed of among their barrels of old Jamaica, or their spacious and awkward seines" and who "incline to entertainments and receptions where dreary platitudes pass for conversation, and well intending men and women, whom nature would not bless with wit, fall asleep and dream of a heaven in which they seem clever forevermore."[2]

The second important group were the "cultivatedly comfortable" who had smaller incomes but were marked by their cultural activity. Browne lumped in this group writers, artists, actors, journalists, and others, whom one cannot properly classify as in society in the generally held sense of that term. They tended to constitute their own society, although there is no question but that in American democratic circumstances there was a degree of overlapping between these two groups.

The third group, "the new rich," says Browne:

are at present stronger and more numerous than ever in New York. They prof-
ited by contracts and speculations during the war, and are now a power in the
metropolis—a power that is satirized and ridiculed, but a power nevertheless.
They are exceedingly prononce, bizarre and generally manage to render themselves very absurd. . . . They have the most imposing edifices on the Avenue,
the most striking liveries, the most expensive jewelry, the most gorgeous furniture, the worst manners, and the most barbarous English. They prejudice plain
persons against wealth, inducing them to believe that its accumulation is associated with indelicacy, pretense and tawdriness, and that they who are materially prosperous are so at the price of much of their native judgment and original good sense. After two or three generations, even the new rich will become
tolerable.[3]

For reasons already discussed political careers were generally closed to
the great majority of the wealthy classes. They were able, thus, to objectify
their superior position only in their private life, and in their charitable and
cultural activities. In the first they could tangibly express their superior
wealth. In the second, they could acquire names as patrons of art, and as
civic and philanthropic leaders.

As a plutocracy lacking political power and a tradition of acquiescence
and recognition, the New York wealthy were insecure politically and socially. They attempted to counteract their political insecurity by setting up
an indirect control over political policy. They attempted to counteract their
social insecurity and assert their superiority along two lines of action. The
first was to intermarry with and participate in the social life of the English
and continental aristocracies. The main creative contribution of the American plutocracy was the development of a highly elaborate and extravagant
social life.

Ralph Pulitzer, son of the New York publisher, brings out the difference
between American and European society rather sharply.

With these [European aristocracies] Society is an intermittent condition cre-
ated by the temporary meeting of persons of permanent rank—persons who
possessed their rank before their association made Society, and retain it after
their separation for the time being ends Society. . . . Instead indeed of having
an aristocracy whose caste is beyond question and beyond change, and whose
mutual hospitalities constitute Society, New York has an "aristocracy" whose
elevation is largely artificial, whose membership is largely arbitrary, and whose
existence vitally depends upon those activities which are known as social functions.[4]

In other words plutocratic social life in New York became an end in itself.
It became the special function of the plutocracy, and not an incidental
recreative activity. It was the means by which the plutocracy was able to
show to itself and to the world its merit and achievement.

The directions which these efforts at objectifying the superior position of the plutocracy took were to elaborate the materials and routines of living in great part patterned after the life of the English aristocracy. They copied manners, styles, dress, the organization of the household, and other aspects of social life from these foreign elements. The imitation of foreign aristocracies was not direct for all elements of the plutocracy. It tended to be more marked for the older and more socially established elements. Within itself the plutocracy was divided into many sets, following birth, nationality origin, occupation, sporting, cultural, and philanthropic interest and lines. Most marked were the barriers between the established social elements and the *parvenus*. The established social elements, besides imitating and maintaining contacts with foreign aristocracies, differentiated themselves from the newer and less fashionable plutocracy by closing their social and private lives to them.

The objectification of the superiority of the plutocracy on the social level took many directions. We shall not discuss in any detail their role in the development of artistic and cultural life in New York City. This identified them (with some justice in a few cases) with the higher values of life. The identification of the plutocracy with artistic and cultural life was objectified in the diamond horseshoe of the Metropolitan Opera, the boxes of the Philharmonic Symphony, the patronage of individual artists and musicians, the large private art collections of Morgan, Frick, and many others, rare book collections, grants of money and service on the boards of educational and cultural institutions, and many other lines of activity. On the social level the effort at distancing, at emphasizing their superiority, took the lines of (1) the elaboration of the materials and routines of living; (2) contact with foreign aristocracies; (3) the formation of fashionable sets following an especially spectacular social life; (4) the organization of numerous social, recreational, and sport clubs; and (5) genealogical research and the formation of associations celebrating ancestry. This chapter is concerned with a description of the content of social life in this "Gilded Era" and with a brief discussion of these modes of differentiation.

The Content and Values of Social Life in the "Gilded Age"

A day by day analysis of the purposes for which social events were given in the New York of this era reveals a society pursuing pleasure with a seriousness and an intentness which made Pulitzer remark, "Beneath the frivolity and flippancy with which Society bedizens itself, like the paint and tights in which a chorus girl must do her work, that Society is transacting deadly earnest business."[5] This pleasurable life was little relieved and little justified by any more serious or constructive purpose. In the era of the limited franchise and the transitional period before the Civil War, social functions in

New York tended to be related to more serious activities, or if not, tended to be the minor and recreative aspects of its social life. In the post–Civil War Era a plutocracy inundated with *parvenus*, wanting in political and social security, expanded this recreative aspect of life into its central activity, its main means of showing its superiority.

In the "Social Season of 1882–83" there were a total of 849 social affairs exclusive of weddings. Only 30, or 4 percent, were given for charitable purposes. Prominent among the purely pleasure affairs were the three Patriarch's Balls, the Balls of the Family Circle Dancing Class, and the Ladies Assemblies, all of which were sponsored by the Astor-McAllister group. The important individual balls were those of Mrs. Pierre Lorillard and Mrs. William K. Vanderbilt.[6] The biggest charity affair of the season of 1882–83 was given for the benefit of the Nursery and Child's Hospital with Cornelius Vanderbilt as President, from which approximately $12,000 was raised, a sum only slightly larger than the cost of the favors at many private balls. In addition to these more important affairs the society record lists 100 smaller dances and entertainments of which only 2 were given for philanthropic purposes. Among the other purely pleasurable social functions recorded were 205 dinner parties, 35 luncheon parties, and 301 receptions and teas.[7]

There were 17 balls and entertainments given by military groups which were attended by "fashion." Among the affairs of intellectual and cultural importance were 36 theater parties, 23 musicals, exclusive of opera, 36 lectures, discussions, and literary readings, and 3 art exhibits. In all, these artistic and cultural affairs constituted only 12 percent of the total number of social events of that season. Among the affairs with a charitable or "benefit" purpose were 3 large balls, 2 smaller dances, 2 musical benefits, 8 theatrical benefits, one literary benefit, one benefit art exhibit, and 12 charitable sewing circle meetings. The charitable social affairs were thus in the main not only a very small percentage of the total number of affairs, but they were in most cases the very minor affairs.

A comparison of the social season of 1900 with that of 1882 reveals a number of interesting changes.[8] One development was the decrease in the number of private receptions recorded in the society pages of the *New York Tribune*. In 1882 these formal private affairs constituted 35 percent of the total number of recorded events. In 1900 the proportion of this type of social affair had decreased to 5 percent. Although this decrease may be accounted for by the failure of the *Tribune* to record such minor events, nevertheless other sources indicate that in large part the decrease was due to the passing out of style of this more conservative and modest entertainment. Social competition had become more severe, and only those capable of giving more spectacular and novel entertainments could survive as leaders.

The proportion of balls and large-scale entertainments had increased from 4 percent to 9 percent; and the proportion of smaller dances and entertainments had increased from 13 percent to 20 percent. This also reflects the increase in large-scale social competition, and a far more spectacular social season.

The center of the fashionable group in this era was Mrs. William Astor, and to a lesser extent Mrs. Stuyvesant Fish, and Mrs. Ogden Mills. The latter two acquiesced in the social leadership of Mrs. Astor. It is important to take note that the primary bearers of American society have been women. They were the animating spirits in the spectacular balls and affairs of this and the later era, which constituted the outstanding events of the social season. In the sphere of sport the men naturally dominated. In the sphere of cultural life the activity was shared, although the men dominated in the important cultural institutions, such as the opera, and Symphony Society, the museums of art and natural history. The causes of this feminine domination of society lay in the very nature and values of society. In an aristocracy where the purely pleasurable functions tend to be incidental to more serious concerns, men naturally play the dominant role. Although the women of the aristocracy are the animating spirits in dances and the lighter aspects of social life, this constitutes only an incidental sphere of activity. In American society on the other hand these pleasurable and recreative activities became the special function of this element. Hence the feminine dominance; and hence the development of a kind of effeminate male social leader such as McAllister or Lehr who made specialties of society. The peculiarly extravagant and naive character of American society is in some measure attributable to this feminine leadership which had no contact whatsoever with the productive aspects of life.

The society pages of 1900 also indicated a great increase in the proportion of sporting events. These constituted only one percent of the season's events in 1882, and increased to 16 percent in 1900. These sport events were dog and horse shows, fox hunts, yacht races, and the like. The development of sport as an integral part of "high social life" thus was greatly accelerated in the two decades between 1880 and 1900. The proportion of charitable affairs had increased to 8 percent in 1900. The number of intellectual and cultural affairs remained roughly constant.

Thus in the latter decades of the nineteenth century, although a small portion of plutocratic social life was devoted to charitable and cultural purposes, its primary emphasis was pure display and pleasure for its own sake, an emphasis which tended to increase from the 1880s on.

The Elaboration of Housing, Dress, Transportation, and Sport

The elaboration of the materials and the routines of living was a special mark of the effort of these wealthy elements to enjoy and display their economic power and social position. The building of large expensive town houses after European styles, and of great estates in the country, the owner-ship of yachts, the hiring of tremendous staffs of servants marked the elaboration of housing. The participant in these wealthy groups ordinarily owned a town house and a country house at one of the exclusive summer resorts. This was the minimum. In addition to these necessities, many owned additional winter houses in South Carolina and Florida, hunting estates and preserves in the Adirondacks, and estates in England, France, Spain and other countries.[9] The possession of an ocean-going yacht was indispensable for water transportation,[10] and for land transportation the hiring of private railroad cars was commonplace. The ownership of carriages of all types, sizes, and varieties, and later, automobiles in the same quantity and diversity for local transportation, and, at present, of aeroplanes, were and are matters of course.[11]

To man these great estates, large bodies of liveried servants were indispensable. Here the American wealthy followed the English pattern, even hiring English servants to supervise their staffs, and in some cases to watch over the manners of their employers. The typical wealthy city household takes from 14 to 20 servants, according to the estimate of a private social secretary to one of these families.[12] The large household naturally requires many more servants than this. And the various estates require their permanent caretakers, gardeners, aside from the staffs necessary during a season's entertainment. The American wealthy class in this period imitated the English nobility in having their servants give annual servants' balls at which their masters were frequently present.

In the sphere of food and drink there was naturally a great elaboration. Private houses had place, facilities, and staffs to serve a hundred guests within short notice. Great wine establishments, fine food stores, and restaurants were supported by their custom. The eating of foods out of season, and of rare foods transported from great distances was also a special mark of power and taste. The ownership of vegetable and flower gardens to supply their own needs was a mark of the gentleman-farmer pretensions of this element.

It would be too tedious to discuss the elaboration of clothing and adornment on the part of this class.[13] These elements could naturally afford to be daring, and it was their taste which was dominant in American clothing styles. Each fashionable matron competed with the other in the ownership of jewelry. Writes Nicholls:

> Let royal coffers be what they may the collective contents of the jewel caskets of the ultra-fashionable sets in New York society approximate closely to $170,000,000. Half a dozen women, Mrs. Astor, Mrs. Vanderbilt, Mrs. Oliver H. P. Belmont, Mrs. Wm. K. Vanderbilt Jr., have a million dollars a piece in jewelry.[14]

Expensive sports, the breeding, racing, and exhibition of blooded horses and cattle, the raising and exhibition of thoroughbred dogs, the playing of racquets, tennis, and golf on their own courts and links, swimming in their own swimming pools, fox and other types of hunting, and polo on their own estates, fencing and many other sports marked the elaboration of sport and recreation. The distinguishing marks of the sporting life of the upper classes was its expensiveness, the large amount of time devoted to it, its tremendous variety, and the special imitation of the British nobility.

Contacts with Foreign Nobilities

Although there was much foreign travel on the part of the pre–Civil War plutocracy, and no doubt occasional intermarriage, this development took on really great proportions following the Civil War. The Social Register of New York of 1892 lists 31 titled individuals. This list is limited to New York, and even for New York is not comprehensive. There no doubt also were cases of intermarriage between wealthy Americans and untitled foreigners. Of these 31 foreign noblemen, 21 were from the French aristocracy, 4 from the Spanish, 3 from the German, 2 from the English, and 1 from the Italian. If the claim of Gustavus Myers is correct,[15] by 1909 500 heiresses had married titled foreigners, taking some $220 million away to Europe. In the Social Register, of 1935, however, only 106 individuals with titles are listed. Since New York City naturally would contribute the largest proportion of heiresses for foreign titled marriages, and since generally these individuals are listed in the Social Register, it seems likely that Myers' figures are exaggerated. At any rate his estimate is given in a footnote without supporting documentation. Titled marriages, however, have been many and frequent as the above Social Register figures indicate. Aside from titled marriages these plutocratic circles have made contact with foreign aristocratic and plutocratic circles through non-titled marriages, through the purchase of foreign estates, through philanthropies, and through participation in the foreign social seasons.

It was in the late nineteenth century that the practice of participation in foreign social seasons was seriously undertaken by many families of great wealth. The comment of the Episcopalian clergymen, Nicholls, is instructive:

> If one has in London the avant heraldry of being an Ogden Mills, a Vanderbilt, a Goelet, an Astor, a Pierpont Morgan, or a Belmont, for instance, the doors of its exclusive drawing rooms swing open sesame. For Americans not covered with International Social and Financial prestige, time, tact and above all ceaseless expenditures of money are requisite.[16]

The society pages of these years record the departure of Mrs. William Astor and others for Europe in March, and their return for the social season in Newport in June and July. The society pages also record the frequent social events given by Wm. Waldorf Astor, the Bradley Martins, and other expatriates as well as travelling American social families in London. The "London Season" became an integral part of the social life of the ultra-fashionable element in New York City.

> Strange to narrate [writes Nicholls] in our free democratic United States, almost within a decade there has sprung up an exclusive social caste as valid at certain European courts as an hereditary titled aristocracy—a powerful class of ultra-fashionable multi-millionaires, who at their present ratio of ascendancy bid fair to patronize royalty itself. Personages there are whom Edward VII well might prefer to his own subjects for dinner companions, and "intime" week-end house parties, to say nothing of their being the recipients of almost royal honors, not only at the palaces of sovereigns, but even aboard their own yachts, thus cheapening thrones in the eyes of subjects—these wearers of American coronets, and American Strawberry leaves.[17]

The Formation of Social Sets

The formation of "sets" in this class follows naturally from the tremendous proliferation of its activities. Each sport had its own group of devotees; each summering place its community feeling, each philanthropy its group of supporters, each ethnic and religious element its loyalties; each sphere of economic enterprise, even each business enterprise effected groupings, loyalties, ties of various kinds and strengths. The consequence of the great increase in the number of the wealthy and the essentially anarchic character of the great number of individual interest groups was a growing need for an organization of the "fashionable." The wealthy were on a treadmill. What constituted arrival, legitimation?

This need for the formation of an exclusive set found its first answer after the Civil War in the organization of the Patriarchs, a social committee of 25 men. These 25 men invited 5 ladies and 4 men to a series of three balls held each year, which came to constitute the main events of the New York social season for two decades. The prime movers behind the Patriarchs were Ward McAllister and Mrs. Wm. Astor, nee Schermerhorn. For younger people McAllister organized the Family Circle Dancing Class which also held a series of dances during the season. It was this group around Mrs. Astor, with Ward McAllister as *arbiter elegantiarum,* that constituted the ultra-fashionable set of the New York plutocracy. Nicholls wrote that it was Mrs. Astor's "court" and not the White House which granted social legitimation in America, that "Newport and not the White House is the Supreme Court of social appeals in the United States."[18]

With Mrs. Astor as queen, the New York–Newport set was built upon wealth, birth, and fashion. McAllister was a kind of court chamberlain whose special capacity lay in devising new forms of entertainment and in examining the qualifications of new aspirants. It generally admitted those with enough money, and with a flair for the fast pace followed by this element, while birth, though an important element, was a secondary factor as McAllister and Nicholls both admit. The social rank of this ultra-fashionable set was determined by its pace and its spectacle. And only those were admitted who had the inclination and the energy and the power to participate in it.

> In Europe [wrote Nicholls] the pleasures of social life are the privileges of social rank which, of course, is founded upon the Brahmin caste of nobility. In America in ultra-fashionable society rank has to be created and kept up by *social functions,* these amenities of necessity being extended to people already bearing the imprimatur of fashion, or meet for elevation to the Golden Caste of Vere de Vere. One's family fixed one's social status under the old time social regime in America. A European upper class finds in society in general and particularly in summer migratory residence and relaxation, a surcease from care and worry. The ultra-fashionable America, on the contrary, finds in society a treadmill from which there is no shuffling out; the giving and attending of a round of social functions which cannot be neglected without imperilling, or more often actually losing caste.[19]

The older Knickerbocker elements also constituted an important set at this time. Their position, distinctly secondary in the public eye, was determined by their birth and their conservatism. It has frequently been maintained that this old Knickerbocker set scorned and snubbed the Newport crowd. If the word of a frank old Knickerbocker is to be taken, "they jumped at the invitation of a Vanderbilt." A sounder interpretation would be that the older set was unable economically to compete with the Astor-Mills-Vanderbilt group and that they rationalized their inferior public position by scorning the more spectacular and wealthier group. Nicholls recommends to climbers of the social ladder, "Whenever you receive a social thud from an ultra-fashionable, fly into the arms of a Knickerbocker."[20]

The Formation of Social Clubs

The great increase in the number of wealthy individuals in New York City was marked by a proliferation of many clubs with convivial, sporting, cultural, intellectual, and political goals. Table 7.1 classifies these social clubs according to their date of organization and purpose.

The tremendous expansion of the club movement in New York City in the latter half of the nineteenth century is revealed by the fact that previous to 1860 the writer has found record of under 20 clubs, while between the years 1860 and 1895 there are readily accessible records of 110, patronized primarily by the wealthy elements. As we have already indicated, the typical club of the pre–Civil War epoch was the cultural or intellectual group; after

TABLE 7.1   The Organization of Clubs in New York City, 1783–1890*

Types of Clubs	Period of Organization					
	1783–1800	1801–1860	1861–1870	1871–1880	1881–1896	Total
Social clubs	1	3	5	7	17	32
Cultural and intellectual clubs	4	2	7	5	13	32
Political-recreational clubs	—	—	2	2	4	8
Religious clubs	—	—	—	2	2	4
Athletic clubs	—	—	1	2	2	5
Horse racing clubs	—	—	1	2	1	4
Hunting clubs	—	—	—	1	2	3
Dog breeding clubs	—	—	—	1	6	7
Cattle breeding clubs	—	—	1	—	—	1
Yacht clubs	—	1	1	3	3	8
Boating clubs	—	2	2	7	2	13
Cycling clubs	—	—	—	1	2	3
Country clubs	—	—	—	—	3	3
Total	5	8	20	33	57	123

*Francis G. Fairfield, *The Clubs of New York City* (New York: H. L. Hunter, 1873); the *Elite Catalogue of Clubs, 1890* (New York: New York Publishing Co., 1890); and miscellaneous sources.

the Civil War these more serious clubs were overshadowed by the many social clubs and athletic and sporting associations. The organization of political clubs, the membership of which was largely plutocratic in character in the post– Civil War period, represents a special form of indirect political participation characteristic of the upper classes, and has been dealt with in Chapter 4.

The purpose of the general social club is to supply a place of congregation with hotel and restaurant services, offering facilities for card playing, billiards, magazine reading, and lounging. The Union Club was organized in 1836, the New York Club in 1845. Both of these clubs were Social Register clubs, that is, were later listed in the Social Register, and hence may be assumed to be relatively exclusive. The Hone Club was also a social club, but had no permanent organization and clubhouse and passed out of existence before the Civil War. Between the years 1861–1870 five social clubs were formed: the Calumet, Downtown Association, Harvard, Harmonie, and Fidelio. The Calumet was similar to the New York and Union clubs in purpose and social composition. The Downtown Club was an eating place for the business men in the financial section of Manhattan. The Harvard was made up of Harvard graduates. These three clubs were listed in the Social Register. The Harmonie and Fidelio were both clubs for the wealthier German Jews but were not listed in the Social Register.

The social clubs formed in the years 1871–1880 were the Knickerbocker, the Metropolitan, Lawyers, the Hoot Club, the Harlem Club, Manhattan Chess Club, and the New York Chess Club. The first three were Social Register clubs; the last four were less exclusive. Sixteen more social clubs were formed in the 1881–1895 period. These were the Hamilton Club of Brooklyn, the Merchants Club, the Tuxedo Club, the Fulton, and Traveller's Home Club, as well as ten clubs restricted to the graduates of universities. These were the Amherst Graduate, the Barnard, the Brown University Graduate, the Columbia Graduate, the University of New York Graduate, the Princeton Graduate, the Trinity Graduate, the Union College Graduate, the Williams, and the Yale Graduate clubs. All of these graduate clubs were listed in the Social Register.

The exclusive Social Register Clubs of this period were:

Union Club	1836
New York Club	1845
Downtown Association	1860
Calumet Club	1869
Knickerbocker Club	1871
Metropolitan Club	1878
Hamilton Club of Brooklyn	1882
Tuxedo Club	1886
Merchants Club	1888

The organization of clubs for intellectual and cultural purposes began at a much earlier date. One writer has found records of four cultural clubs formed before the nineteenth century. These were the Drone Club, the Euterpean, the Philharmonic, and the Columbian Anacreontic societies, the last three, musical societies.[21] In the period 1801–1860 two cultural and intellectual clubs were formed, the Kent and the Century clubs. The first was a lawyer's club devoted to the discussion of serious topics. The Century Association was an artistic and literary club, forming an art gallery and founding a magazine. Seven cultural and intellectual clubs were organized in the decade of the Civil War. These were the Lotos, the Travellers, the Palette, the Mendelsohn Glee Club, the Progress Club, Sorosis, and the University Club. Of these only the Lotos and the University clubs were listed in the Social Register. Five cultural and intellectual clubs were formed in 1871–1880, the Arcadian, and Eccentric clubs, the Freundschaft Society, the Salmagundi, and the New York Press Club. None of these was a Social Register club; their memberships were either German as in the case of the Freundschaft Society or else drawn primarily from the ranks of professional artists, journalists, actors, and the like.

Twelve additional cultural and intellectual groups were formed in the period 1881–1895. These were the Aldine Club, devoted to literature and art, the Author's Club, the Players Club (actors and laymen), the Electric Club (the study of electricity), the Grolier Club (bibliophile), the Kit Kat Club (professional painters), the Mendelsohn Glee Club, the Narragansett Club (literary), the Orpheus Society (music), the Quill Club (writers), and the Owl, Cosmos, and Commonwealth clubs, the last three being general intellectual discussion groups. Of these twelve clubs the Aldine, Authors, Grolier, and Players clubs were Social Register clubs.

The cultural and intellectual clubs of New York society which were given Social Register listing were:

The Century	1847
University Club	1865
Lotos Club	1870
Authors Club	1882
Grolier Club	1884
Players Club	1887
Aldine Club	1889

Clubs combining recreational with avowed political purposes were first organized in the decade of the Civil War. The Union League Club, formed in 1862, was the first of these. It has always been the stronghold of Republicanism in New York City. The Manhattan Club for Democrats was formed two years later. The Army and Navy Club was formed in 1871, and the Republican in 1879. In the 1880s and 1890s four political associations were organized. These were the Reform, the City Reform, and the Federal Club (Republican), and the Democratic Club. Of these all save the Federal Club were listed in the Social Register. The Reform Club, the City Reform Club, and the City Club, organized later, were non-partisan political reform groups, while the others were partisan groups. The movement for political reform largely sponsored by these wealthy elements was thus fairly well institutionalized by the 1860s, and the listing of reform clubs in the Social Register indicates that the revolt against political corruption was socially legitimated.

The records list four religious clubs, organized from the 1870s to the 1890s. These were the Catholic Club of New York, listed in the Social Register; the Church Club, also listed in the Register; and the Clergy and Congregational clubs, neither of which were Social Register clubs.

The period following upon the Civil War was also marked by a tremendous proliferation of athletic and sporting clubs. The first of such clubs organized were the yachting and boating clubs. The New York Yacht Club was first in 1844, and was followed by the Columbia Yacht Club in 1869, the Seawanhaka Yacht Club in 1871, the Hudson River Yacht Club in 1874, the Larchmont in 1880, and the American and Harlem Yacht clubs in 1883. Of these, four were listed in the Social Register: the New York, American, Larchmont, and Seawanhaka-Corinthian.

A host of boating and canoe clubs arose in these decades—two in the years before the Civil War, two in the decade of the Civil War, seven in the decade 1871–1880, and two in the period 1881–1890. None of these was given Social Register listing. This is largely due to the fact that boating clubs involved a relatively small outlay of money, and hence were accessible to individuals of lesser wealth.

The first horse-racing association, the American Jockey Club, was formed in 1866 by the banker August Belmont and the stock speculator Leonard W. Jerome. This was followed in 1879 by the Coney Island Jockey Club in which Jerome was also influential, the Driving Club of New York for trotting-horses in 1880, and the New York Jockey Club in 1888. Although the membership of these horse-racing groups were recruited largely from the wealthy elements, none of the clubs was included in the Social Register.

Cattle- and dog-breeding clubs also arose in the decades following the Civil War. The American Jersey Cattle Club was organized in 1868. Annual horse shows exhibiting the blooded stock of the stables of the wealthy began to take place in the 1890s. The Westminster Kennel Club was formed in 1878, and the American Kennel Club in 1884. The Fox Terrier, the Mastiff, the St. Bernard, the Spaniel, and the Collie clubs were all formed in the 1880s. Of these dog and cattle breeding clubs only the Westminster Kennel Club was listed in the Social Register.

Clubs for indoor athletics, called athletic clubs in the table, were organized in the 1870s and the 1880s. The New York Athletic Club was formed in 1868, followed by the American and Manhattan in 1877, and the Berkeley Athletic and Berkeley Ladies Athletic clubs in 1888 and 1889. Of these only the New York Athletic Club was listed in the Social Register.

Three hunting clubs originated in these years. These were the Meadow Brook Hunt Club, the Washington Heights Gun Club, and the Adirondack League Club. Of these only the Meadow Brook, a Long Island fox-hunting group, still in existence, was given Social Register listing.

Country clubs, devoted to riding, golfing, tennis, swimming, and the like, originated in the last two decades of the nineteenth century. Clubs of this type were the Country Club, the Westchester Country Club, and the Essex County Country Club. All three of these are Social Register clubs. Three cycling clubs were also formed between the 1880s and 1890s, but were not listed in the Social Register. The Fencers Club, formed in 1883, is still listed in the Social Register. Among other special sporting clubs sponsored by these exclusive elements was the Coaching Club, which endeavored to keep up the pageantry and color of the English stage coach by holding annual stage coach parades in and around New York City during the 1880s and 1890s.

The period from the Revolution to the 1890s was also marked by the formation of many ancestral associations, that is, clubs based primarily on birth. The aristocratic Society of the Cincinnati was formed in 1783 and exists at the present time, its membership restricted to the descendants in the male line of the officers of the Continental Army. The St. George Society, consisting of the descendants of the English settlers, and the St. Andrew Society were also formed in the years before 1800. During the nineteenth century a large number of these ancestral associations were organized. Prominent among these groups were the Sons of the American Revolution, the Society of Colonial Wars, the Colonial Dames, and the Colonial Dames of America, the Descendants of the Colonial Lords of the Manor, the Daughters of the Cincinnati, the Holland Society, the St. Nicholas Society, the Huguenot Society, the New England Society, the Southern Society, the Mayflower Descendants, the Society of the War of 1812, the Society of the Scions of the Colonial Cavaliers, the Society of Descendants of the Colonial Governors, and a number of others. These associations of birth are societies of aristocratic pretense, and arose mainly in the latter half of the nineteenth century following upon the frenzied genealogical research sponsored and subsidized by the wealthy classes.

Notes

1. Junius Henry Browne, *The Great Metropolis: A Mirror of New York* (Hartford: American Publishing Co., 1869), p. 31.

2. *Ibid.*, p. 33.

3. *Ibid.*, pp. 35–36.

4. Ralph Pulitzer, *New York Society on Parade* (New York and London: Harper Bros., 1910), pp. 1–3.

5. *Ibid.*, p. 4.

6. A description of the Vanderbilt ball of 1882 by a contemporary observer may serve to give the reader a sense of the elaborateness of some of the tremendous entertainments. "The home of Mr. and Mrs. William K. Vanderbilt, at the northwest corner of Fifth Avenue, and Fifty-Second Street, was thronged with a brilliant company in the evening at the first fashionable fancy dress ball which has been given in New York for a number of years. The Ball probably equalled if it did not excell, in beauty and attractiveness any similar entertainment ever given in the city. Any dreams of splendor by a passer-by would have been more than realized could he have caught a glimpse of the rooms inside, where beautiful women and distinguished men promenaded through the halls, formed groups in the various rooms, made charming pictures on the stairways or mingled in the waltz, quadrille, or minuet. Louis Quinze and Mary Queen of Scots might almost have felt at home in the company, unless they happened to run across too correct copies of themselves. A countess might be seen walking with a Marchioness, or a duke with a Venetian lady, and indeed the combinations of imitated rank and beauty were endless where so many powdered wigs were graciously bowing, so many pairs of bright eyes flashing in rivalry of the jewels of their owners, and so much talking, dancing, and promenading were enjoyed. Mrs. Vanderbilt was assisted in receiving the company by her sister Mrs. Yznaga, and Lady Mandeville, formerly Miss Yznaga. From 600 to 800 people were present, but owing to the large rooms there was little discomfort from crowding. The dancing was begun with the quadrille, the participants in which gathered in the gymnasium, and marched down the broad winding staircase making a lovely effect in their various costumes. . . .

"A crowd of commoners gathered outside the house and waited three hours. A squad of policemen were there to maintain order. . . . At twenty minutes past ten the first carriage stopped with a business air in front of the awnings. The door was opened by a footman and out stepped a stout gentleman in all the glory of silk stockings, knee breeches, cloak, sword, and laces. Then a rustle, next a pretty silk slipper upon the carriage step, and then the fair damsel herself looking, with her high head-dress plentifully bepowdered, her court dress of rich silk and her flashing diamonds, like a vision from the court of one of the Georges. The beginning was now made and with ever increasing rapidity the carriages drove up and discharged their beautifully attired occupants, and those in the front rank of the spectators had passing before them a brilliant pageant of Knights, nobles, ladies, characters from history and fiction, and pretty little creatures from the world immortalized for the nursery by Mother Goose.

"On entering, powdered footmen with knee breeches, like the London 'Jeames' came forward to meet the guest, and the ladies were directed up a vast marble staircase whose splendid white effect with stained glass windows everywhere, recalled the Milan Cathedral. Vastness is the first impression in this truly magnificent house, and splendor is the second impression, and luxury is the third impression. The great state bedroom, into which the ladies were ushered, had a four poster bed, hung with tapestry quite as gorgeous as any state bed in a royal palace in the days of the most luxurious Queen of France. The wood carving, the gilding, the furniture, the hangings were all regal. Out of this state bedroom opened a dining room lined with mirror. On that mirror was painted branches of apple blossom so that it was a bewildering bower of brilliancy and spring. In this room was also a bath tub of onyx or alabaster fit for Undine to bathe in. The dining table was also a slab of onyx, and all the appointments were of silver. It is a dream of loveliness. Here sat a little nun, in the full dress of her order, and flitting past her were the gayest costumes possible. Another large room with two little brass beds in the French style opened out of this room. Maids in pretty caps and national costumes of Brittany and Sweden attended the ladies. . . .

"The end of the dining room is a stained glass window of immense dimensions representing the meeting of Francis I and Henry VIII on the Field of The Cloth of Gold. It had exactly the effect of another fancy ball going on in another room, and added infinitely to the effect of the glittering pageant which was going on below. . . . Retracing our steps to the grand staircase again, and meeting a beautiful French Marquise in white satin on the way, who spoke cordial words of welcome, the wanderer descended the stairs and found the hall below already full of knights, courtiers, and princes, waiting for their ladies. The guests were shown to a Francois Premier Salon, where stood Mr. Vanderbilt, dressed as the Duke de Guise, and looking well in that courtly costume, Mrs. Vanderbilt as a Venetian Lady, Lady Mandeville, as a Princess du Croi, in black velvet, both looking marvelously well, received the guests. The whole wainscotting of this beautiful apartment was brought from a chateau in France. On the walls hung three French Gobelin tapestries, a century old but in the brilliance and freshness of their coloring seemingly the work of yesterday." *Social Season of 1882–83* (New York: the *New York Tribune*, 1883), pp. 159 ff.

7. *Ibid.*

8. Data for the 1900 social season were gathered from the weekly summaries of society events in the *New York Tribune.*

9. Ferdinand Lundberg, *America's 60 Families* (New York: The Vanguard Press, 1937), p. 418.

10. *Ibid.,* p. 432.

11. *Ibid.,* p. 441.

12. This estimate is based upon confidential information from a private social secretary.

13. Lundberg, *op. cit.,* p. 444.

14. Charles W. D. Nicholls, *The 469 Ultra-Fashionables of America* (New York: Broadway Publishing Co., 1912), p. 55.

15. Gustavus Myers, *Great American Fortunes* (Chicago: C. H. Kerr, 1910), II, 274.

16. Nicholls, *op. cit.,* p. 83.

17. Ibid., p. 83.

18. *Ibid.,* p. 9.

19. *Ibid.*

20. *Ibid.,* p. 34. These conclusions are also based upon interviews.

21. W. Harrison Bayles, "Old Taverns of New York," *Journal of American History,* XXVII (1933).

Part Three

Politicians Under Democratic Conditions

8

Federal
Office-Holders

THE RISE OF A DEMOCRATICALLY SELECTED political leadership made essential a rapid adjustment on the part of the economic controlling classes. The perennial problem of the business leadership came to be that of maintaining a safe political situation for themselves. Historically this exercise of influence has shifted from the rather crude practice in which wealthy entrepreneurs journeyed to legislatures with suitcases of greenbacks and distributed them among amenable legislators or officials, to the acquisition of the services of "key politicians" and instruments of political pressure to maintain them in political safety.

The political elite under democracy tended on the whole to be amenable to this situation. In the most part consisting of lawyers and smaller entrepreneurs, they were not generally animated by political convictions and objectives of a general character. Political office came to be viewed less as the representation of the interests of groups in the population or the representation of the interests of the whole, but generally as a means of self-aggrandizement, through the perquisites of office, or through coming into contact with the "right" people, the wealthy themselves, or the bosses who had already established the right contacts.

Historically lawyers have played an increasingly dominant role in American politics. Tocqueville saw in this dominance of the lawyer the main safeguard against democratic excesses.

> The more we reflect upon all that occurs in the United States, the more shall we be persuaded that the lawyers, as a body, form the most powerful, if not the only counterpoise to the democratic element. In that country we perceive how eminently the legal profession is qualified by its powers, and even by its defects, to neutralize the vices which are inherent in popular government. When the American people is intoxicated by passion or carried away by the impetuosity of its ideas, it is checked and stopped by the almost invisible influence of its legal counsellors, who secretly oppose their aristocratic propensities

to its democratic instincts, their superstitious attachment to what is antique to its love of novelty, their narrow views to its immense designs, and their political procrastination to its ardent impatience.[1]

Professional advocates lawyers tend to be infrequently animated by convictions of their own, but generally tend to advocate the cause, which pays their fees. As entrepreneurs they generally identify themselves with other entrepreneurs, and generally hope as the summation of their careers to become associated with the most powerful entrepreneurs, that is, to achieve the status of great corporation lawyers. More particularly the English and American lawyers have tended to be conservative because of the emphasis upon precedent in the Common Law.

Besides the lawyers the next largest group represented among politicians are the smaller entrepreneurs—especially promotional enterprisers such as real estate and insurance salesmen, or those with large personal clienteles such as saloon-keepers, or those entrepreneurs whose businesses make political connections specially profitable, such as building contractors, coal and oil dealers, truckers, and the like.

The primarily legal and middle class character of the professional politicians under democracy tended to identify them psychologically with the plutocracy. But the identification was not purely psychological in those outstanding cases in which political bosses were able to rise through politics into big business status by means of public franchises and rights.

The consequence of the fact that the politicians were not recruited from the wealthiest sections of the population has been the comparatively low prestige level of public life in America. The term "comparatively" is used, since it must not be forgotten that on the whole the politicians sought and achieved power and prestige within lower class groups, primarily the immigrant, laboring, smaller middle class, and lesser agrarian groups. But in terms of the general stratification of prestige in America the politicians have on the whole been rated as on a lower level than the more influential private occupations.

In his studies of attitudes toward the public service in Chicago, Professor Leonard D. White discovered that

> employment by the city of Chicago apparently tends to command the respect of the immature, the uneducated, the foreign born, and the laboring people. Among persons of maturity, of judgement, substantial education, native to Chicago, high in the economic and business world, a position with the city of Chicago is normally rated as one of low prestige.[2]

In a later study, nationwide in scope, he found again that generally for the United States as for Chicago, the degree of esteem accorded to city employment tended to coincide with occupational and economic stratification;

that is, the lower middle and lower classes tended to be more favorably impressed by city employment, and the upper classes unfavorably impressed by it, with the middle classes occupying an intermediate position. His second investigation found that federal employment was viewed more favorably than state employment, and state employment more favorably than municipal.[3] Although his investigations were directed at the prestige of the administrative levels, his general findings are probably applicable to the political level as well.

The low prestige level of municipal employment in Chicago he attributed to two conditions: (1) "distrust of the general conditions under which work is performed by the city,"[4] in other words the consequences of being dominated by political machines; and (2) "the continued abstention of the well-to-do business elements from active participation in the city's affairs."[5] Of these two causes of the low prestige level of public employment it is contended here that the second is basic, although the conditions of employment are without question also of great importance. Let us put the question in the following form: If the moral level and the efficiency of public office were raised, would it raise its prestige level, and if so, to what degree? That it would be raised somewhat there can be no question. But how much? White views the problem of prestige from the point of view of the "pulling power" of the public service. The ideal situation in the underlying philosophy of his investigation is one in which the public service draws the best of the community talent. What are the objective conditions which would make this possible? If dishonesty and inefficiency were eliminated from the public service, if the conditions of the public service were to become more stable, there is no question but that its pulling power would be increased, that it would draw talent from wider elements of the population. But the pulling power of the public service must be viewed as relative to the pulling power of private occupations, relative to the objective potentialities of private business and professional life. For as long as private activity offers greater rewards to individual endeavor it will be superior to public activity as a competitor for talent.

The "volume" of emulation directed into the various channels of social activity is determined by (1) the relative influence or power which these activities offer—their rewards, in other words—and (2) the objective chances of achievement in those spheres. A situation is possible in which a sphere of activity offers the greatest influence and power, and in which the chances of achievement are high; and second, one in which the sphere of activity offering the greatest influence is relatively closed to new entries. In America business activity has been the sphere of activity offering the greatest rewards in power and esteem. This is attributable to (1) the constitutional limitations upon the powers of government in America; (2) the great national and human resources of the country; and (3) the new techniques of economic exploitation developed in the industrial revolution.

Since the rewards have been highest in business activity it therefore follows that business would pull the best talent. Since political activity in America has been legally limited in its scope, and since the conditions of political competition make for instability and dependence upon political organizations and machines, it would naturally follow that politics would not attract those elements whose chances of achievement in business activity are high and whose social status is therefore relatively stable.

As the upper ranges of the entrepreneurial classes become more fixed or self-perpetuating, a situation will arise in which the sphere of activity offering the greatest rewards will tend to become closed to new entries. This situation will result in an enhanced pulling power of the public service; for, although the rewards will still be highest in business, the objective chances of rising to this controlling class will be decreased. Thus, while the prestige of the public service will rise, it will still be relatively lower than that of the upper business class.

But the decreasing chances of entry into the upper business classes reflects a situation which has deeper consequences for the relative influence and pulling power of the economic and political spheres. The rise of an upper business class, increasingly self-perpetuating in character, means that on the whole the economic resources of the country are owned, and the potentialities of exploitation under the obtaining system of exploitation has reached a ceiling. Since material human aspiration continues (unless repression and the substitution of non-material rewards are resorted to) and since aspiration in the sphere of business activity becomes increasingly blocked, the resort to political means will increase. To put this concretely, since the lower middle and lower classes will be unable to improve their economic situation by individual economic effort, there will be a tendency toward a politicization of their activities. That is, they will seek as groups and through group pressures (i.e., political or potentially political) to improve their economic situation. This group action on the part of the lower middle and lower classes will be directed toward restricting the power of the economic controlling classes and toward spreading the chances of economic betterment more equally in the population. This movement, signs of which are clearly to be observed today, will have far-reaching consequences for the prestige and influence of politics and the public service. For by breaking those legal limitations upon the scope of political activity it will tend to undermine the exclusive privileges and powers of the economic controlling classes. And the prestige and pulling power of politics will increase in proportion to the degree to which the powers of the economic controlling class are restricted or destroyed.

The increased threat to the exclusive powers and privileges of the upper business classes may have other consequences which will affect the power and prestige of political life. A threat to the power of the upper classes inevitably increases the volume of their political activity. If in response to this threat they should succeed in entering increasingly the political and administrative services, this will also mean a heightened prestige level and pulling power of the public service.

However in a situation of mass democracy the possibility for an increased personal entrance into politics on a great scale of the upper business elements are small. Strategically this would be poor if not impossible politics. The alternative is a mass movement deriving its major support from the middle and lower middle classes designed to destroy the "left" labor organizations, a movement which would seek and perhaps gain exclusive or totalitarian powers. This too would inevitably mean an increased prestige level of politics, since such a movement would necessarily have to exercise increasingly strict controls over political and economic life.

The materials presented by L. D. White are of a social psychological character describing the attitudes of various classes and groups of the population toward the public service. The materials discussed in the three succeeding chapters are intended to describe the actual class composition of various types of political office-holders from New York City, the intention being to show the relationship of the class composition of elected office-holders in the three levels of government to the general esteem in which these levels of the government service were held. On the basis of White's study we would expect to find a higher participation of the wealthy classes on the federal level, a smaller participation on the state level, and the smallest participation on the municipal level. The theory upon which this hypothesis is based is that the degree of the participation of the wealthy classes in the various levels of government and types of offices would vary with the prominence and power of the offices. Because of the prestige already enjoyed by the wealthy by virtue of their economic power, the plutocracy would be attracted primarily to the very outstanding offices, leaving to the lower classes the bulk of the less prominent offices. For the moment we exclude crisis situations. These are discussed specially in Chapter 12.

For the analysis of the social composition of federal office-holders the biographies of 251 federal officials holding office between the years 1860 and 1935 were collected and studied. Comparisons were made chronologically and between the holders of the various federal offices.

Birthplace[6]

Of the 198 federal officers upon whom information of this kind was available, 177, or 89 percent, were native born, and 21, or 11 percent, were foreign-born. This compares with 91 percent native born for business leaders and 98 percent for society leaders. Only 30 percent of the federal officers were born in New York City as compared with 34 percent for business leaders and 70 percent for society leaders. Those federal politicians born outside of New York City came largely from New York State, the New England states, the Middle Atlantic and South Atlantic states. In respect of territorial origins federal politicians are similar to business leaders, being recruited largely from the eastern seaboard states, and different from society leaders, the great majority of whom were born in New York City. Of the foreign-born federal politicians the largest number came from Ireland, and the next largest from Germany.

It is noteworthy that all except one of the executive and cabinet officers were born in the United States. Of these, 14 were from New York City or State, and 10 from the New England states. The largest number of New Englanders in this group of federal officers held office in the 1860–1890 period. Of the 79 diplomatic officers from New York City on whom this information was available, 70 were native born. The 9 foreign-born were from Germany, Canada, Ireland, France, Turkey, and the Dutch East Indies. Hector De Castro, United States Consul General to Rome in 1897, was born in Turkey. Jacob Gould Schurman, president of Cornell University, and Minister to Greece and Montenegro in 1912 was born in Freetown in the Dutch East Indies. He was, however, of German origins. Half of the diplomatic officers were from New York City and State. A relatively large number also came from the New England, the Middle Atlantic, and the southern seaboard states.

With one exception all of the United States senators were native born. Robert Wagner, present United States Senator from New York, was born in Germany. Nine of the 10 native born were from New York City or State and the Pennsylvania and New Jersey area.

The office of congressman was more frequently accessible to immigrants. Thus 10, or 18 percent, of the total number were foreign-born. Of these 5 were Irishmen and 2 were Scotch. All of the members of the federal judiciary for whom these data were available were native born. They came largely from New York City and State and from New England.

In summary, data on birthplace indicated that federal officers were similar to business leaders in that large numbers came from areas outside of New York City and State. They also point out that the office of Congressman was most accessible to the foreign-born. Federal officers generally derived from the eastern seaboard states. The proportion of New Englanders among federal politicians, although high in the early periods, has been decreasing.

Nationality Origins

There are fewer second generation natives among federal politicians than among business leaders, the ratio being 70 percent to 81 percent. The foreign-born or first generation natives were primarily Irish, German, and Jewish of various nationality origins. The executive and cabinet officers from New York City with a single exception were all native of native stock. Oscar Straus, secretary of Commerce and Labor in 1906–1909, was a Jew of German origin. Eighty-two percent of the diplomatic officers were native born of native stock. The largest foreign-born or first generation native born element among diplomats were Jews. And 6 out of the total of 7 Jews were of German origin. Jews are in themselves a stratified group. Those of German origin came to the United States first and were established by the time of the arrival of their non-German co-religionists.

Eight of the 11 United States senators were native of native stock; 3 were of foreign origin. Two were from Ireland and 1 from Germany. United States congressmen included the largest number of foreign born individuals. Of the 51 upon whom these data were available, only 17 or 33 percent were native born of native stock. Thirty-seven percent were of Irish origin, 10 percent of Jewish, and 10 percent of German origin. All 5 of the Jewish congressmen were of Russian, Polish, or Hungarian origin, that is, the later Jewish immigrations. The Jewish congressmen are all to be found in the 1935 period, whereas the immigrant stock represented in the 1880–1890 period were primarily Irish and German. Seventy-four percent of the federal judges during this period were native of native parentage. This group included Supreme Court Justice Benjamin Cardozo who comes of the older Portuguese Jewish stock, the forbearers of which came to America in pre-Revolutionary times. The other federal justice of Jewish origin is United States District Court Judge Grover Moscowitz.

The statistics of nationality origin indicate that of all federal offices that of United States congressman was most accessible to newer immigrant stocks. In terms of nationality origins federal politicians are far more heterogeneous in origin than New York society leaders, and slightly more so than business leaders.

Occupational Composition

As compared with business leaders and society, federal politicians included a larger proportion of individuals from the professions—66 percent. Twenty-six percent were in the *rentier* or big business class, and 8 percent were in the category of Other Non-Professional Self-employed. This latter group is made up of small shopkeepers, building contractors, of real estate and insurance agents, and the like. Four of the total, or 2 percent, were *rentiers;* 10, or 5 percent, were officers of banking, investment, and insurance corporations; 4 percent were officers of railroad and utility enterprises; 9 percent were publishers or editors or both; 4 percent were in manufacturing enterprises; and 2 percent were in commercial corporations.

Among the non-professional self-employed the real estate and insurance agents constituted the largest element, with building contractors, shopkeepers, and the like, following in number.

The largest profession represented was the legal profession. It constituted 52 percent of the total number of federal politicians. The next important professional element were academicians who constituted 5 percent of the total. Physicians, writers, journalists, engineers, clergymen, and social workers made up the total.

Of the five groups of federal officers represented here, three were made up entirely of corporation or firm executives and professionals. Only among senators and United States congressmen was there any representation of the smaller entrepreneurial class. Executive and cabinet officers from New York City during the years 1860–1935 were recruited entirely from the classes of firm or corporation executives and professionals: 25 percent from the first, and 75 percent from the second. Of the 7 officers of corporations holding executive or cabinet positions, 2, Thomas L. James, Postmaster General in the first Cleveland administration, and president of the Lincoln National Bank in New York City, and Robert Bacon, Secretary of State in 1909 and a member of the banking house of Morgan, were officers of financial and other business institutions. Two were officers of railroad companies, 2 of manufacturing corporations, and 1 of commercial corporations.

Of the 15 lawyers holding executive or cabinet office, 5 held many corporation offices. These corporation lawyer politicians were William Collins Whitney, Secretary of the Navy in 1885, who held office in 14 banking, railroad, and insurance corporations; Charles Stebbins Fairchild, Secretary of the Treasury in 1887–1889, who held offices in 12 banking, investment, railroad, and insurance corporations; Benjamin Tracy, Secretary of the Navy in 1889, who held office in 6 corporations of various kinds. Elihu Root, Secretary of State in 1905, held office in 6 banking and insurance corporations; and William Gibbs McAdoo, Secretary of the Treasury in Wilson's cabinet, who was an officer of railroad corporations. Two of the 28 cabinet and executive officers were engaged in the teaching of law either primarily or in addition to practice. Harlan Fiske Stone, Dean of the Columbia Law School, was Attorney General in the Coolidge administration, and Charles Evans Hughes, Secretary of State during the Harding and Coolidge administration, was Special Law Lecturer at Cornell and New York law schools.

As a group, executive and cabinet officers from New York City were recruited from the classes of big business and the lawyers. More than a third of the lawyers were directly connected with large corporations. Many of the others were no doubt associated with large corporations in advisory and professional capacities. With but a few exceptions the executive and cabinet officers were drawn from the more powerful occupational and economic groups in New York City.

Diplomatic officers also were drawn entirely from the classes of wealthy business men and the upper levels of the professions. The proportion of officials in large enterprises was larger than that of executive and cabinet officers—37 percent. Of the 30 officials of corporations or firms 15 were publishers, or publishers and editors, 4 were *rentiers,* 5 had interests in transportation and utility corporations, 3 were in manufacturing corporations, and 2 in banking, insurance, and investment corporations. Many of the lawyers, who constituted the large majority of the professionals were also primarily interested in large corporations. Eight of the 51, or 16 percent, of the professionals in the diplomatic service were associated with universities in administrative or professional capacities; 5 were writers, and 3 were journalists. The predominating elements among diplomats were wealthy business men and lawyers, these two elements constituting 79 percent of the total number concerning whom these data were available.

Of the 11 United States senators 2 were corporation officials, 1 a building contractor, 7 were lawyers, and 1 a physician. Edwin D. Morgan, elected to the United States Senate in 1863, was a wealthy wholesale grocer; Edward Murphy Jr., United States Senator in 1893, was a partner in a large brewery establishment. William Calder, elected to the United States Senate in 1916, was a building contractor.

Fifteen, or 25 percent, of the congressmen from New York City came from the smaller entrepreneurial elements. Of these 15, 8 were real estate and insurance agents, 4 were building contractors, and 3 small retailers. The House of Representatives was the only federal body to which these elements had access. Twenty-five percent of the New York City congressmen also were recruited from the firm or corporation executive element. Of these 15, however, 12 were from the 1880–1890 period, indicating that while the occupational status of congressmen was relatively high in these early years, during the last decades it was considerably lower. Over 50 percent of the congressmen were from the professions. Forty-three percent were lawyers. Judging by their occupations it is clear that the office of congressman was more accessible to middle and lower middle class elements.

Naturally all of the federal judges were lawyers. Their economic and social status will be discussed at later points in this chapter.

The general tendency has been toward a decrease in the proportion of big business men holding federal office. Dividing the federal politicians into those holding office within the years 1860–1910 and those holding office in 1910–1936, we find that the proportion of firm or corporation executives has decreased from 24 percent to 18 percent. Smaller entrepreneurs have increased from 6 percent to 10 percent, and professionals from 70 percent to 72 percent. Singling out federal officers for the period 1930–1936 we find that the decrease in the big business representation has been even greater. Thus only 12 percent of these contemporary federal officers held large corporate offices, while 14 percent were smaller entrepreneurs, and 74 percent professionals.

Degree of and Ramifications of Economic Activities

The economic status of federal politicians is to be judged not only from their occupations but from their additional economic interests and holdings. An analysis of these figures showed that 42 percent of the federal politicians in the sample had such affiliations, as compared with 87 percent for our selection of business association officers. Forty-three percent of these affiliations were in the fields of banking, investment, and insurance; 26 percent were in utilities and transport companies; 19 percent in manufacturing corporations; and 5 percent each in real estate and building corporations, and commercial firms. These proportions are very similar to those for business leaders. The average number of other business offices for business leaders was 6.5 as compared to only 1.1 for federal politicians.

Of the five groups of politicians, that of cabinet and executive officers was most active economically. The average number of offices or directorships for executive and cabinet officers was 3.2. United States senators were next highest with 1.1 business offices. Diplomats had an average of only .7, and judges only .3. Another index to the degree of economic activity is the proportion of executive to directorial positions. The proportion for business leaders was 29 percent executive offices to 71 percent directorial. For federal politicians the proportion was the same. Thus while there were fewer very active business men among federal politicians, those who were tended to be as frequently in active executive control as business leaders.

The number of federal politicians holding corporate offices has been decreasing. The group of federal politicians holding office at the present time are less influential in the business world than individuals holding the same offices have been in the past. The executive and cabinet officers holding office in the years 1860–1890 had an average of 2.7 economic affiliations; those holding office between the years 1890–1910 had 5.5 affiliations; those holding office between 1910 and 1930 had 1.8 affiliations; and those holding office in the last six years had .6 affiliations. This trend does not hold for diplomatic officers, who have risen from .5 in the years 1860–1890 to 1.4 in 1930–1936. The incumbent United States senators from New York City have no corporate offices at the present time. The average number of business affiliations of congressmen has decreased from 1.2 in 1880 to .9 in 1930–1936, and that of United States judges from .4 to .3 for the same periods.

Education

A slightly larger proportion of federal politicians had college educations than business leaders, the ratio being 79 percent to 76 percent. Four percent of the federal politicians had only grammar school education, 14 percent only high school education or its equivalent, and 3 percent had some college training, but had not completed it. Thus 21 percent of the total had no college training whatsoever. Of the 153 having college training, 110, or 71 percent, had professional training. In almost every case this was training for the law degree. Eight percent of the college-educated federal politicians had received higher academic degrees—Master of Arts or Doctor of Philosophy—while only 3 percent had received honorary degrees. These summary figures will later be compared with those for state and local politicians.

All of the executive and cabinet officers holding office between the years 1860–1936 had at least a high school or preparatory school training. Four had only such training and no more; one had some college training but had not received his degree; and 23 had received their degrees. Nineteen of these had received professional degrees, in all cases law degrees. One, Henry L. Stimson, Secretary of State in the Hoover administration, had received the M.A. degree, and one, Charles E. Hughes, Secretary of State in the Harding and Coolidge administrations, had received eleven honorary degrees. The number of executive and cabinet officers not having college educations has decreased from 2 out of 9 in 1860–1890 to none out of 5 in 1930–1936.

Of the 74 diplomatic officers for whom educational data were available, only 7 had not had college training. Sixty-seven had college degrees. Of these, 39 took professional degrees, in practically every case the law degree. Seven had higher academic degrees, and one an honorary degree. All of those diplomatic officers lacking college education had held office in the 1860–1890 period.

The educational characteristics of United States senators are roughly similar to the preceding groups. Three had no college education whatsoever but these held office before 1930. Eight had college educations, 6 of this group having professional degrees. Five of these degrees were in law, and 1 in medicine.

Congressmen had the highest number of individuals lacking college education. Five had only grammar school education, 14 only high school education, and 5 had not completed their college training. Twenty-three of the 32 with college educations had taken professional degrees, in most cases the law degree. Five of the congressmen holding office in 1935 had only high school educations. These data substantiate the preceding generalizations that the office of United States congressman was more accessible to the less advantaged elements of the population. All of the federal judges had college education, and all had taken the law degree. Five had taken higher academic degrees, and 2 had received honorary degrees.

The differences in educational background were not only to be found in the level of education of federal officers, but in the institutions they attended. For the group as a whole Columbia University was the most frequently attended institution; Harvard was second; Yale third; New York University fourth; and City College of New York fifth. We have already found business leaders and society leaders attending most frequently Harvard, Columbia, Yale, Princeton, and New York University. While business and society leaders tended to be concentrated in these older traditional universities, federal politicians attended a large number of other universities, including a relatively high proportion of municipal, state, and parochial institutions.

For federal executive and cabinet officers Columbia, Harvard, and Yale were the most frequently attended institutions. Since Columbia is located in New York City, this institution might be assumed to be accessible to a larger element of the New York population, including the middle classes, and those from the lower classes able to work their way. But the fact that there were so many Harvard and Yale graduates in their number indicates that on the whole these officials came generally from elements of the population financially able to send their sons away to college. The proportion is almost exactly the same for diplomatic officers. The advantages enjoyed by the diplomatic officers in their youth are also indicated by the fact that 6 of them had studied abroad at the University of Berlin, 3 at the University of Göttingen, and 2 at the University of Paris.

There were no Harvard graduates among the United States senators from New York City, and none from Columbia. Three had been educated at Yale; 3 at New York University; and 2 at the City College of New York. Of the congressmen 11 graduated from Columbia, 6 from the parochial College of St. Xaviers, 4 from the Municipal College, 4 from New York University, and only 3 from Harvard and 2 from Yale. Congressmen and senators, from the point of view of the educational institutions which they attended, had been less advantaged as a group than executive and cabinet officials, and diplomatic officers. Eighteen of the 26 federal judges had graduated from Columbia, Harvard, and Yale in the order of frequency named. In terms of educational advantages they are on a par with cabinet and executive officers and diplomats.

Social Register Inclusion[7]

One way of determining the degree to which politicians are recruited from the "socially legitimated" elements of the population is to discover the proportion listed in the Social Register. We have already seen that 57 percent of our selection of business leaders were listed, as compared with almost universal inclusion for society leaders. Forty-one percent of the total number of federal politicians holding office between 1860 and 1936 were listed in the Social Register. The significance of this figure will emerge when compared with the percentages of inclusion for state, local, and party politicians. Judging by the decrease in the number of inclusions the proportion of federal politicians from the socially legitimated classes has been lowering in the last 75 years. Thus in 1860–1910, 44 percent of the federal politicians in our selection were in the Social Register. In 1910–1936 this proportion decreased to 35 percent, and for those federal politicians holding office in 1930–1936 the percentage is even lower—25 percent. Important differences in Social Register inclusion appear upon examination of the totals for the various groups of federal politicians. The proportions included in the Social Register for executive and cabinet officers, federal judges, United States senators, and diplomats has been relatively high, while that of United States congressmen has been relatively low.

For each group of officers the tendency has been a decrease in the number of inclusions. The proportion for executive and cabinet officers has decreased from 89 percent in 1860–1890 to 40 percent in 1930–1936; that of diplomats from 56 percent in 1890–1910 to 40 percent in 1930–1936; that of United States senators from 50 percent in 1860–1890 to none in 1935; and that of federal judges from 80 percent in 1903 to 50 percent in 1935. Over the whole period, however, it is clear that federal executive and cabinet officers, diplomats, and judges tended to be recruited more frequently from the socially legitimated elements of the population than congressmen and senators.

Types of Social Affiliations[8]

An analysis of the social affiliations of federal politicians also indicated that this group was not on the same social level as the business and society leaders. Thus only 60 percent of the federal officers belonged to social clubs, as compared with 88 percent for business leaders and almost universal affiliation for society leaders. Five percent of the federal officers belonged to fraternal orders, as compared with 3 percent for business leaders. Seventeen percent of the federal politicians belonged to ancestral associations, as compared with 29 percent for business leaders and 39 percent for society leaders. On the average, federal politicians belonged to 3.1 social clubs, as compared with 4.2 for business leaders and 6 for society leaders.

Almost all—90 percent—of the executive and cabinet officers were affiliated with social clubs. Seventy percent of the diplomatic officers, 63 percent of the United States senators, and 73 percent of the federal judges belonged to social clubs, while only 25 percent of the congressmen were so affiliated. Only 9 percent of the congressmen holding office in 1935 had such affiliations, indicating again the fact that the office of congressman particularly in recent years has been accessible to individuals of lower status. This is borne out also by the fact that the largest number of individuals affiliated with fraternal orders were to be found among United States congressmen.

Twenty-one percent of the executive and cabinet officers belonged to ancestral orders and associations, as compared with 15 percent for diplomatic officers, 45 percent for senators, 20 percent for United States judges, and only 11 percent for congressmen. Of the congressmen holding office at the present time none had such affiliations.

The relatively low social status of congressmen is again to be discovered in the average number of social club memberships per person. Thus, while the average executive and cabinet officer belonged to 5.6 social clubs, the average diplomat to 3.5 clubs, the average senator to 4.7, and the average federal judge to 2.5 clubs; the average congressman belonged to only 1.3 social clubs. The average number of social clubs per congressman has been decreasing. Those holding office in 1880–1890 belonged to 1.7 social clubs; while those holding office in 1935 belonged to only .5 clubs.

Club List[9]

A general comparison of the club memberships of business leaders, society and federal politicians brings out a number of differences in social affiliation between these groups. Thirteen percent of the federal political office-holders belonged to the aristocratic Union Club as compared with 67 percent for society leaders, and 12 percent for business leaders. Only 7 percent of the federal politicians belonged to the Knickerbocker Club as compared with 4 percent for business leaders and 56 percent for society leaders. Federal politicians belonged more frequently to the Metropolitan Club of Washington, which is no doubt attributable to the long residence of the federal office-holders in Washington. Federal political office-holders included proportionately as many exclusive "general club" members as the selection of business leaders.

In the sphere of "achievement and occupational" social clubs federal political office-holders were on the whole more frequently represented than business leaders. Thus 24 percent of the federal group were members of the Century Club, and 15 percent were members of the Lawyers Club (cf. Table 8.1). Society leaders were more frequently affiliated with the Century and the University clubs than either of the other two groups.

As might be expected, business leaders were more frequently affiliated with luncheon clubs than either of the other two groups. Only 8 percent of the federal political office-holders were affiliated with the Downtown Association and 2 percent with the City Midday.

The representation of federal politicians in the group of art and culture clubs is slightly smaller than that of the business and society leaders.

Business leaders were more frequently affiliated with political clubs of the type of the Union League and Republican clubs, even more frequently than federal politicians. Thirty-one percent of the business leaders belonged to the

TABLE 8.1 Percent of Memberships in Classified Types of Clubs for Business and Society Leaders and Federal Political Office-Holders from New York over the Period 1860–1935*

Name of Club	Percent Membership of Business Leaders	Percent Membership of Society Leaders	Percent Membership of Federal Politicians
General Social Clubs			
Union	12	67	13
Knickerbocker	4	56	7
Metropolitan	30	51	30
Metropolitan (Washington)	4	5	14
Tuxedo	5	20	5
Harmonie (German Jewish)	3	—	1
Achievement Social Clubs			
Century	19	32	24
University	14	23	20
Lawyers	13	8	15
Engineers	3	—	1
University (Washington)	—	—	1
Luncheon Clubs			
Downtown Association	18	13	8
City Midday	4	4	2
India House	4	4	2
Recess	4	—	—
Art and Culture Clubs			
Players	5	13	5
Commonwealth	2	—	—
Grolier	3	11	2
Lotos	7	3	4
National Arts	6	2	4
Authors	2	—	4
Ardsley	3	—	—
Political Clubs			
Manhattan (Democratic)	8	7	7
Union League (Republican)	31	8	15
National Democratic	1	2	3
National Republican	6	—	10
City	12	6	4
Reform	7	2	2
Fraternal Orders			
Masons	3	—	3
Elks	—	—	3
Knights of Pythias	—	—	1
Knights of Columbus	—	—	1
B'nai Brith	—	—	1

(*continues*)

TABLE 8.1   (*continued*)

Name of Club	Percent Membership of Business Leaders	Percent Membership of Society Leaders	Percent Membership of Federal Politicians
Sport and Athletic Clubs			
Riding	12	21	7
Racquet and Tennis	11	33	5
New York Yacht	10	28	6
Piping Rock	4	14	2
Turf and Field	4	12	3
Jekyl Island	4	4	—
New York Athletic	3	2	3
Westchester Country Club	3	11	5
Creek	2	—	—
Baltusrol Golf	2	2	—
Deepdale Golf	2	4	—
Meadow Brook	2	9	2
St. Andrews Golf	2	3	—
Larchmont Yacht	2	4	—
Seawanhaka Yacht	2	12	—
South Side	2	11	2
Links	2	6	—
Hangar	2	4	—
Sleepy Hollow Country	2	—	1
Montclair Golf	1	—	—
Brook	1	8	1
River	1	5	—
Automobile	1	—	—
Knollwood	1	—	—
Rockaway Hunt	1	6	2
National Golf Links	1	10	—
Oakland Golf	1	—	—
Westminster Kennel	—	8	—
Garden City Golf	—	6	—
Essex Fox Hounds	—	2	—
Chevy Chase (Washington)	—	—	6
Crescent Athletic Association	—	—	1
Riding (Washington)	—	—	1
Racquet (Washington)	—	—	1

*New York Chamber of Commerce, *Annual Report, 1870; ibid.,* 1900; *ibid.,* 1935; New York Clearing House Association, *Annual Report, 1894; ibid.,* 1935; New York Merchants Association, *Annual Report, 1906; ibid.,* 1931; Union Club, *Yearbook, 1870; ibid.,* 1900; *ibid.,* 1935; Knickerbocker Club, *Yearbook, 1872; ibid.,* 1932; Metropolitan Club, *Yearbook, 1892; ibid.,* 1935. Mrs. Astor's set was taken from Charles W. DeLyon Nicholls, *The 469 Ultra-Fashionables of America*

(*continued*)

TABLE 8.1 (*continued*)

(New York: Broadway Publishing Co., 1912); the list of Subscribers to the New York Junior Assembly was taken from the *New York Herald Tribune*, Dec. 8, 1935, Society Section. Biographical data were taken from E. Vale Blake, *History of the Tammany Society* (New York: Souvenir Publishing Co., 1901); *Appleton's Cyclopedia of American Biography*, edited by James Grant Wilson and John Fiske (New York: D. Appleton Co., 1888); Moses Yale Beach, *The Wealth and Biography of the Wealthy Citizens of New York*, 1842–1855 (New York: published by the *New York Sun*); *Dictionary of American Biography*, 1928–1937, edited by Dumas Malone (New York: Charles Scribner's Sons); Charles Lanman, *Biographical Annals of the Civil Government of the United States* (Washington: James Anglin, 1876); Lanman, *Dictionary of the United States Congress* (Washington: Government Printing Office, 1864); Henry Hall, *America's Successful Men of Affairs* (2 vols.; New York: the *New York Tribune*, 1895–1896); Marguerita Aulina Hamm, *Famous Families of New York* (2 vols.; New York: G. P. Putnam's Sons, 1902); Moses King, *Notable New Yorkers of 1896–1899* (New York: M. King, 1899); *The National Cyclopedia of American Biography* (New York: J. T. White and Co., 1906); Lyman Horace Weeks, *Prominent Families of New York* (New York: The Historical Co., 1897); *Who's Who in America, 1899–1936* (Chicago: A. N. Marquis Co.); *Who's Who in Our American Government* (Washington, 1935); *Who's Who in Government* (New York: Biographical Research Bureau, 1930); *Who's Who in Jurisprudence* (Brooklyn: John W. Leonard Corp., 1925); *Who's Who in Commerce and Industry, 1936* (New York: Institute for Research in Biography, Inc., 1936); *Who's Who in Finance and Banking, 1911–1925* (New York: Who's Who in Finance, Inc.); *Who's Who in New York City, 1904–1929* (New York: Who's Who Publications, Inc.); *Who's Who in the East* (Washington: Mayflower Publishing Co., 1930); *Who's Who in the Nation's Capital, 1934–35*, edited by Stanley H. Williamson (Washington: Ransdell, Inc.); *Directory of Directors in the City of New York, 1898–1927* (New York: The Audit Company of New York); *Poor's Register of Directors of the United States, 1928–1937* (Babson Park, Mass.: Poor's Printing Co.); *Social Register New York, 1889–1936* (New York: Social Register Association). Where the publisher is not given it may be assumed that the organization cited is the publisher; where the date of publication is not given it may be assumed to be the year for which the work is cited.

Union League Club, as compared to 15 percent for federal political office-holders. More of the federal politicians belonged to the National Republican Club than business leaders. In the reform political clubs—the City and the Reform—business leaders again were more frequently represented than federal politicians. This is largely to be accounted for by the fact that these types of political clubs, with the exception of the National Democratic and the National Republican clubs, tend to be limited to individuals of wealth and business importance, or individuals from the higher levels of political life.

Three percent of the business leaders belonged to the Masons, as compared with 3 percent for federal politicians. However, there were a number of other fraternal orders with which federal politicians were affiliated, so that on the whole federal politicians were more frequently represented in this type of organization.

Federal politicians were far less frequently affiliated with sport and athletic clubs than either business or society leaders. The club to which the largest proportion of federal political office-holders belonged (7 percent) was the Riding Club. Others having a few memberships were the Racquet and Tennis, the New York Yacht, Piping Rock, Turf and Field, New York Athletic, Westchester Country, Meadow Brook, the South Side Athletic, Sleepy Hollow Country, the Brook, Rockaway Hunt, Chevy Chase (of Washington), the Crescent Athletic Association, and the Riding and Racquet clubs of Washington.

As a group federal politicians included as many individuals affiliated with exclusive social clubs and achievement clubs as business leaders; and both were far below the society group. There were far fewer memberships in art and cultural clubs and sport and athletic clubs for federal politicians.

A comparison of the club memberships of individual groups of federal politicians indicates that on the whole executive and cabinet officers were most frequently affiliated with these types of organizations. Nine, or 32 percent, of the executive and cabinet officers belonged to the Metropolitan Club, as compared with 10, or 12 percent, for diplomatic officers, 2, or 18 percent, for senators, 5, or 8 percent, for United States representatives, and 3, or 12 percent, for United States judges. Twenty-five percent of the executive and cabinet officers were members of the aristocratic Union Club, as compared with 15 percent for diplomatic officers, 18 percent for senators, 6 percent for United States representatives, and 4 percent for federal judges. An analysis of general social club memberships indicates, then, that executive and cabinet officers, diplomats, and senators included a relatively larger representation of individuals included in these exclusive social organizations.

The representation of these various groups of federal politicians in the group of achievement social clubs is distributed in roughly the same manner as that of general social clubs, with executive and cabinet officers, diplomats, senators, and judges frequently affiliated with such organiza tions as the Century, University, and Lawyers clubs, and congressmen infrequently affiliated.

The group of diplomats had the largest number of memberships in artistic and cultural clubs. This seems to square with other conclusions drawn elsewhere as to the frequent entrance of exclusive society elements into the diplomatic service. The larger proportion of wealthy business men among executive and cabinet officers accounts for the large representation of this group in the luncheon clubs. As was pointed out above, congressmen were most frequently affiliated with fraternal orders. The two groups most frequently represented in sport and athletic clubs were the executive and cabinet officers and the diplomats, with United States representatives and judges having the smallest number of affiliations. Executive and cabinet officers were again most frequently represented in political social clubs, with senators and diplomats following in percentage of individuals with such affiliations.

A description of the trend in club membership for federal political office-holders substantiates the conclusions drawn above as to the decreasing number of prominent business men and society leaders among federal politicians. The federal officers were divided into three groups: those holding office in 1860–1910, in 1910–1936, and 1930–1936. For the group of general social clubs we find a general decrease. Membership in the Metropolitan Club has decreased from 20 percent in 1860–1910 to 7 percent in 1910–1936, to 2 percent in 1930–1936. Membership in the Union Club has decreased from 19 percent in 1860–1910 to 4 percent in 1930–1936. Membership in the Metropolitan Club of Washington has increased from 10 percent in 1860–1910 to 19 percent in 1910–1936, and has dropped to 8 percent in 1930–1936.

Membership in the group of achievement and occupational social clubs has remained roughly constant. The Century Club membership has changed only from 24 percent in 1860–1910 to 21 percent in 1930–1936. University Club membership has increased from 16 percent in 1860–1910 to 26 percent in 1910–1936, and decreased to 17 percent in 1930–1936.

Membership in artistic and cultural clubs shows a considerable decline in memberships, with only three clubs represented in the 1930–1936 period, and those with only 2 percent memberships. Membership in luncheon clubs shows a slight increase. Thus the Downtown Club had an 8 percent membership for federal political office-holders in 1860–1910 and a 12 percent membership in 1930–1936.

Fraternal order affiliations for federal politicians show an increase. Thus there was only a 1 percent membership in this type of organization in 1860–1910, while in 1930–1936 we find a 12 percent membership for the Masons, 10 percent for the Elks, and 6 percent for the Knights of Pythias.

Membership in upper class political partisan and reform clubs shows a decided decrease. Thus only 2 percent of the 1930–1936 group of federal political office-holders were members of the Union League Club as compared with 8 percent in 1910–1936 and 22 percent in 1860–1910. Membership in the Republican Club has decreased from 12 percent in 1860–1910 to 6 percent in 1930–1936. Membership in the Democratic Manhattan Club has remained roughly constant with 7 percent in 1860–1910 and 6 percent in 1930–1936, which is attributable to the incumbency at the present time of a democratic administration. Membership in the City and Reform clubs shows a slight decrease. The decrease in the number of Union League Club members among federal political office-holders is attributable to the defeats of the Republican Party, since we find in the period 1910–1936, during which time the two parties enjoyed fourteen years of office, that the number of Union League Club members was only 8 percent, as compared with 22 percent in 1860–1910, during which time the Republicans were in power with the exception of the Cleveland administration.

Membership in exclusive sport and athletic clubs shows a general decrease. The Riding Club in 1930–1936 has only a 2 percent representation as compared with 10 percent in 1860–1910. Membership in the New York Yacht Club shows a decrease from 7 percent to 2 percent. The same is true for most of the sport and athletic clubs.

In general the trend in club membership points to a decrease in the number of exclusive club memberships for federal politicians, which is attributable to the decreasing proportion of individuals from the more powerful economic classes holding that type of office.

Admission to ancestral associations is based upon descent from socially esteemed groups in the population. Fewer federal politicians were affiliated with these types of associations than business or society leaders. Eight percent of the federal politicians belonged to the Sons of the American Revolution, as compared with 13 percent for society leaders and 9 percent for business leaders. Only .4 percent of the federal political office-holders belonged to the Pilgrims, as compared with 6 percent each for business and society leaders. Four-tenths percent of the federal political office-holders belonged to the St. Nicholas Society, as compared with 4 percent and 12 percent for the business and social leadership respectively. In the Society of the War of 1812, the Society of Mayflower Descendants, and the Holland Society the proportion of these groups represented was roughly the same.

In all, the federal officials in this selection had 56 memberships in ancestral associations. Diplomats had by far the highest representation with 32 memberships. Fifteen percent of the diplomats belonged to the Sons of the American Revolution, as compared with 18 percent for senators, 6 percent for congressmen, 4 percent for judges, and none for cabinet and executive officers. Although congressmen were as well represented in these associations as executive and cabinet officers, senators, and judges, all of the congressmen with these affiliations held office in the 1860–1890 period.

A tabulation describing the trend in membership in these organizations for federal politicians indicated a decrease. Only three associations were represented in 1930–1936, and these had only a few federal politicians as members. None of the executive and cabinet officers, only 1 of the diplomats, 1 of the senators, none of the congressmen, and 2 of the federal judges holding office in the 1930–1936 period were members of ancestral associations. This does not necessarily mean that the families of old stock are no longer contributing federal office-holders. Frequently individuals eligible for such membership fail for various reasons to join. It would, however, be justifiable to conclude not only from these data, but from materials presented above that there has been a decided decrease in the federal political office-holding of individuals of old American stock from New York City.

Philanthropic Activities[10]

Another characteristic function of the wealthier elements has been found to be philanthropic activity, the financial support and direction of charitable, cultural, educational, and religious institutions. Sixty-three percent of the selection of business leaders and 46 percent of the society leaders held philanthropic office, as compared with 25 percent for federal political office-holders. Business leaders held on the average 2.1 philanthropic offices, society leaders 1.2, and federal political office-holders .5. A comparison between groups of federal politicians shows that 40 percent of the executive and cabinet officers and judges held philanthropic offices as contrasted with 29 percent for diplomats, 27 percent for senators, and only 7 percent for congressmen. Executive and cabinet officers held the largest number of such affiliations, with an average of .8, diplomats next with .7, senators third with .6, judges fourth with .5, and congressmen last with .1 (cf. Table 8.2).

The trend in philanthropic affiliations shows an increase from 20 percent in 1860–1910 to 34 percent in 1910–1936, and 33 percent in 1930–1936. There has been a corresponding increase in the average number of affiliations from .2 in 1860–1910 to .8 in 1910–1936 to .6 in 1930–1936. It has already been indicated that philanthropy is an activity generally characteristic of wealthy individuals. The qualification must be made that there is a stratification of philanthropic institutions and activities, some being sponsored entirely by the socially elite, as the New York Metropolitan Opera, some sponsored by wealthy individuals generally, and some smaller scale nationality and religious philanthropies being sponsored by the wealthy or well-to-do in those nationality and religious groups. Hence a decrease in the number of big business men and society leaders in federal political office would not necessarily result in a decrease in the number of federal political office-holders engaging in philanthropy (cf. Table 8.3).

TABLE 8.2   Philanthropic Offices Held by Federal Political Office-Holders*

	Executive and Cabinet	Diplomats	Senate	Congressmen	Judges
Percent holding such offices	40	29	27	7	40
Average number of such offices	.8	.7	.6	.1	.5

*Names of federal officials during the period 1860–1892 were taken from the *Tribune Almanac*, 1860–1892 (New York: *New York Tribune*) and after 1892 from the *World Almanac*, 1892–1935 (New York: the *New York World*, and later the *New York World Telegram*). [Where publication dates are not cited it may be assumed they are the years for which the publication was consulted.] In the typewritten manuscript the data following are in tabular form in Appendix B. Biographical data were taken from E. Vale Blake, *History of the Tammany Society* (New York: Souvenir Publishing Co., 1901); *Dictionary of American Biography*, 1928–1937, edited by Dumas Malone (New York: Charles Scribner's Sons); Charles Lanman, *Biographical Annals of the Civil Government of the United States* (Washington: James Anglin, 1876); Lanman, *Dictionary of the United States Congress* (Washington: Government Printing Office, 1864); *The National Cyclopedia of American Biography* (New York: James T. White and Co., 1898); *Who's Who in America* (Chicago: The A. N. Marquis Co., 1899); *Who's Who in Our American Government* (Washington, 1935); *Who's Who in Government* (New York: Biographical Research Bureau, 1930); *Who's Who in Jurisprudence* (Brooklyn: John W. Leonard Corp., 1925); *Who's Who in New York City*, 1904–1929 (New York: Who's Who Publications, Inc., 1930); *Who's Who in the East* (Washington: Mayflower Publishing Co., 1930); *Who's Who in the Nation's Capital*, 1934–35, edited by Stanley H. Williamson (Washington: Ransdell Inc.); *Directory of Directors in the City of New York*, 1898–1927 (New York: The Audit Company of New York); *Poor's Register of Directors of the United States* (Babson Park, Mass.: Poor's Printing Co., 1928); *Social Register New York*, 1889–1935 (New York: Social Register Association).

Channels of Selection of Federal Political Office-Holders[11]

Thus far we have been concerned primarily with the social class origins and characteristics of federal political office-holders. It is also of considerable importance to compare their political experience and background with that of other types of politicians. This last comparison will be made in later chapters. At the present we are mainly concerned with the differences in political background between the various groups of federal office-holders. The 205 federal politicians upon whom these data are available held 286 offices, or an average of 1.4 offices per person. Of these, 43 percent were federal offices, 34 were state offices, and 23 percent were local offices.

United States senators have been the most active politically of the groups treated here. All of these have held other political offices, the average for

TABLE 8.3   Trend in Philanthropic Activity of Federal Political Office-Holders*

	1860–1910	1910–1936	1930–1936
Percent with such offices	20	34	33
Average number of offices	.2	.8	.6

*Names of federal officials during the period 1860–1892 were taken from the *Tribune Almanac*, 1860–1892 (New York: *New York Tribune*) and after 1892 from the *World Almanac*, 1892–1935 (New York: the *New York World*, and later the *New York World Telegram*). [Where publication dates are not cited it may be assumed they are the years for which the publication was consulted.] In the typewritten manuscript the data following are in tabular form in Appendix B. Biographical data were taken from E. Vale Blake, *History of the Tammany Society* (New York: Souvenir Publishing Co., 1901); *Dictionary of American Biography*, 1928–1937, edited by Dumas Malone (New York: Charles Scribner's Sons); Charles Lanman, *Biographical Annals of the Civil Government of the United States* (Washington: James Anglin, 1876); Lanman, *Dictionary of the United States Congress* (Washington: Government Printing Office, 1864); *The National Cyclopedia of American Biography* (New York: James T. White and Co., 1898); *Who's Who in America* (Chicago: The A. N. Marquis Co., 1899); *Who's Who in Our American Government* (Washington, 1935); *Who's Who in Government* (New York: Biographical Research Bureau, 1930); *Who's Who in Jurisprudence* (Brooklyn: John W. Leonard Corp., 1925); *Who's Who in New York City*, 1904–1929 (New York: Who's Who Publications, Inc., 1930); *Who's Who in the East* (Washington: Mayflower Publishing Co., 1930); *Who's Who in the Nation's Capital*, 1934–35, edited by Stanley H. Williamson (Washington: Ransdell, Inc.); *Directory of Directors in the City of New York*, 1898–1927 (New York: The Audit Company of New York); *Poor's Register of Directors of the United States* (Babson Park, Mass.: Poor's Printing Co., 1928); *Social Register New York*, 1889–1935 (New York: Social Register Association).

each senator being 3.2 other political offices. The largest number have been state offices, primarily executive and legislative, the second largest, local offices, and last in number, federal offices. The two senators holding office at the present time have been the most active in politics of all the senators, having held an average of 5.5 political offices.

The second most active group politically have been executive and cabinet officers. This group held on the average 2.9 political offices. All of the executive and cabinet officials had held other offices. Most of their other political offices were held in the federal government, and these in turn were largely in the upper levels of the executive establishment. State offices were next in importance, and here too the largest number were in the executive branch of state government. Only 5 of the offices held by executive and cabinet officers were on the local level of government, and these in most cases were offices on school boards, and commissions of various kinds. This indicates clearly that executive and cabinet officers do not work up from the ranks politically, but generally are drawn directly into the state and federal levels of government from some relatively influential position in private life.

Diplomatic officers comparatively speaking were rather inactive in politics previous to their choice as diplomats. Thus each diplomat held on the average .9 political offices. Sixty-six percent of the diplomats holding office in the years between 1860 and 1890 had held some other office, while only 33 percent of those holding office in the period 1930–1936 had held such office. These data indicate that diplomats have generally been drawn from private life after relatively little political service, and that this tendency has been growing in recent years. Most of the offices held by the diplomats were in the federal service, the next largest in the state service, and the smallest number in the local service.

United States congressmen, as a rule, did not have long political records, the average congressman having held only 1.5 offices. The average number of political offices held by congressmen has decreased from 1.7 in 1860–1890 to 1 in 1935. The largest number of offices held by congressmen was in local government. Of a total of 18 offices held by contemporary congressmen only 2 were in the federal government, 10 in the state, and 7 in the local government agencies. Of the 10 state offices 9 were legislative, and of the 7 local offices 4 were legislative, that is, in the state senate, assembly, and municipal council. Over two-thirds of the contemporary congressmen passed their apprenticeships in the state legislature and the municipal council. This is true also for the earlier group of congressmen. In contrast the lines of advancement for executive and cabinet officers seem to be more generally from some other branch of the federal and state administrative and executive services, or from some influential status in private life. The diplomats of the present time in most cases have been taken directly from private life. In the earlier periods, particularly in the years between 1860 and 1890 diplomats were a much more active political group, being drawn primarily from federal and state executive and legislative offices.

Federal judges are the least active group politically. The 21 judges holding office in 1935 had held only 9 other political offices. Six of these were federal and 3 were state offices. Thus federal judges even more than diplomats tend to be drawn directly from private life, in many cases from influential law practices.

The general conclusions to be drawn from this study of the biographies of federal political office-holders from New York City are that they include a fairly large proportion of individuals from the wealthy classes of the population. This proportion, however, has been decreasing. In Chapter 4 this same tendency was pointed out. Nevertheless, comparatively speaking the number of individuals from the wealthy classes holding federal office is high, and as we shall see in the succeeding two chapters, far higher than the proportion on the state and local levels.

Within the group of federal political office-holders executive and cabinet office has been most frequently held by wealthy entrepreneurs, and corporation lawyers. These elements of the population also contributed a high proportion of diplomats, federal judges, and senators. The office of congressman was most accessible to the middle and lower middle classes of the population.

Notes

1. Alexis De Tocqueville, *Democracy in America,* trans. by Henry Reeve (New York: A. S. Barnes and Co., 1862), I, 304. For a keen analysis of the role of the lawyer in politics see Max Weber, "Politik als Beruf," *Gesammelte Politische Schriften* (Munich: Drei Masken Verlag, 1921), pp. 414 ff.
2. Leonard D. White, *Prestige Value of Public Employment in Chicago* (Chicago: University of Chicago Press, 1929), p. 144.
3. White, *Further Contributions to the Prestige Value of Public Employment* (Chicago: University of Chicago Press, 1932), pp. 65 ff.
4. White, *Prestige Value of Public Employment in Chicago,* p. 146.
5. *Ibid.,* p. 151.
6. Names of federal officials during the period 1860–1892 were taken from the *Tribune Almanac,* 1860–1892 (New York: *New York Tribune*) and after 1892 from the *World Almanac,* 1892–1935 (New York: the *New York World,* and later the *New York World Telegram*). [Where publication dates are not cited it may be assumed they are the years for which the publication was consulted.] In the typewritten manuscript the data following are in tabular form in Appendix B. Biographical data were taken from E. Vale Blake, *History of the Tammany Society* (New York: Souvenir Publishing Co., 1901); *Dictionary of American Biography,* 1928–1937, edited by Dumas Malone (New York: Charles Scribner's Sons); Charles Lanman, *Biographical Annals of the Civil Government of the United States* (Washington: James Anglin, 1876); Lanman, *Dictionary of the United States Congress* (Washington: Government Printing Office, 1864); *The National Cyclopedia of American Biography* (New York: James T. White and Co., 1898); *Who's Who in America* (Chicago: The A. N. Marquis Co., 1899); *Who's Who in Our American Government* (Washington, 1935); *Who's Who in Government* (New York: Biographical Research Bureau, 1930); *Who's Who in Jurisprudence* (Brooklyn: John W. Leonard Corp., 1925); *Who's Who in New York City,* 1904–1929 (New York: Who's Who Publications, Inc.); *Who's Who in the East* (Washington: Mayflower Publishing Co., 1930); *Who's Who in the Nation's Capital,* 1934–1935, edited by Stanley H. Williamson (Washington: Ransdell Inc.); *Directory of Directors in the City of New York,* 1898–1927 (New York: The Audit Company of New York); *Poor's Register of Directors of the United States* (Babson Park, Mass.: Poor's Printing Co., 1928); *Social Register New York,* 1889–1935 (New York: Social Register Association).
7. *Ibid.*
8. *Ibid.*
9. *Ibid.*
10. *Ibid.*
11. *Ibid.*

9

State
Office-Holders

FROM WHAT SOCIAL CLASSES of New York City were state-elected office-holders in contrast to federal office-holders recruited? What differences were there in the class origins of the various state officers—governors, judges, state senators, and assemblymen—holding office in the decades between 1860–1935? What general transformations have occurred in the social composition of these office-holders from the earlier to the present period? These three problems constitute the theme of the present chapter.

Birthplace[1]

Eighty-five percent of the 196 state officers concerning whom these data were available had been born in the United States, as compared with 89 percent native born for federal political office-holders. State political office-holders, however, were more frequently natives of New York City; 61 percent of the state officers were indigenous to New York as compared with only 30 percent for federal officers. A relatively large proportion of federal office-holders (17 percent) were New Englanders, while relatively few of the state politicians (5 percent) were from these areas. Pennsylvanians, New Jerseyans, and Southerners were also better represented among federal officers than state politicians.

Taking each group of state officers separately we find that governors from New York City were 100 percent native. Relatively few governors—only 4 out of 13—were natives of New York City. The largest number came from New York State, and from the New England states. As far as birthplace is concerned, governors show a similar distribution to federal executive and cabinet officers, diplomats, senators, and federal judges.

Ninety-four percent of the state senators were natives. Over two-thirds were natives of New York City. The proportion of natives of New York is even greater for assemblymen. The proportion for state judges is similar to

154

that of governors. The largest foreign element among state offices was the Irish, the next largest German and Austro-Hungarian. There were fewer Irish and more Germans among the federal politicians.

The trend in territorial origin is toward an increase in the number of American native born, and an increase in the number of native New Yorkers in state politics. This is largely attributable to the fact that the tendency in American population in the last 30 years or so has been toward stabilization.

Nationality Origins

A much larger proportion of second generation native born Americans are to be found among federal politicians than among state officers, the proportion being 70 percent to 22 percent. Federal politicians thus are largely of the older stock, while the great majority of state politicians are of foreign parentage. Forty-four percent of the state politicians were of Irish origin to only 12 percent for federal politicians. Seven percent of the federal politicians were Jews, while more than twice as many of the state officers were Jews. Jewish state political office-holders also were in almost all cases of non-German origin, but derived from the newer Russian, Polish, Bohemian, and Hungarian immigrations. In other words, Jewish state officers were largely recruited from the less advantaged and less established Jews.

Eighty-five percent of the governors were of older American origins. A large number of the judges (36 percent) were also of native derivation. Only 8 percent of the state senators and 9 percent of the assemblymen were natives of native parentage. Sixty-five percent of the state senators, and 53 percent of the assemblymen were Irish in origin. Of the judges only 26 percent were Irish. The largest number of Jews were to be found among state judges, assemblymen, and senators in the order named. The remaining 16 percent of the state politicians were German, Italian, English, Scotch, and Negro. Briefly the governors and judges included a far larger proportion of the older stock than state senators and assemblymen.

Occupational Composition

The differences in influence and prestige enjoyed by federal and state political office-holders is brought out clearly through an examination of their occupations. We have already seen that 26 percent of the federal officials were derived from the class of owners and directors of large economic undertakings. Only 4 percent of the state officers were recruited from this powerful element of the population of New York. There were no employees among federal politicians; 5 percent of the state officers derived from this class. There was also a far larger proportion of smaller entrepreneurs among state officers than among the federal group—the percentage being 22 percent for state, and 8 percent for federal officers. The proportion of members of the professions in these two levels of government is approximately equal, 66 percent for federal and 69 percent for state political office-holders. There is, however, an important difference in the composition of the professional elements in state and national politics. Fifty-two percent of the total number of federal officers were lawyers to 65 percent for state officers. Among federal politicians there was a far larger representation of academicians, writers, and journalists.

Occupational differences between types of state officers were also found. Six of the 13 governors were recruited from the class of financial and industrial entrepreneurs, while only one, Alfred E. Smith, came of the smaller entrepreneurial class. The big business men governors from New York City were Samuel J. Tilden, who as a railway counsel amassed a fortune of seven million dollars; Alonzo B. Cornell, who inherited his father's interests in telegraphic corporations; Roswell Pettibone Flower who amassed a fortune of four million dollars in railroad manipulations and in brokerage and banking; Levi P. Morton who rose from the dry goods business to banking; and Herbert Lehman, who succeeded in the control of his father's banking business. The balance of the governors were prominent lawyers, with the exception of Theodore Roosevelt who would class as a *rentier,* writer, and professional politician.

Ninety-eight percent of the New York state senators were self-employed, but only one (3 percent) was a large corporation officer. Forty-two percent were smaller entrepreneurs. Twenty-one percent were real estate and insurance agents, and 21 percent were miscellaneous entrepreneurs. The balance were members of the professions—in 20 out of 22 cases, lawyers.

The occupational composition of New York assemblymen was roughly similar to that of state senators with the important exception that 10 percent of the assemblymen were employees to only 3 percent for senators. The office of assemblyman seems thus to have been accessible even to poorer elements of the population. Naturally all of the state judges were lawyers. As such, however, they were not an unstratified group. At a later point, distinctions have been drawn between these groups in terms of their other economic positions and social affiliations.

The trend in the occupational composition of governors and judges has not varied in any particular way in the last forty years or so. For senators and assemblymen a separate trend tabulation has been made, which indicates first that, whereas 7 percent of those holding office in 1870 and in 1892 had been large corporation officers, none of this class held such office in 1935. The proportion of employees also has decreased from 14 percent to 3 percent. There has also been a considerable increase in the number of lawyers and a decrease in the number of smaller entrepreneurs. Thus state senators and assemblymen now are recruited almost entirely from among lawyers, with a few of such office-holders from the smaller entrepreneurial element. The increase in the number of lawyer politicians is to be attributed to the special advantages enjoyed by this profession in the struggle for political office.

Other Business Affiliations

As a group federal political office-holders are far more active in business than state politicians. In addition to the facts brought out in the previous tabulation, a far larger number of federal officers held offices in business corporations of various kinds than state politicians, the proportion being 42 percent for federal officers to only 25 percent for state officials. An analysis of the trend, however, indicates that whereas the proportion of federal officers with offices in corporations outside their main office has decreased from 55 percent in the period 1860–1910 to 32 percent in 1910–1936, that of state officers has increased from 24 percent to 28 percent in the same periods. This decrease in the number of those having directorships or executive offices in corporations was not uniform for all groups. Executive and cabinet officers experienced only a small decrease, while senators and congressmen decreased approximately to one-third of their earlier proportion. Among federal officials there has been a marked decline in the economic power of senators and congressmen, while the other occupants of offices have continued generally on the same level of economic power.

The increase in the number of individuals with corporation offices of various kinds among state officers is largely attributable to the changing composition of state assemblymen who constitute almost half of the total number of state officers. Twenty-three percent of the assemblymen of 1935 held such corporate offices, as compared with 12 percent in 1892. This raised level of assemblymen is largely attributable to the increase in the number of lawyers. Lawyers more than small entrepreneurs and certainly more than salaried employees are likely, by virtue of their contacts and skills, to be chosen to the boards of smaller banks, industries, and building and real estate corporations.

Considerable differences were found between federal and state political office-holders in the nature of the corporate offices held. Fifty-two percent of the offices held by state politicians were of an executive character, while only 29 percent of those held by federal officers were of this character. What is not brought out in this tabulation is the fact that the corporations in which the federal officials were interested were on the whole far greater in capitalization than those of the state officers. In the smaller corporation there is rarely much differentiation between the executive officers and the board of directors. In most cases the executive officers constitute the majority, if not the whole number of directors. Certain other differences emerge in a comparison of the business activities of federal and state officers. The greater prominence of the federal officials in the business world is further borne out by the fact that they held on the average 1.1 corporation offices, while state officers held on the average only .5 offices.

There are also considerable differences in the spheres of business in which these two groups were mainly interested. A larger proportion of the federal officers were interested in banking, investment, and insurance corporations, the proportion being 43 percent to 36 percent. Thirty-nine percent of the business interests of state officers were in manufacturing corporations to only 19 percent for federal officers. While only 5 percent of the corporate offices held by federal officers were in real estate and building corporations, such offices constituted 14 percent of the total corporate offices of state officers. Federal officers were far more frequently interested in utility and transport companies than state officers, the ratio being 26 percent to 7 percent. Thus in addition to the fact that federal officers on the whole more frequently held corporate offices, they were also found to hold offices in the corporations of larger capitalization—in banks, investment, and insurance companies; telegraphic, power, gas companies; and railroad, air and bus lines. More than half of the business affiliations of state officers were in the field of smaller manufacturing enterprises and real estate and building corporations. Even the fairly large number of banking, investment, and insurance offices held by state politicians will be seen at a later point to have been in smaller corporations and firms.

A comparison of the business interests of the various types of state officers indicates again the difference in economic status of governors as over against senators and assemblymen. The average governor held 1.4 corporation offices to 1.0 for senators, .2 for assemblymen, and .6 for judges. Further the governors proportionately were more frequently interested in the greater corporations of the country. Alonzo B. Cornell, governor of New York in 1891, was a director of the Chicago and North Western Railway, the New York Central, and the Michigan Central Railway corporations. Levi P. Norton, governor in 1894, was trustee of the Atlantic Mutual, the Equitable, and the Washington Insurance companies, as well as president of the Fifth Avenue Trust, the Guaranty Trust, and other banking corporations. Herbert Lehman, incumbent governor, is a director of eight corporations, including Jewel Tea Company and the Studebaker Corporation.

Among the state senators in 1892 only two had influential business connections, William L. Brown, president and director of the Ball Electric Company, and George W. Plunkett, director of the Riverside Bank. Among the economically influential senators in 1935 were Edward J. Coughlin, who held twenty-five offices in rubber and subsidiary corporations; James J. Crawford, director of the First National Bank of Brooklyn, and the Knickerbocker Fire Insurance Company; and James A. Garity, director of the Yonkers National Trust Company.

Among the 41 assemblymen holding office in 1892 there were 5 with corporation affiliations. Among these were Thomas F. Byrnes, director of the Merchants Bank of Brooklyn; Percival Farquhar, director of the Cuban Electric Company; George L. Ward, secretary and director of the Faraday Electric Company, and of the New York Lines Company; and James L. Wells, director of the Twenty-Third Ward Bank. Among the contemporary assemblymen were Bernard Austin, secretary of the Patent Steel Bond Equipment Company; Edward P. Doyle, officer of seven subdivision, realty and building, and loan corporations; Maurice A. Fitzgerald, vice president and director of subdivisions; Daniel MacNamara Jr., counsel and trustee of the Fort Hamilton Savings Bank of Brooklyn; William Schwartz, president and director of the Schwartz Ornamental Glass Works, Inc.; William J. Sheldrick, vice president and director of the North River Chemical Bank; and Albert D. Schanzer, counsel and director of the Dewey State Bank.

Among the early judges were Morgan J. O'Brien, appellate judge in 1903, trustee of the Equitable Life Assurance Corporation and director of the Stock Quotation Telegraph Company; George L. Ingraham, vice president and director of the Phoenix Insurance Company; Francis M. Scott, director of the Empire City Fire Insurance Company; and Henry Bischoff, Jr., director of the Union Square Bank. Miles Beach, Supreme Court judge in 1903, was a member of a law firm which represented the Gould and Vanderbilt interests. Among the contemporary state judges with important business interests are Kenneth O'Brien, son of Morgan J., and director of the Stock Quotation Company, the Commercial Cable Company, the Postal Telegraph Company, and a number of other corporations; Irving Untermeyer, a director of 8 realty, manufacturing, publishing, and railway corporations. Others are Richard P. Lydon, director of real estate corporations; Louis A. Valente, director of the Bowery and East River National Bank of New York; Timothy A. Leary, secretary and director of the Inter-Seas Commercial Company; and William T. Collins, director of the Times Square Trust.

This enumeration brings out clearly the greater size and influence of the corporations with which the governors and judges are affiliated, as over against those of senators and assemblymen. The firms of the latter, with a few exceptions, were of smaller capitalization.

Education

The differences in the level of education between federal and state officers are not particularly large. Twenty-four percent of the state officers had gone no further than high or preparatory school to 21 percent for federal officers. Seventy-nine percent of the federal politicians had college education, to 76 percent for state officers. The larger number of lawyers among state officers is reflected in the proportion taking professional degrees or taking practical study for admission to the bar. Thus 82 percent of the college graduate state officers had taken professional degrees or had served apprenticeships in law offices after the completion of college work, to 71 percent for federal officers. More of the federal officers had taken higher academic degrees and had received honorary degrees, the proportions being 8 percent to 5 percent and 3 percent to 2 percent respectively. The relatively large number of individuals with only high school education among state officers were in almost all cases (37 out of 43) senators and assemblymen; while among federal officers they were largely congressmen.

The educational differences between state and federal politicians are to be found not so much in the level of their education, but rather in the nature of the educational institutions attended. It has already been pointed out that the five universities most frequently attended by federal politicians were Columbia, Harvard, Yale, New York University, and Brown in the order named. State politicians on the other hand attended Columbia, Fordham, New York University, New York Law School, and City College of New York. Yale and Harvard were sixth and seventh on the list. This reflects the differences in economic origin, social status, and tradition between federal and state politicians. The first frequently attended the traditional upper class schools, the second attended most frequently the parochial, public, and professional colleges in the immediate vicinity of New York.

Viewing groups of state officers separately we find governors differentiated from other groups. With one exception the governors were educated at Columbia, Harvard, Yale, Union, Amherst, Brown, Colgate, and Williams. Although there were a large number of Columbia graduates among senators and assemblymen the most frequently attended institution for these groups was Fordham, a Catholic institution. Next in order for these groups were New York University, City College of New York, both public universities, and the New York Law School. The judges fell between governors and state legislators in terms of the exclusiveness of their educational institutions. Fordham, the New York Law School, and City College of New York were frequently attended, but Yale was also represented.

Social Register Listing

The differences in social status between federal and state officers are clearly brought out by the relative numbers included in the Social Register. Forty-one percent of the federal officials had received this social recognition to only 11 percent for state officials. The trend in Social Register inclusion is also of interest. We find in both cases a decreasing tendency, among federal officers from 44 percent in 1860–1910 to 25 percent in 1930–1935, while for state officers the decrease is from 23 percent in 1860–1910 to 7 percent in 1910–1936. Both substantiate the generalization as to the decreasing participation of the upper classes in politics in the last thirty years or so, but in the case of state officers this decrease is more marked. However, treating state politicians as a homogeneous group obscures important differences.

Thus 7 of the 13 governors (or 54 percent) were listed in the Social Register, and 30 percent of the state judges were given this mark of recognition. Only 5 percent of the state senators were so recognized, and 3 percent of the assemblymen. The New York state judges have shown a marked decrease in Social Register listing, from 52 percent in 1903 to only 12 percent in 1935. This is to be attributed to the increase in the number of Jews and Catholics and individuals from the later immigrations in the state judiciary.

Types of Social Affiliations

Even more marked are the differences in types of social affiliations between federal and state officers. Sixty percent of the federal political office-holders belonged to social clubs as compared with only 38 percent for state officers. The average federal officer held 2.5 social club memberships to only .9 for the average state officer. State officers were affiliated more frequently with fraternal orders than federal officers, the proportion being 23 percent to 5 percent. The proportion of federal officers holding membership in ancestral associations was more than twice that of state officers. Social Register inclusion, membership in social clubs and ancestral associations are among the socially differentiating characteristics of the American upper classes. Fraternal order affiliations are the characteristic recreational and convivial affiliations of the middle and lower classes.

But it is again necessary to point out the fact that governors entirely and state judges in part also derived frequently from the upper class and enjoyed the same status and social recognition. Thus 69 percent of the governors and 80 percent of the judges belonged to social clubs, to only 26 percent for senators and 17 percent for assemblymen. The average governor belonged to 5.1 social clubs, the average judge to 2.0, while the average senator belonged to only .3, and the assemblyman to .2. Only one of the 13 governors belonged to fraternal orders; 18 percent of the judges had these affiliations; while 26 percent of the senators and 37 percent of the assemblymen were so affiliated. The distribution of ancestral association membership indicated similar proportions. An examination of the trend in social affiliations shows a general decrease in the number of those possessing upper class social affiliations.

Club List

A comparison of the club memberships of state and federal officers indicates again the lower social status of the state political office-holders. Only

3 percent of the state officers belonged to the Union Club, as compared with 13 percent for federal politicians; none of the state officers belonged to the Knickerbocker, as compared with 7 percent for federal officers. While only 6 percent of the state officers belonged to the Metropolitan, 30 percent of the federal officials were members. Only one percent of the state officers belonged respectively to the Metropolitan of Washington, the Tuxedo, and the Cosmopolitan, as compared with 14 percent, 5 percent, and 8 percent respectively for federal officials.

State officers also were rarely affiliated with the group of achievement and occupational social clubs, having only 5 percent membership in the Century, 3 percent in the University, and 4 percent in the Lawyers, as compared with 24 percent, 20 percent, and 15 percent respectively for federal politicians.

Federal officials also had a larger representation in the luncheon clubs. State officers had only a 1 percent membership in the Downtown Club, while federal officials had an 8 percent membership in the Downtown Club, and 2 percent each for the City Midday and the India House.

The same is true for the art and culture clubs. Here state officials had only a 3 percent membership in the Lotos, and 1 percent in the Ardsley, while the federal officials had small representations in the Players, Grolier, Lotos, National Arts, and Authors.

In the group of political clubs the memberships varied. Thus state officers had much larger representations in democratic clubs, with 13 percent membership in the Manhattan, and 12 percent membership in the National Democratic Club, as compared with 7 percent and 3 percent respectively for federal officers. The federal officials had a 15 percent membership in the Union League Club, as compared with only 5 percent for the state officers. Republican club memberships showed a similarly high representation of federal officials. This points only to the fact that the Republican Party was more frequently in the saddle in Washington than in Albany. Insofar as the leadership of the Republican Party tends to be more frequently recruited from the upper classes, the larger percentage of Republicans among federal politicians reflects a larger representation of upper class elements in federal politics. There was a slightly higher membership of federal officers in the City and Reform clubs than for state officers.

Since membership in fraternal orders and lodges of various kinds is a typical social affiliation for the middle and lower middle classes, we would expect a higher representation of such memberships for state officers. Such is clearly the case. Twelve percent of the state officers belonged to the Elks, as compared with only 3 percent for federal officers. Ten percent of the state officers were affiliated with the Masons, to only 3 percent for federal officers.

Federal officials were more frequently represented in exclusive sporting and athletic associations. Seven percent were members of the Riding Club as compared with none for the state officers; 5 percent were in the Racquet and Tennis, as compared with .5 percent for state officers. Four percent of the state officers were members of the New York Yacht Club, as compared with 6 percent for federal officers. Both groups were equally represented in the New York Athletic Club. In the balance of the athletic clubs, state officers in no case had higher than 1 percent membership.

Important differences emerge in a comparison of the types of club memberships of the various types of state officers. None of the state senators and only 1 percent of the assemblymen were members of the exclusive general social clubs, while both governors and state judges in a number of cases were represented in these associations. Eight percent of the governors and 9 percent of the state judges were members of the Union Club. Eight percent of the governors and 20 percent of the judges were members of the Metropolitan Club. Only 1 percent of the assemblymen were members of the Metropolitan.

There is a similar membership distribution in the group of achievement and occupational social clubs. Sixteen percent of the governors and 15 percent of the judges were members of the Century, 8 percent of the governors were members of the University, and 9 percent of the judges were included in this organization. Sixteen percent of the governors and 12 percent of the judges were members of the Lawyers Club as compared with none for members of the state legislature.

Sixteen percent of the governors belonged to the Downtown Association, a luncheon club, compared with 1 percent for the assemblymen, and none for the judges. The distribution of the membership of the art and culture club shows 8 percent of the governors members of the Ardsley, and 9 percent of the judges in the Lotos, while the assemblymen had only 1 membership in both organizations.

Governors and judges were far more frequently members of the group of political clubs than members of the state legislature. Eight percent of the governors, and 50 percent of the judges were members of the Manhattan Club, while none of the members of the state legislature were affiliated with this organization. There were no legislators in the National Democratic Club, while the governors and judges had an 8 percent and a 24 percent membership respectively. Thirty-one percent of the governors and 13 percent of the judges were members of the Republican Union League Club. The governors had the highest representation in the City and the Republican Clubs.

The distribution of fraternal order membership among state officers shows a large representation among the state legislators and a small one among the governors and judges. Twenty-one percent of the senators and 18 percent of the assemblymen were members of the Elks, while none of the governors and judges were members of this organization. Thirteen percent of the senators and twelve percent of the assemblymen were Masons, as compared with 8 percent for governors and 5 percent for judges. With two exceptions, the Knights of Columbus and the Friendly Sons of St. Patrick, governors and judges had no further memberships in fraternal orders.

Only one assemblyman was a member of a sporting club, and this was not an exclusive club. Governors and judges were in a number of cases affiliated with these exclusive sporting organizations, judges far more frequently than governors.

The trend in club membership for state politicians indicates on the whole a considerable decrease in the proportion of exclusive club memberships. There were no Union Club members in the group of state officers holding office in 1930–1936; only 3 percent of the state officers were members of the Metropolitan Club in 1930–1936, as compared with 11 percent in 1860–1910. Other decreases or increases were slight.

The number of memberships in the achievement and occupational social clubs has also decreased considerably in the last thirty or forty years. Thus in the 1860–1910 period 10 percent of the state officers were affiliated with the Century, while none are so affiliated in the contemporary period. Slighter decreases are recorded for the University and Lawyers Clubs.

In the art and culture group of clubs there has been a slight decrease; membership in the Lotos Club has decreased from 4 percent in the early period to 2 percent in 1930–1936, and in the Ardsley from 1 percent in 1860–1910 to none in the contemporary period.

The trend in political club membership has varied with the individual clubs. Thus membership in the Manhattan has decreased from 25 percent in the early period to 4 percent in 1930–36. On the other hand, membership in the National Democratic Club has increased from 3 percent in 1860–1890 to 11 percent in 1930–1936. Membership in the Union League Club has decreased considerably, while that of the Republican Club has decreased but to a lesser extent. It would seem justifiable to conclude, however, that membership in the "better" political clubs—the Manhattan and the Union League—has decreased considerably.

On the other hand, the number of those with fraternal order affiliations has increased substantially. In the 1860–1910 period only 4 percent of the state officers belonged to the Masons; and the only other order represented was the Friendly Sons of St. Patrick with a 1 percent membership. In the 1910–1936 period the Elks, Masons, and Knights of Columbus alone had 24 percent, 16 percent, and 15 percent memberships respectively among state officers. As was pointed out previously, almost all of these were among the state legislators.

The percentage affiliated with various sporting and athletic clubs has decreased in practically all cases. Eight percent of the state officers in 1860–1910 belonged to the New York Yacht Club, as compared with none in 1930–1936. Although the proportion of state officers in the other athletic clubs listed in the table never was high, still in almost all cases it is smaller in the 1930–1936 period than in the earlier years. These data indicate clearly a decrease in the proportion of members of fashionable clubs among state officers, and an increase in the number of those having affiliations with the middle and lower middle class fraternal orders.

Federal officers belong to ancestral associations far more frequently than state officials. There were 56 memberships among the first and 23 among the second. The societies with more than 2 memberships among state officers were the St. Nicholas Society, the Society of Colonial Wars, and the Sons of the American Revolution. With two exceptions the members of these organizations were governors and state judges.

Philanthropic Activities

There were more "philanthropists" among federal groups than among the state officers, the ratio being 25 percent to 17 percent. State officers were more frequently officers of charitable organizations, while federal officers held office more frequently in cultural and educational institutions. The charitable organizations with which state officers were most frequently associated were in most cases denominational institutions, while those of the federal officials were in the more prominent secular, charitable, cultural, and educational institutions.

Seven of the 13 governors had philanthropic affiliations, and 24 percent of the judges, to only 8 percent and 9 percent respectively for senators and assemblymen. All of the philanthropic offices held by senators and assemblymen were charitable in character, while a considerable number of those of the governors and the judges were in educational philanthropies of various kinds. Here again governors and state judges appear to be more like federal politicians in their social characteristics.

Other Political Offices

Although an equal number of state officers and federal officers had held other political offices (55 percent in both cases), there were important differences in terms of the degree of political activity and the levels of government in which these offices were held. Thus the average federal officer held 1.4 political offices, while the average state politician held only .8. Only 18 percent of the total number of offices held by state politicians were in the national level of government, as compared with 43 percent for federal officers. Thirty-four percent of the federal political offices were in state government, to 45 percent for state officers; and only 23 percent of the offices held by federal officers were held in local government, as compared to 37 percent for state officers.

These differences in political activity and political prominence are to be attributed to two general causes. First, state officers as a group are younger men. But possibly more important, for the general run of state politicians it is ordinarily impossible to rise any higher than state office, and in a few exceptional cases to congressional office. Barriers of greatly increased competition, prestige, money, and ability stand in the way. Governors stand out as an exception among state officers. Eighty-five percent of these had held other political offices; on the average they had held 2.8 political offices. Thirty-nine percent of these offices were on the national level of government; and these federal offices were of the most influential sort, in the cabinet, the diplomatic service, and in the Houses of Congress. Forty-two percent of the other political offices held by the governors were state offices, and here too almost all of these were either executive or legislative state offices. Only 19 percent of the offices held by the governors were in local government; and in most cases these were in the local judiciary, or in the many local commissions and boards.

Eighty-four percent of the state senators had held other offices, but most of these offices were in state and local government. Only 7 percent were federal offices; and all of these were the smaller appointive jobs, given as a reward, no doubt, for faithful party service. The federal offices held by state senators were United States Marshal, deputy collector of the port of New York, and receiver of taxes in New York. Almost all of the state offices held by the senators were in the assembly. A relatively large number of the offices held by senators were in local government (31 percent). Most of these were in the municipal council and in the administrative branch.

State assemblymen were the least politically active of all of the groups. Only 22 percent had held other offices, the average number of offices being only .3. Almost half (48 percent) of these offices were in local government. At first sight the large percentage of federal offices held by assemblymen is rather surprising; but in the first place 7 of the 8 were held by the assemblymen of 1892, and in most cases these were the less important patronage appointments. The assemblymen held such federal offices as Assistant United States District Attorney, United States Paymaster in New York, deputy revenue collector, deputy collector of the port of New York, and the like. The great majority of the offices held by assemblymen on the state and local levels of government were also of this lesser appointive type.

State judges were an extremely active group politically, 91 percent having held other political offices. On the average they had held 1.2 political offices. All the federal offices held by state judges were in the House of Representatives. A considerable number of judges had held state legislative and administrative offices, and a large number also were active in the local administrative services.

The details discussed on the preceding pages bring out important differences in the social origins, economic, cultural, and social status, and the degiec and scope of political activity of federal and state politicians, and between the various types of state politicians from New York City. The facts clearly support the generalization that state politicians as a group originate generally from the newer immigrant stocks, have less economic power, do not enjoy the educational advantages, are excluded from society lists and exclusive clubs, do not so frequently perform the traditional "aristocratic" function of "largesse," and have had shorter political experience than federal office-holders.

Among state officers the governors and judges were found to be exceptions. Governors particularly tended to derive from the same social class, and have characteristics similar to federal executive and cabinet officers, diplomats and federal judges. State judges were found to be a more mixed group, some deriving from and having the characteristics of the middle and lower middle classes, and others belonging to the advantaged elements of the New York community.

The data that have been offered describing the trend in recruitment to state office indicate on the whole a large decrease in the number of individuals coming from the upper social and economic classes. On the other hand there has been no rise whatsoever in the number of individuals coming from the lower classes. State office, and primarily state legislative office, has become increasingly the target of the political ambitions of the lawyers and the smaller entrepreneurial classes.

Notes

1. The statistical data upon which the present chapter is based appear in tabular form in the typewritten version of the thesis in Appendix C. For these tabulations lists of governors were taken from *The World Almanac, 1935* (New York: *New York World Telegram*, 1935); lists of state senators and assemblymen for 1870 from *The Evening Journal Almanac, 1870*, compiled by S. C. Hutchins (Albany: Weed Parsons and Co., 1870), pp. 87–104; lists of state judges, *ibid.*, 1870–1880; lists of state senators and assemblymen for 1892 from *The World Almanac, 1892* (New York: Press Publishing Co., 1892), pp. 320–321; for judges for 1903, *ibid.*, 1903, pp. 437–438; for lists of state senators, assemblymen, and judges for 1935, *The World Almanac, 1935*, pp. 468 ff. Biographical data were taken from the following sources [where date of publication is not given, it is assumed to be for the years cited]: *The Evening Journal Almanac*, 1870; *The New York Red Book*, 1892–1935 (Albany: J. B. Lyon); *Who's Who in New York City*, 1904–1929 (New York: Who's Who Publications, Inc.); *Who's Who in Jurisprudence* (Brooklyn: John W. Leonard Corp., 1925); *Who's Who in Government* (New York: New York Biographical Research Bureau, 1930); *Directory of Directors in the City of New York*, 1898–1927 (New York: The Audit Company of New York); *Poor's Register of Directors of the United States*, 1928–1937 (Babson Park, Mass.: Poor's Printing Co.); *Social Register New York*, 1889–1935 (New York: Social Register Association).

10
Municipal
Office-Holders

PREVIOUS COMPARISONS HAVE SHOWN federal politicians in New York, with the notable exception of congressmen, to be recruited frequently from the upper economic and social classes. State politicians were found on the whole to be recruited from the middle and lower middle classes, with the notable exceptions of governors and, in many cases, state judges whose social characteristics placed them in the class of federal executive and judicial officers, and hence in the upper classes in terms of prestige, economic influence, and "connections." Federal congressmen and state legislators were seen generally to be recruited from the less influential elements of the population—the smaller entrepreneurial classes and the less influential strata of the legal profession. The present discussion is intended to describe the social status of municipal office-holders and party officers and delegates.

Unfortunately considerably less material on the background of municipal officials was available. This in itself is an indication of the lack of prominence of the general run of this type of political office-holder. The scarcity of material also raises the question as to whether or not those cases which were available were not a favorable selection, and hence unrepresentative of municipal officials as a group. This possible error has been taken into consideration in the conclusions drawn from the available material. With one exception data were available on the whole "universe" of mayors of New York City. Only data on nationality origins, occupations, and social status as measured by Social Register inclusion were available for aldermen of New York City. But as far as these characteristics were concerned, data on a sufficient number (from 60 percent to 100 percent) were forthcoming to justify generalization for the universe. It is in the case of municipal judges that the criticism of too favorable a selection can be made. Generalizations concerning this group of political officers are therefore qualified in the text.

Mayors[1]

As leaders of the municipal party tickets it is to be expected that mayors would not be "run of the mine" local politicians. Chosen in many cases to lend prestige and respectability to the party lists, mayoralty candidates have been frequently recruited from among those bankers, industrialists, and merchants of New York City interested in seeking political offices through motives of prestige, reform, or both, or the advantages of a political or economic nature which might be gained through the powers of the office. It is to be expected, then, that mayors as a group would be similar in their social characteristics to governors, federal executive officers, senators, and federal judges. Thus only 3 mayors out of 26 (11 percent) were foreign-born. Twelve (46 percent) were born in New York City, 6 in New York State outside of New York City, and 5 (19 percent) in the New England and Middle Atlantic states. The three mayors holding office since 1930, McKee, O'Brien, and La Guardia, were all native New Yorkers, although the last spent his boyhood in the Southwest.

In their nationality origins the mayors were also similar to the upper class politicians. Thus 17 (65 percent) were natives of native parents. This proportion is less than that of federal executive, cabinet, diplomatic, and judicial officers and governors, but was considerably higher than that of United States congressmen, and state senators and assemblymen. The trend in mayoral recruitment, however, has been in the direction of greater representation of newer nationality elements. Thus the mayors holding office between the years 1860–1890 were, with two exceptions, natives of native parentage, while in the years 1910–1930 only 1 out of 7 fell into this category.

Mayors of New York in the last seventy-five years derived from only two occupational classes of the community: officers of large corporations and enterprises, and the legal profession. Nine out of the 13 holding office between the years 1860–1890 were large entrepreneurs, in all cases in banking, commercial, and manufacturing enterprises. The remaining 4 were lawyers. Since 1890, with three exceptions, mayors have been professional politician lawyers. Thus in terms of economic status as well, mayors fall into the class of federal officers, exclusive of congressmen. They also show the same trend toward increasing representation of individuals of lower class origins. Among the big business men mayors of earlier New York were the wealthy manufacturers, Edward Cooper, Abram Hewitt, Havemeyer, and Wickham, the bankers George Opdyke and Franklin Edson, the shipowner William R. Grace. The years 1860–1910 were the high point for mayors in terms of their class derivations. Hylan, Walker, O'Brien, and La Guardia have come of middle and lower middle class elements.

These points are brought out again in an analysis of the business affiliations of mayors. Nine of the 13 mayors holding office between the years

1860 and 1890 held other business offices. Between them they held a total of 55 directorships. William Grace, the shipowner and merchant, held 13 directorships in banking, insurance, and shipping corporations; Peter Cooper in 5 industrial, mining, and banking corporations; Abram Hewitt in 15 such enterprises; and Havemeyer in 8. The largest number of other business affiliations held by mayors in the 1860–1890 period were in the field of banking, investment, and insurance. Utilities and transportation enterprises were also very well represented. Next in order were manufacturing corporate offices. For the period 1890–1910 three of the 5 mayors held such positions. The average number of business affiliations held by mayors during these two periods indicates that the earlier mayors were more powerful economically. Thus the average mayor of the period 1860–1890 held 4.2 directorships or executive offices, while the average for the 1890–1910 period held 2.8. The lower class origin of the later mayors of New York is brought out clearly by the fact that of the 8 mayors holding office between 1910 and 1935 none held such business positions.

Nineteen of the 25 mayors had college educations, and 13 received law degrees. The proportion of lawyers among mayors has increased from 4 out of 12 in the 1860–1890 period to 9 out of 13 in the years between 1890 and 1935. In respect of this trend mayors show the same developments as other political office-holders generally. The university most generally attended by mayors was Columbia, 8 of the 25 having studied there. Three attended New York University, 2 the New York Law School, 2 Princeton, 2 Manhattan College, and 2 Fordham. The schools attended by mayors were thus on a slightly lower level of esteem than those of federal executive officers, federal judges, and governors.

The social status of mayors as measured by Social Register inclusion and types of social affiliations points also to their derivation from the upper levels of the population. Fourteen of the 27 mayors were included in the Social Register. Later mayors, however, have generally not derived from these esteemed layers of the population. Thus since 1910 only 1 out of 8 mayors has been a Social Registerite. The social affiliations of mayors indicate that they are an only slightly less active group socially than federal executive officers, federal judges, and governors. Thus 16 of the 26 belonged to social clubs. But they were affiliated on the average with only 2.9 social clubs, to 5.6 for federal executive officers, 3.5 for diplomatic officers, and 5.1 for governors. Six belonged to ancestral associations of the types discussed above. Three fraternal order memberships were held by mayors in the 1910–1935 period; while all 6 of the ancestral association memberships were held by mayors in the 1860–1910 period. This again bears out the point of the change in the composition of mayors from merchants, bankers, and industrialists enjoying great wealth and social esteem to lawyers of relatively undistinguished origin.

The same general tendencies are again brought out in a more careful examination of the social affiliations of mayors. Mayors of the earlier period belonged in may cases to exclusive social clubs, such as the Metropolitan, the Century, the Downtown Association, the University, Union, Tuxedo, Racquet and Tennis, and Riding clubs. Those of the later period not only had far fewer affiliations, but those they had were less exclusive socially. A number of the early mayors also belonged to such societies of descendants of the early settlers as the St. Nicholas Society, the Sons of the American Revolution, the Society of Mayflower Descendants, the Holland, and Huguenot societies.

The proportion of mayors engaging in philanthropy indicates similarities to federal executive officers and judges and governors. Thus 8 of the 26 mayors were officers of philanthropic institutions of various kinds. The largest number of these were in educational institutions.

An examination of the other political offices held by mayors of New York City indicates that the earlier mayors held fewer offices than the later ones. The average mayor of the 1860–1890 period held only .9 offices, while the average mayor in 1910–1930 held 1.8, and the average 1930–1936 mayor held 2.3. The early mayors then were largely derived from the wealthy elements of the population, who were elected after relatively little political service and ordinarily returned to private life after their mayoralty. The later mayors, on the other hand, fell more into the class of professional politicians, recruited from the less established elements of the population. As a group, mayors were less active politically than federal executive officers and governors. They were taken in the early period from private life to lend their prestige and financial support to party tickets or as leaders of reform coalitions, and then returned to private life. The later mayors have derived increasingly from the professional politician class.

Local Judges[2]

As has already been pointed out, insufficient material was available on the group of local judges to justify as complete a characterization as has been given of mayors and other types of political office-holders. However, the material that is available permits certain general characterizations. The group of local judges upon whom some data were available were the 18 judges of the Court of Common Pleas and the Superior Court of New York City for the year 1870; for 1901–1903 the judges of the Court of General Sessions for New York City, the judges of the City Court and Municipal Court, in all a group of 24; for 1935 there were 100 judges of the City Court, County Court, General and Special Sessions courts, the Children's Court, the Magistrates and Municipal courts. For the contemporary group of judges biographical information was especially incomplete.

The 1870 group of local judges were in 7 out of 12 cases born in New York State, outside of New York City. Only 2 were foreign-born. For the 1903 group 8 out of 15 were native New Yorkers, and 4 were foreign-born; 2 were from Ireland, 1 from Germany, and 1 from Canada. For the contemporary group of 100 judges data were available for only 24. Of these 24, 9 were born in New York City, 6 in New York State, and 3 in New England. The high representation of individuals outside of New York City is attributable to the too favorable selection of the available sample. Common observation indicates that the municipal judiciary is largely dominated by the lawyers of the newer immigrations—largely the Irish and the Jews. This will come out at later points in the discussion.

Nationality was concluded from definite information as to birthplace or origin and affiliations with nationality organizations where this type of information was available. In the majority of cases for the contemporary selection, however, only the name, occupation, and business activities were available. In most of these cases it was thought justifiable to conclude nationality from the name. Generally these names were clearly peculiar to nationality groups; where there was doubt the case was excluded. This nationality tabulation indicated that of the early 1870 group of judges 11 out of 14 were native born of native parents, 1 was Irish, 1 German and 1 French. For the 1903 group, out of 16, 9 were Irish, 2 Jewish, 3 German, and only 2 were native born of native parents. For the 1935 group, where most of the guessing from names was resorted to, it was found that some 34 out of 91, or 37 percent, were of Irish origin, 25 percent were Jewish (of the later non-German Jewish stock), and 9 percent were German in origin. For the rest of the cases nationality origin was doubtful.

Naturally the judges were with few exceptions lawyers. As has been brought out many times, however, lawyers are an extremely heterogeneous group. These particular groups of lawyer municipal judges included a number of combination lawyer-business executives. Thus of the 18 in the 1870 group 2 held offices in corporations. In 1903, 2 out of 24 held such offices; and in 1935, 7 out of 100 were executive officers or directors of corporations or firms. One of the 1870 judges with such business affiliations was Judge George M. Van Hoesen of the Court of Common Pleas, a descendant of an old Dutch family, who was a trustee of the Holland Trust Company and a director of the Philadelphia and Brigantine Railroad Company. Judge Miles Beach of the Court of Common Pleas was a member of a firm that represented the Gould and Vanderbilt interests. He himself, however, held no corporate offices. Superior Court Judge James C. Spencer was president and director of the Florida Ocean and Gulf Canal Company. In the 1903 group there was judge of the Court of General Sessions Warren W. Foster, who served as director of the American Light and Traction Company, the Bonanza Gold Mining Company, the Southern Light and Traction Company, and the Western Gas Company. City Court Justice George F. Roesch served as counsel for the German Exchange Bank.

In the contemporary group of local judges New York County Judge George Whitney Martin is a director of the American Salamandra Corporation and the North Star Line Insurance Company. County Judge Alonzo G. McLaughlin is a trustee of the Fort Hamilton Savings Bank of Brooklyn. Judge Frank F. Adee is secretary and director of the Long Island Finance Company, the Queensboro Chamber of Commerce, and counsel and trustee of the Savings Bank of Ridgewood. Judge of the Court of General Sessions Francis X. Mancuso is director of the Atlantic State Bank, and chairman of the board of the Harlem Bank of Commerce. Children's Court Judge James J. Conway is a trustee of the Long Island City Savings Bank. City Magistrate Alexander Brough is director of the Franklin National Insurance Company of New York, and of the Transcontinental Insurance Company. City Magistrate Louis B. Brodsky is treasurer and director of a Park Avenue building corporation.

With these exceptions the judges in these three periods were predominantly from those elements of the legal profession not associated with big business, and hence may be said to be from the middle and lower middle classes. The proportion of judges associated intimately with big business has decreased since the earlier periods.

That the local judiciary on the whole tends to be recruited from the less influential and esteemed elements of the population is again demonstrated in the number of Social Register inclusions. Of the 18 local judges holding office in 1870, 5 were Social Registerites. Among these were judges of the Court of Common Pleas Charles H. Van Brunt, who was a member of the Manhattan and the New York Yacht clubs and the St. Nicholas Society; Joseph Francis Daly, son of a British Naval Captain, member of the Metropolitan, Democratic, Lawyers, Manhattan, Catholic, Players clubs, and the Southern Society; George M. Van Hoesen, member of the Union, St. Nicholas, Democratic clubs, and the Holland Society; and Miles Beach, associated with Vanderbilt and Gould, a member of the Union and Manhattan clubs. Of the Superior Court judges of 1870 only Samuel Jones was a Social Registerite. He was listed as a member of the Union Club. Of the 24 local judges holding office in 1901–1903 only one was listed in the Social Register. This was Rufus B. Cowing, a member of the Union League and the Merchants clubs.

Among the 100 contemporary local judges only 5 were listed in the Social Register. Frederick Kernochan, graduate of St. Marks and Yale, a philanthropist and member of the Knickerbocker, Manhattan, Tuxedo, and Church clubs, served as Chief Justice of the Court of General Sessions. Charles Cooper Nott, Jr., graduate of Williams and Harvard Law School, a member of the University and Century clubs, is a judge of the Court of

General Sessions. William Young, graduate of Cornell, and husband of a daughter of the old Schermerhorn family, also is a Social Registerite and a justice of the Children's Court. Joseph Eugene Corrigan, graduate of Seton Hall and Columbia Law School and member of the Calumet and Racquet and Tennis clubs, is a city magistrate. And George Leal Genung, Cornell graduate and member of the University, Sleepy Hollow Country, Sons of the American Revolution, Pilgrams, and York clubs, served from 1917 to 1937 as a justice of the municipal court.

Proportionately this enumeration reveals a considerable decrease in the number of individuals from the more influential and esteemed elements of the population in the local judiciary from a little less than one-third in 1870 to only 5 percent in 1935. Although sufficient data are not available to justify definite quantitative judgments, we may assume that the great majority of the contemporary local judiciary, being middle class or lower middle class in social status, are most frequently affiliated with fraternal orders, and more rarely affiliated with social clubs. Very few are affiliated with ancestral associations. For some 24 on whom data are available, we find the Elks, the Democratic and Republican clubs, the Masons, the Knights of Columbus, the Friendly Sons of St. Patrick, and the Knights of Pythias the most frequent affiliations.

Nine of the 24 judges upon whom these data were available held offices in philanthropic organizations. These 24, however, are too favorable a sample to be considered as representative of the entire group of local judges. The proportion, in all likelihood, if the data were available, would be far smaller. In summary, therefore, we may conclude that the local judges, and especially those of the present time, with a few exceptions, are middle class in status and economic influence, and that the tendency in the last decades has been toward an increasing representation of these lower class elements in the local judiciary.

City Councilmen[3]

For members of the Council of New York City only information as to occupation, inclusion in the Directory of Directors and in the Social Register was available. This type of information, however, is sufficient to come at an estimate of their economic and social status. In 1900 the president of the Borough of Manhattan, James J. Coogan, was a real estate owner and operator. Bronx President L. F. Haffen is listed as a commissioner, no doubt an appointive public office. Brooklyn President Grout was a lawyer; and George Cromwell, president of the Borough of Queens, was a prominent business man and socialite. Taking the borough presidents and aldermen together, making a total of 30 out of 33 on whom data were available, a total of 23 was found to fall into the class of self-employed. Two borough presidents, Coogan and Cromwell, fell into the class of large entrepreneurs. Sixteen were smaller entrepreneurs. Three of these were building contractors, 2 real estate and insurance agents, and 6 were liquor dealers. The remaining 5 included a poultry dealer, a furniture dealer, a brewer, a plumber, and a door manufacturer. The remaining 5 self-employed were lawyers. There was a group of 7 employees, including a train dispatcher, a sales agent, a secretary, and an individual who was listed in the City Directory as a manager. The remaining 3 employees were appointive public employees with no other occupation given.

In 1936 there were 65 aldermen from the boroughs of New York City. Occupational information was available for 44. Of these, 25, or 49 percent, fell into the self-employed group. Only 1 of the self-employed, T. J. Sullivan, was in the class of larger entrepreneurs. Twelve, or 24 percent, were smaller entrepreneurs. Seven of these were either real estate agents or insurance agents or both. Five were miscellaneous smaller entrepreneurs; 1 was a printer, 1 a service station owner, 1 a partner in a lunch room chain, and 1 an owner of an electrical supply concern. Twelve, or 24 percent, were in the professions, 10 of whom were lawyers, 1 a physician, and 1 an engineer. Twenty-six, or 51 percent, fell in the class of employees. Seven of these had been privately employed, 1 as a secretary of the Van Owners Association of Greater New York, 2 were salesmen, 2 were insurance agents, 1 a minor manager of a typewriting company, and 1 a superintendent of a real estate firm. For 19, only appointive public offices were given as occupations. These included 14 city clerks, a city dockmaster, a combustible inspector for the fire department, and a chief inspector.

New York aldermen therefore on the whole tend to be recruited from among the smaller entrepreneurs, with liquor dealers, real estate and insurance dealers, and building contractors predominating, from the lawyers (smaller lawyers, as we shall see later) and from the salaried employees, the largest percentage of which apparently are professional political jobholders—individuals who possibly from youth have "fed from the public trough." Since 1900 the proportion of self-employed has increased from 23 percent to 51 percent. The composition of the self-employed also has changed considerably. There were no liquor dealers in the Board of Aldermen serving in 1936, while there were 7 in 1900. There were also no building contractors. The number of real estate and insurance agents has increased from 3 to 7. There has also been an increase in the number of lawyers from 5 in 1900 to 10 in 1936. The proportion of professional political jobholders in the municipal council has increased from 3 in 1900 to 19 in 1936.

Six of the 33 aldermen and borough presidents holding office in 1900 were listed in the Directory of Directors of 1903 as holding office in corporations. Borough President of Richmond, George Cromwell, was a director of the Hanover Fire Insurance Company; Randolph Guggenheimer, president of the

Council, was a director of the Yorkville Bank and attorney and director of the Empire State Surety Company; Harry C. Hart was director of a paint and oil company and president of a copper mining company. Stewart M. Brice was director of the Coal Creek Mining and Manufacturing Company and the Washington County Railroad Company; John J. Murphy was secretary and director of the Anti-Slip Horseshoe Company; Adolph C. Hottenroth was treasurer and director of the Sandrock Realty Company and director of the United States Title Guaranty and Indemnity Company. David Van Hostrand was a director of the Flushing Bank. Thus 18 percent of the borough presidents and municipal councilmen of 1900 were listed in the Directory of Directors of New York City as officers of corporations. The period around 1900 in New York City was marked by considerable interest and activity in municipal politics on the part of the respectable and wealthy elements—a movement which culminated in the election of the fusion mayor, Seth Low, in 1902. This probably explains the relatively large degree of personal participation in municipal office on the part of the wealthier classes.

In 1936 the proportion of aldermen holding corporate offices has decreased to 6 percent. Only 4 out of 65 aldermen held offices in corporations exclusive of their main positions. Michael E. Pelligrino was a director of a small bank. Max Gross was treasurer and director of a realty company. James B. Allen was director of the Federation Bank and Trust Company. John J. McCusker was director of a building and loan company. This tabulation again bears out the fact that the proportion of economically influential individuals in the New York City Council has decreased in the last thirty years.

With but few exceptions none of the aldermen of either 1900 or 1936 were listed in the Social Register. Three out of the 33 (9 percent) borough presidents and aldermen holding office in 1900 were Social Registerites. James J. Coogan, president of the borough of Manhattan, was listed in the Social Register and was a member of the exclusive Turf and Field Club. Borough president of Richmond, George Cromwell, a Yale graduate, was listed in the Social Register and was a member of the University, Union League, Republican, Harvard, Downtown, City, and the Richmond County Country clubs. Stewart M. Brice, Harvard graduate and Social Registerite, was listed as a member of the Knickerbocker Club, the New York Athletic Club, the Colonial Club, and the Metropolitan Club of Washington. In the 1936 group of aldermen, only one, A. Newbold Morris, Yale graduate and attorney, was listed in the Social Register. He was a member of the Racquet and Tennis, the Downtown, the National Golf, and the River clubs, and of the Society of Colonial Lords of the Manor.

In general summary the New York City aldermen of the last thirty or forty years are largely middle and lower middle class in terms of their occupational and economic characteristics and their social status. A relatively high representation of economically influential and esteemed elements in the council of 1900 may be attributed to the reform movement of that period.

This description of municipal elected office-holders shows that mayors in contrast to judges and municipal councilmen have historically been most frequently recruited from the wealthier elements of the population. In recent decades, however, New York mayors have derived from the class of lawyer-professional politicians.

Notes

1. A list of the mayors of New York City was taken from the *New York World Almanac, 1935* (New York: *New York World Telegram*, 1935), p. 471; biographical data were taken from the *Dictionary of American Biography*, edited by Dumas Malone (New York: Charles Scribner's Sons, 1928); *The National Cyclopedia of American Biography*, 1898 (New York: James T. White and Co.); *Who's Who in America*, 1899–1936 (Chicago: The A. N. Marquis Co.); *Who's Who in Government* (New York: New York Biographical Research Bureau, 1930); *Who's Who in New York City*, 1904–1929 (New York: Who's Who Publications, Inc.); *Directory of Directors in the City of New York*, 1898–1927 (New York: The Audit Company of New York); *Poor's Register of Directors in the United States*, 1928–1937 (Babson Park, Mass.: Poor's Printing Co.); *Social Register New York*, 1889–1935 (New York: Social Register Association).

2. For lists of New York City judges, *Trow's New York City Directory*, compiled by A. Wilson, Part III, *City Register* (New York: John F. Trow, 1870); for lists of judges in 1901–1903, *Trow's General Directory of the Boroughs of Manhattan and Bronx* (New York: Trow Directory Printing and Bookbinding Co.), see section "City and Borough Register." For lists of judges in 1935 see *The World Almanac, 1935* (New York: *New York World Telegram*, 1935), pp. 468, 474, 475; for biographical data, *Who's Who in Government* (New York: Biographical Research Bureau, 1930); *Who's Who in Jurisprudence* (Brooklyn: John W. Leonard Corp., 1925); *Who's Who in New York City*, 1904–1929 (New York: Who's Who Publications, Inc.); *Directory of Directors in the City of New York*, 1898–1927 (New York: The Audit Company of New York); *Poor's Register of Directors of the United States*, 1928–1937 (Babson Park, Mass.: Poor's Printing Co.); *Social Register New York*, 1889–1935 (New York: Social Register Association).

3. Lists of members of the Municipal Council for 1900 were taken from *Trow's General Directory of the Boroughs of Manhattan and Bronx, 1900* (New York: Trow Directory, Printing, and Bookbinding Co., 1900), section "City and Borough Register"; for 1936 names of municipal councilmen were taken from *The World Almanac, 1936* (New York: *New York World Telegram*, 1936), p. 470. Biographical data were taken from *Trow's General Directory*; from the *New York City Directory, 1932* (New York: R. L. Polk, Inc.); *The Directory of Directors in the City of New York*, 1898–1927 (New York: The Audit Company of New York); *Poor's Register of Directors of the United States*, 1928–1937 (Babson Park, Mass.: Poor's Printing Co.); *Social Register New York*, 1889–1935 (New York: Social Register Association).

Part Four

Plutocracy and Insecurity

11

The "Moralization" of Social Life in Response to Protest

Under democracy we have seen that the wealthier classes withdrew from the personal control of politics, substituting indirect pressures, and tended to develop an extravagant, elaborate, and irresponsible social life. This indirect control over politics, and these irresponsible attitudes were maintainable only as long as normal situations prevailed. In crises of various kinds the plutocracy was forced to exercise more personal controls and establish more personal connections with politics, and adopt more responsible attitudes in their social life. The present chapter treats of the transformations in plutocratic social life as a consequence of the growing labor and agrarian unrest following the closing of the frontier. The succeeding chapter treats of the reactions of the wealthier classes to political crises of various kinds.

If it was great wealth, and distance from political and economic realities, which made for the spectacular triviality of the life of the plutocracy in the so-called Gilded Age, it was the growing volume of labor and agrarian unrest after the passing of the frontier which made it question its values early in the twentieth century. In his address as retiring president of the American Historical Association in 1911, Frederick Jackson Turner, looking back upon the changes America had undergone in the two decades following the announcement of the Bureau of the Census of the disappearance of the frontier, said:

> The revolution in the social and economic structure of this country during the past two decades is comparable to what occurred when independence was declared and the Constitution was formed, or to the changes wrought by the era which began a half a century ago, the era of Civil War and Reconstruction.[1]

The revolution which Turner was describing was the tremendous urban development, consequent upon the great expansion in industry, the growth of mammoth industrial enterprises, and the political, social, and moral consequences of these changes. Turner did not, as is sometimes suggested, attribute all of these developments to the passing of the frontier. He also emphasized the role played by technique, both in the narrow and the organizational sense, in the rise of the new American economy and politics. But the passing of the frontier was of the greatest significance both directly and indirectly in precipitating a political ferment in the lower industrial and agrarian classes.

The existence of free lands had performed the function of a safety valve not so much in the direct provision of escape for dissatisfied laborers but through forcing employers to keep up wages in order to maintain an adequate labor market in the cities.

> In earlier times [writes a contemporary historian] the frontier had served as an automatic regulator of labor conditions, including industrial wages, which had to be maintained at a level attractive enough to induce laborers to remain rather than seek the available cheap farm lands. The inevitable substitute for such a regulator was increasing emphasis upon organization among industrial labor groups, and an intense struggle between these groups and the capitalists, who likewise were effectively organized.[2]

Not only labor organization and ferment resulted from these fundamental economic transformations, but more radical movements with avowed political and revolutionary aims resulted from industrialization, the concentration of industrial control, and urbanization.

> It is not surprising [wrote Turner] that socialism shows noteworthy gains as elections continue; that parties are forming on new lines; that the demand for primary elections, for popular choice of senators, initiative, referendum, and recall, is spreading, and that the regions once the center of pioneer democracy exhibit these tendencies in the most marked degree. They are efforts to find substitutes for the former safeguard of democracy, the disappearing free lands. They are the sequence to the extinction of the frontier.[3]

Agrarian unrest followed as well from the so-called extinction of the frontier. The arbitrary powers of the industrial and railroad barons resulting in high and discriminatory freight rates, high prices for industrial commodities, and the wholesale corruption of legislatures, and democratic processes, resulted in a swelling volume of protest against the monopoly capitalists of the East. And the absence of free lands made more difficult the escape from these difficulties. At the time of Turner's address the "insurgent west" was "demanding increase of federal authority to curb the monopolies, for the sake of the conservation of our natural resources, and the preservation of American democracy."[4]

The hypothesis is proposed here that it was this swelling volume of protest against monopoly, and against the irresponsibility of the plutocracy which forced the wealthier classes in this era to justify their social functions in terms other than pleasure and diversion. The fashionable set, even before the days when the consequences of the closing of the frontier were felt, was criticized both from within and without, but these occasional criticisms were not strong and continuous enough to disturb the life and standards of the fashionable group. One of these earlier critics, Abram C. Dayton, contrasting the life of the Gilded Age with that of the period of Knickerbocker dominance, trumpeted a plea and a warning to these bearers of extravagant social life:

> For mercy's sake, fair and beloved American ladies, do set your faces against this reckless riot in extravagant display, this Vanity Fair. Turn your thoughts inwardly for a moment and reflect. Serious thought may perhaps induce that moderation which will continue itself even in this railroad age. Vie not with the mushrooms that spring up in a night, and wither if they be not promptly gathered. The test of social elevation is a moderate tone of conduct, for that marks a mind secure in its own strength and equal to the destiny to which heaven has invoked it.[5]

Frederick Townsend Martin, writing at a considerably later date, also contrasted the trivial society of his time with that of his boyhood:

> Perhaps [he said] as I write, my mind will carry me back to the days before these new phenomena transpired; and I shall be moved to write of social America in the days of its true glory, before the glitter of tinsel and the tawdry finery of mere wealth overlaid it. For that is the background against which stand out in all their hideousness the empty follies of the idle rich and the vapid foolishness of the ultra-fashionable in America today.[6]

On the fly leaf of the copy of his book which he gave to the New York Public Library, Charles W. De Lyon Nicholls, Episcopalian clergyman, and a commentator on the life of the "469 Ultra-Fashionables," wrote, "The social game—is it worth the candle?"[7]

The internal criticism of the earlier period was ineffective in and of itself. The criticism of the Knickerbockers and the more conservative elements were on the whole an ineffective deterrent. And in many cases their sincerity was to be doubted. For the scions of the older families, many of whom had but small incomes, were in many cases happy to lend the legitimacy of their names to the holders of newer fortunes. After all, they could not but follow the example of the European aristocracies members of which descended in great numbers upon the daughters of wealthy Americans.

The latter decades of the nineteenth century were marked by the growing labor movement and by the eloquent espousal of the cause of the lower classes by journalists and publicists. Some of the wealthy began to see in the passage of the Sherman Law of 1890, in the passage of the Interstate Commerce Act, in the Homestead strike, the Haymarket Riot, the Ludlow Massacre, the secret revolutionary orders in the Knights of Labor, symptoms of "a revolt on the part of a subjugated people against the hardships of industrial slavery."[8] The reaction of the press and the population to the famous Bradley Martin Ball of February, 1897, illustrates this growing protest against the extravagant life of the wealthy.

"On the night of the ball," says one writer, "there was a meeting of the 19th Century Club at Sherry's to discuss the question of 'Culpable Luxury.'"

> Inasmuch [said President John A. Taylor, in opening the meeting] as the two of your lecture committee were not invited to the Bradley Martin's Ball they thought it might be well to hold an overflow meeting here tonight and make it a subject of discussion. I take it that luxury is that which somebody else has, and that we, ourselves, cannot afford, but that is a matter to be left to the gentlemen who will discuss the question for us.[9]

Two lecturers, Professor Franklin H. Giddings of Columbia, and John Graham Brooks of Boston, then proceeded to criticize the extravagance of the Bradley Martin Ball and other large-scale social affairs.

On the day after the ball the *New York Tribune* referred to the criticisms of an Episcopalian clergyman, Reverend Rainsford:

> A new turn was given to the anticipation of the public, however, by the utterance of one of the city's clergymen, who was not only among the best known of the metropolitan wearers of the cloth, but whose congregation included many of the most fashionable and wealthy citizens of New York. This clergyman, the Rev. Dr. Rainsford, Rector of St. George's Protestant Episcopal Church, while disclaiming any desire to attack the propriety of the Bradley Martin Ball in particular, declared that all exhibitions of wealth and its lavish use were much out of place in hard-times during the present. Dr. Rainsford furthermore said that he had advised some of his parishioners against countenancing the Bradley Martin Ball by attending it. This utterance naturally provoked a storm of comment, for and against, which did not die away up to the day of the ball.[10]

Many of those who attended received threatening letters. A participant was quoted as having said: "It was the most delightful entertainment I have attended in years. The one thing which destroyed some of our pleasure was the fear that some disturbing crank would carry out the threats made to the different people at the ball."[11] So concerned were the givers of the ball over the popular event that one hundred police were called to keep order on the streets outside of the Waldorf.

The writing of the muckrakers at the turn of the century, Upton Sinclair's satires in the beginning of the twentieth century, works such as those of

Henry Demarest Lloyd[12] began seriously to influence the thinking of elements of the plutocratic group. Frederick Townsend Martin, himself a banker socialite, in his *Passing of the Idle Rich* described these reactions with much eloquence, and with a sense of impending tragedy. He spoke of a changed tone in exclusive club conversations and social gatherings.

> I do not say that it is general, this tendency to take seriously the social, industrial, and economic questions of the day. In my own case, I do know that up to a very few years ago none of these problems bothered me very much. I know that very rarely did I hear the question raised as to the permanence of the conditions under which we lived within our social barriers. Nobody, in my world, considered the problem of industry his own; and every one drifted onward through the years secure in the conviction that in the end everything was going to be alright.[13]

The most important single cause for this changing attitude, Martin thought, was the changed attitude of the "working classes themselves toward the rich."

> For, more assiduously than anything else in this world, we, the wealthy, seek the praise and admiration of the crowd. It may seem a strange confession from a member of the wealthy class, but it is true. . . .[14]
>
> When the 19th century closed, America worshipped great wealth. It sanctified its possessors. It deified the hundred-millionaires. In five years time America has learned to hate great wealth.[15]
>
> Some day, perhaps in the twenty-first century, some Carlyle, sitting in the shade of elms before an old country house, will head another chapter "Printed Paper," and describe the war made with words upon the crumbling ideals and ideas of an age. He will tell how a nation from worshipping wealth on Monday learned to hate it on Saturday. He will relate how it came that myriads of poor, blessing the alms-giver as they fell asleep in low hovels and crowded tenements, awoke with their hearts full of bitterness and hatred for those whom they had worshipped. He will humorously describe how the plutocracy itself, alarmed beyond power of expression, sought to disgorge its ill-gotten gains upon the multitude.[16]

This changed attitude on the part of the lower classes, journalists, and even important political leaders, such as Theodore Roosevelt, LaFollette, and others, at first amused, and later outraged the plutocracy and society.

> Finally—and here lies the heart of the matter—we began to read these outpourings of the popular sentiment very seriously indeed. They came, at last, from sources that we dared not disregard. Instead of mere muckracking expeditions they assumed the proportion of crusades. Instead of the frantic mouthings of mere sensation-mongers, there confronted us in the columns of the press, and in the more sedate and orderly pages of the magazines, the speeches of a President, or sane, sober editorials written by men who knew

both sides, and who commanded our respect as well as the respect and admiration of the crowd. We recognized—those of us who thought, saw, and felt—that instead of being a passing phase, as we had dreaded or hoped, this change of popular sentiment was the beginning of a revolution.[17]

Elements in the wealthy classes began to read. "Even the most violent and anarchistic of the publications that pretend to portray the facts of the class relationships have thousands of readers among the very wealthy."[18] Five years before, Martin went on, it would have been possible to count on the fingers of one's hands the men in the wealthy classes who read "the literature that comes from below. . . . Today it is a common occurrence to hear in the best clubs of New York wealthy men discussing with intense earnestness and real economic sense articles of which they would never have heard five years ago."[19]

Martin explained that in many cases it was not the actual feeling of danger, or threat to their position, but that "our armor of self complacency and self satisfaction has been pierced, and our pride has been wounded."[20]

Behind the writings of the muckrakers, writers, and editors, the speeches of Roosevelt, and the progressive politicians were

the forces of labor and poverty forming new lines upon the plains and hill sides. We see them lashed to new fury by the whip of rising prices; we hear the stern, stentorian voices of their tribunes calling them to battle for their lives and liberties; we smell the reek of them as they crowd from the dusty mines and sweaty factories.[21]

Posing the magnitude and seriousness of the problem confronting America, and the necessity for appeasement for the lower classes, Martin claimed:

Today we of the class that rules, that draws unearned profits from the toil of other men, know full well that the time is almost here when there must be a true accounting. The fortunes that have been made are made; and that is all of it. The fortunes that are in the making through misuse of political power, through extortionate exploitation of the people, and the people's heritage, through industrial oppression and industrial denial of the rights of men—these must be checked. Tomorrow in this land, the door of opportunity must be again unsealed. We cannot go back and create more free land to take the place of the millions of acres thrown away by a lavish, stupid, careless, traitorous government. We cannot fill again the plundered mines of Michigan or Montana or Pennsylvania. We cannot clothe the hills of Maine and Michigan again with pine, or the broad bottoms of Ohio with walnut. We cannot turn backward the hands of the clock, or re-create the economic factors that have been eliminated to make of their fragments the wealth and the social world today enjoyed by the exploiters and their descendants.[22]

One of the consequences of this attack upon the plutocracy was the decrease in the number of idle *rentiers*. Social pressures in the plutocracy emphasized work. Not only men but women felt it necessary to justify their lives in some measure by work. The women engaged in charitable or cultural activity on a scale greater than ever before. "The very first direct result of the growing consciousness of conditions," wrote Martin, "throughout the country is a sudden growth in the volume of money devoted to charity, and a sudden and quite extraordinary increase in the personal interest shown by the wealthy in the matter of reform."[23] Martin did not consider charity as a solution of the economic and social problem in America. He viewed it "only as an index to the times," a symptom of the fact that the wealthy were becoming concerned with the problem of adjustment.

Martin, writing during the last years of the Taft administration deprecated the attitude among the wealthy that the conservatism of Taft meant the passing of the danger to the upper classes. More clearly than most, he sensed the rise of a new era, and remarkable for one growing in the stifling atmosphere of his social group, he sensed the causes of this transformation. There were no more new lands; the resources of the country were almost entirely owned; the lower classes had no future save that which they would seize from the owning classes.

> The days of the idle rich in America are as a tale that is told. Tomorrow in this land there will be one of two things: either an evolution or a revolution. Either by one of those characteristically swift and marvellous changes for which the history of our race is noted, the class which I represent will again be merged into and assimilated by the body of the nation, as it was half a century ago, or we shall stand face to face with the forces of anarchy, socialism, trade unionism, and a hundred other cults that either do represent, or claim to represent the spirit of this mighty people, and we shall re-enact in this land some of the most terrible tragedies in history.[24]

The special bearers of the gaudy tradition, the "400" or the "150" around Mrs. Astor, continued to function as an exclusive social group until the death of Mrs. Astor in 1908. A number of women competed for the succession. Among them were Mrs. Ogden Mills, by birth a Livingston. According to Wecter,[25] she was too exclusive a type to be able to integrate the eligible wealthy about her. Mrs. Oliver Hazard Perry Belmont, previously the wife of William K. Vanderbilt, was the most spectacular hostess of the time, although insofar as novelty and imagination were concerned Mrs. Stuyvesant Fish was her equal.[26] These three women became the great hostesses of New York and Newport after the death of Mrs. Astor. However, they were animated by a different spirit than Mrs. Astor. Mrs. Ogden Mills was far too exclusive to achieve real dominance of the wealthy social set of New York City, Mrs. Belmont began in the first decade of the twentieth century to devote herself to "causes,"[27] and Mrs. Stuyvesant Fish carried the giddiness of this class in this era to its extreme with her "dog dinner parties" and similar spectacular extravagances. Mrs. Fish was also less exclusive than Mrs. Astor, and hence tended to break down the barriers that had previously existed.

The ultra-exclusiveness of Mrs. Mills, the search for causes and justifications on the part of Mrs. Belmont, and the bohemianism of Mrs. Fish were symptoms of the bankruptcy of this society entirely devoted to extravagant display. Under the pressure of popular criticism, and the rising feminist movement, a number of society women began to search for a more meaningful way of life. The logical direction for justifying their lives was charity and art patronage.

The entrance into active philanthropic and charitable work on the part of society women was made possible and even encouraged by the movement for the emancipation of women which insisted that women leave the privacy of their homes and enter into the "world's work." That this movement touched these elements is illustrated by the fact that Mrs. Belmont became actively identified with the suffragette cause.

The development of a feeling that the rich and the well-born must in some way justify their privileges and power resulted in the founding of the Junior League. The first Junior League was founded in New York in 1901 by Mrs. Charles Cary Rumsey, daughter of Edward H. Harriman. Its purpose according to its founder was to find work for society girls and to engage in experimental philanthropic activities. That it has wandered far from its purpose is indicated by the fact that the founder of the New York Junior League shortly before her death criticized the emphasis placed upon its club house and social activities.

The New York Junior League is the only league which does not require some philanthropic or cultural work on the part of its membership. Nevertheless there are strong influences making some philanthropic activity, if only the contribution of money, unavoidable. The writer was informed by officers of the Junior League that in the lives of most of its members, fresh out of the finishing schools, the philanthropic purposes of the Junior League are distinctly secondary. Sincere interest in charitable work on the part of its membership is the exception. Young upper class girls join because of the prestige of the League, the advantages of the club house, and contacts with the membership. Membership in the Junior League is largely taken for granted for daughters of the wealthy. Some *parvenus* are excluded, and Jews are rarely admitted.

The strength of the philanthropic impulse of the New York Junior League raises the general question of the nature of the philanthropic motivations of the wealthier classes. In what measure is this philanthropic activity a sincere philanthropic impulse, and from an objective point of view, in what measure are these philanthropic efforts directed toward fulfilling the most pressing social needs?

As to the sincerity of the motivation it can only be said that most wealthy women engage in philanthropy because of the social patterns of their class. This is one of the most important fields in which social prestige is to be gained, and it also is a method of associating with women of greater wealth and prestige. That there are many wealthy women who engage in philanthropy out of devotion to what they deem socially and culturally necessary work goes without saying. The philanthropic motive is a mixed one. In some it is mere imitation and striving for social prestige; in others it is sincere interest.

From an objective point of view, that is, from the point of view of the social consequences of their activities, this upper class philanthropy must be evaluated in terms of the degree to which these philanthropies meet urgent needs, in the order of their urgency. Before answering this question, a prior one must be raised. What is the nature of the social education of these wealthy women? The older generation of women, now dominant in social-philanthropic life, almost universally have not gone to college. Their only higher education has been gained in the finishing school, through travel and tutoring. The finishing school naturally emphasizes those qualities and skills most valued in young women by the wealthy classes. These are manners, culture (in the sense of knowledge of the history of painting, or training for dilettante participation in the arts), English language and literature, foreign languages with special emphasis upon French, sports, and athletics. A society debutante sincerely and effectively interested in economics, politics, and sociology is at the present time an extremely rare combination.

Once the purpose for which a sum of money is determined by the grantor, the power to carry out this purpose is left in the hands of a board of directors or trustees. These boards are usually made up of wealthy and prominent business and professional men. Since the execution of philanthropic work in art and in charity has been placed more and more in the hands of experts, the actual policy-making role of such boards has become greatly limited. Their policy-making functions have largely been reduced to procuring additional financial support, negativing suggestions of the professional staff, determining the allocation of funds and manipulating the securities for the purpose of increasing or safeguarding income. Associated with these male boards are ladies' auxiliaries, which play the special role of securing money largely through social affairs.

The major function of society and the plutocracy in philanthropy is the procuring of funds. The decision as to what the money is to be spent for is largely determined by professionals. A typical method of procuring funds for charity and philanthropy is by giving benefit balls, or entertainments of various kinds. By this means the society woman combines her social with her philanthropic function, or better, justifies the former in terms of the latter.

The entrance of women into active work outside the home made practically impossible the older type of exclusiveness. For the means of maintaining exclusiveness for the exclusive pleasure set had been the privacy of the home, that is, the power of the hostess to invite only those whom she chose to invite; and the objectives of social entertaining which were the display of money, power, taste, and imagination to those whom she viewed as worthy of being impressed.

The role of the society woman once actively engaged in philanthropy and charity inevitably influenced her choice of friends, her contacts and associations. As a philanthropist eager to secure the maximum support for her pet charity, she gradually was forced to evaluate people almost entirely in terms of their power to aid her cause financially. In the earlier stages of this large-scale movement into charity and philanthropy and "causes" there was, no doubt, an attempt to exclude *parvenus,* Jews, and other undesirable elements from participation in society philanthropic enterprises. But the pressing need of money and the competition with other women philanthropists inevitably forced the hand of these socialites and made it necessary for them first to nod, then to smile, and possibly later genuinely to welcome and associate with these newer and formerly undesirable elements. There are, of course, still in existence pet charities and philanthropies to which admission is largely on an exclusive basis, but for the greater charitable and philanthropic enterprises, the basis of admission is almost purely plutocratic.

The World War was also an important shaping influence in breaking down barriers and in emphasizing the necessity for some legitimation of the social life of the plutocracy. Extravagant social life was considerably checked during the war years. One society reporter commented:

> The social season jogs along through days of quiet but not of repose, for everybody seems to be doing "their bit." War has smashed the usual routine, which many hoped would continue as in the past. Outside of the weddings and an occasional dance, everything has been going on in a most desultory manner. At present there seems to be little hope of "society as usual."[28]

Debutante affairs were dropped; and there was some fear on the part of the commentator that the ordinary charities would suffer because of the emphasis upon war charities. Recurring to the dullness of the season the social reporter remarked:

> Society women who have sons at the war camps or already in France cannot be blamed for shirking social duties. And there are scores of women and girls who are so engrossed in war relief work that they have no time for social relaxation.[29]

The crisis of the war and patriotic propaganda tended to reduce the strength of sectional and class differences, temporarily, in America. This influence carried on the pre-war trend, emphasized by the entrance of the society woman into philanthropy, of breaking down the social exclusiveness of the eligible wealthy. A social reporter referring to the Thanksgiving celebrations spoke of the fact that many exclusive hostesses invited to dinners soldiers in New York City whom they did not know. There was a considerable shortage of men; and cases were recorded of hostesses who were forced to send their butlers on the streets to pick up all the uniformed men they could find. A case of this last minute recruitment was described by the social reporter:

> Two former cowboys from Wyoming, big, sturdy fellows, members of the Sunset Division at Camp Mills, had only been in town for two hours, for the first time too, when they found themselves seated at a delicious course dinner at the Hotel St. Regis. With a hundred others they had been asked into the hotel after the invited hundred and fifty had failed to appear by a turkey dinner recruiting squad stationed at Fifth Avenue and Fifty-Fifth Street.
>
> The assembled men from the farms and ranches of the far west adapted themselves to the circumstances with remarkable ease, and a society woman who glimpsed the scene took occasion to remark that they were the best-mannered group of men she had ever seen. The two cowboy soldiers declared that it was an event to be remembered all their lives, and they looked awestruck when informed that they were dining within a stone's throw of the homes of John D. Rockefeller, William K. Vanderbilt, and other prominent men.[30]

Other important influences which have shaped the values of plutocratic social life have been prohibition, the prosperity of the twenties, and the present depression. Prohibition began the tradition which has culminated at the present time in the so-called cafe society. It drove many individuals of the upper classes out of their homes or the better hotels and recreation places into the adventures and random contacts of the speakeasies. The prosperity of the later twenties had the further effect of throwing up a new plutocratic group which gained contact with the older circles on the speakeasy fringe and through common philanthropic work.

The depression of 1929 and the years following has had the effect of further identifying the social life of the plutocracy with charitable activity. As an example of the effect of crisis conditions upon social life, it was found that in 1930 and 1931 the society columns were recording unemployed benefits in the place of the normal affairs. Thus, a Women's Emergency Unemployment Relief Committee with Mrs. August Belmont as chairman was appointed. A number of dances and card parties were given to benefit the unemployed. A benefit Horse-Race Meet was held at Colonel E. R. Bradley's Idle Hour Farm. Mrs. Clarence Mackay gave a recital for the benefit of a suburban relief fund. A Venetian Fete, Fashion Show and Supper Dance was given for the benefit of the Emergency Relief Committee. Thus many of the customary social activities of the plutocracy were justified in these years of crisis by turning in a part of the proceeds for the benefit of the unemployed.[31]

The depression not only caused a further increase in benefit social activities but affected the financial situation of the wealthier classes considerably. This tended further to eliminate strongholds of exclusiveness. Thus many of the social clubs experienced serious losses of revenue through declining membership and were forced to relax their standards of admission in order to survive. The same was true for philanthropic and cultural institutions such as the opera and the symphony. These as well as other institutions were under pressure to admit to directorships or boxes purely on the basis of power to pay. These financial stringencies accounted for a further attack upon exclusive groups.

The depression brought a third factor making for a more "moral" social life and a less exclusive one. This was the increase in lower class protest and organization due to increased unemployment. The deepest years of the recent crisis drove fear into the hearts of the wealthier circles. The psychology of "after us the deluge" pervaded a not inconsiderable element. This increased pressure of the lower classes upon the upper served to further emphasize the philanthropic content of social life as a self-justification and as a public justification, and had the important consequence of tending to unify the wealthier classes in response to a situation of threat.

The Season of 1935

A comparison of the content of social life in the earlier period with that of 1935 reveals this shift in emphasis from a primarily social life to a social philanthropic one. We find first that in 1935 the proportion of individual social affairs has decreased to 39 percent as compared with 64 percent in 1900 and 79 percent in 1882. Most modern social affairs of sufficient importance to be reported in society columns whether purely social or philanthropic in their objectives are given under group rather than private auspices. The proportion of philanthropic social affairs or benefits has increased from 4 percent in 1882 to 8 percent in 1900 to 28 percent in 1935. The proportion of intellectual and cultural affairs reported in the society pages has remained roughly the same, having been 12 percent in 1832–1883, 13 percent in 1900, and 13 percent in 1935.[32]

These figures must be qualified by the fact that the society editor places his own interpretation upon social events, decides whether they are to be given much space or little, and determines which types of events are to be publicized. While he, no doubt, selects, he tends generally to reflect the emphases and the evaluations of society itself. It is possible to conclude, therefore, that present day society emphasizes its philanthropic-social function and tends to subordinate its purely social and convivial functions.

This is further substantiated when we examine the types of social events and their objectives in detail. We find thus that the proportion of large-scale events given under individual auspices has decreased from 38 percent in 1900 to 7 percent in 1935; and that the proportion of philanthropic or benefit large-scale social events has increased from 5 percent in 1900 to 44 percent in 1935. The same tendency is to be found in the case of smaller scale dances and entertainments. Thirty-two percent of these in 1935 were given for philanthropic purposes, as compared with 9 percent in 1900.

The individual social events of the present day are largely minor social events, such as dinners, luncheons, or smaller balls and entertainments at summer residences. It is in this sphere where exclusiveness of the type illustrated in the earlier Astor set can be maintained. But even here it is difficult to maintain it since the society woman is driven by her outside activities into random contact with newly rich and non-wealthy elements. Contact in the form of asking money or favors leads to more intimate contact; and more intimate contact tends to break down barriers of birth, and sometimes even of wealth. Thus the general tendency in society has been to break down differentials, and to determine social rank almost entirely on the basis of wealth. This is not entirely true as we shall see at a later point; but the tendency has been in this direction. And this tendency has followed from the increasing emphasis upon charitable, philanthropic, and other forms of work among society women. Charitable and philanthropic work has thrown men and women of wealth and birth out of the security of small and relatively easily maintained coteries into the larger plutocracy.

This breakdown of barriers has had important consequences. It is humanly impossible for a member of the New York plutocracy to be on intimate terms with or even know superficially all the other members of the plutocracy. The Social Register of New York alone contains 27,000 names, and there are at least twice as many not in the Social Register but having considerable wealth. The destructions of barriers of birth, taste, and individual choice in the plutocracy has had the consequence of making relationships between the members of this larger plutocracy superficial and impersonal. The larger plutocracy is broken up into hundreds of little philanthropic, social, cultural, and sporting cliques. These are so numerous that the rank of these sets is difficult to determine. Though individual families, groups, and clubs are accorded general prestige among the plutocracy, it has become impossible to maintain a central set, widely publicized and generally envied, such as was the Astor clique of pre-war days. And as has been pointed out this is in large part attributable to the importance of charitable and philanthropic work in upper class circles. The stability of Mrs. Astor's clique lay in its primarily convivial way of life. Social competition was engaged in for the goals of spectacular but private entertainment for its own sake. Contemporary society competition is directed toward social philanthropic goals, a movement which has produced its typical institution, "the benefit social affair," the nature of which tends to eliminate all principles of admission save the possession of wealth.

Social Specialists

The absence of an integrating set in the New York plutocracy and its tremendous size and heterogeneity has had the consequence of making extremely difficult the problem of determining one's own social rank and the rank of others. The individual wealthy family seeking to launch its daughter in a debut finds the problem of determining whom to invite difficult. Were the family to invite only those whom they know, they would touch only random groups of the plutocracy, and hence would limit the "marriage market" as well as detract from their own prestige and that of their daughters. Thus the very size of the plutocracy, the nature of the relations among its members, and the social compulsion to entertain on a great scale have been responsible for the rise of social specialists.

There have been social specialists in New York society for many years. Indeed at a very early time there were men-about-town who devoted themselves wholeheartedly to giving and attending social functions, and to determining who shall be viewed as in the *bon ton,* and who shall not. Among the early functional equivalents of the modern social secretary was Isaac Brown, the famed sexton of Grace Church, who in the decades of 1850–1870, when society attended Grace Church *en masse,* operated from a peculiarly fortunate vantage point. Weddings, at that time the typical occasions for large-scale entertaining, took place under his direction. As sexton of Grace Church he was looked to by society for information, gossip, and advice, as to what to wear, whom to invite, and the like. He played a specially important role for *parvenus* who found in him a source of information as to who was worth while associating with, what to wear, how to comport themselves, and how barriers were to be overcome.

A later functional equivalent for the modern social secretary was Ward McAllister. Closely associated with Mrs. Astor who supplied the legitimation of wealth and birth, McAllister rapidly became in the seventies and the eighties an amateur social specialist, devising forms of entertainment, determining, under the aegis of Mrs. Astor, social rank, and supplying advice for anxious *parvenus.*

The growing need for professional social specialists in a situation of mobility, heterogeneity, and impersonality led ultimately to the rise of a new, powerful, and fairly lucrative social profession, that of the social secretary. In 1922 Miss Juliana Cutting, one of the first of these commercialized social arbiters, went into business. Born of an old and wealthy family herself, the need of money, her social connections, and experience turned her naturally into this line of work. Her main function lies in compiling and keeping up to date "stag lists"[33] which are furnished at a price to families with debutante daughters or otherwise wishing to entertain on a large scale. Her lists are graded and furnished to families of different social status and potentialities, at different prices. In addition to determining largely who is to be invited to large-scale affairs, Miss Cutting furnishes advice as to place, decorations, ceremonial, orchestras, and the like. In many cases she manages an affair completely from beginning to end, taking, in addition to fees, a percentage of the total cost of the affair. To newer families and indeed even to old, Miss Cutting's social power is great. A family must schedule its affair long in advance in order not to conflict with Miss Cutting's calendar. Newer families turn to her for advice as to deportment and dress. Miss Cutting, thus, as the outstanding social secretary approaches to being the social arbiter of New York City.

Miss Cutting is not alone in her profession. Her colleagues—Tappan and Tew, and Mrs. Fanshawe, and a number of social secretaries who specialize in advising wealthier Jewish elements—all have in common good birth, social contacts, and experience. The need for money in every case turned them into this type of work. The professional social secretary performs two functions: For the more established elements in New York City she performs a primarily secretarial role although even here her advice is frequently controlling. For the less established elements she defines the norms of good society as well as performing the secretarial and administrative functions. The social secretary is the product of a large, heterogeneous, and mobile plutocracy. For newcomers she defines the norms of refined society, and for both these elements and the established groups, she supplies the lack of personal friendship and acknowledged rank. The entrepreneur social secretary is to be distinguished from the private social secretary, who performs private secretarial functions for active society women.

There are other social specialists who have arisen as a result of the changed orientation and anarchy of good society. The society page and its special editors, reporters, and columnists is not a product of the post–World War period but rather received its great impetus in the post–Civil War days when newspapers began to discover the "copy" value of the affairs of the wealthy. It has now become a standard section of the American newspaper playing to the publicity needs of the plutocracy and the curiosity and envy of the lower classes. Society editors and reporters, unlike social secretaries, are a heterogeneous group. Some are of good and wealthy birth, but a large number are not. The society journalists as a group also enjoy considerable social power. By their selection and interpretation of social affairs they have a great part in shaping the social image of the upper classes, which tends to be emulated by the lower classes. It is also within their power to make and break society groups and individuals through the means of more and less publicity. Because of the size, mobility, heterogeneity, and the consequent lack of facilities of communication between wealthy groups, individuals in society necessarily resort to the society pages for their information. It is thus possible for a society editor to bring *parvenus* within the focus of attention of established elements, and thus enhance their social position, and on the other hand within limits, to disestablish other elements by failing to refer to them, or by referring to them infrequently.

The boredom and increasing informality of the plutocracy in New York has given rise to such a social specialist as Elsa Maxwell who plays the special role of bringing into contact the jaded wealthy, and actors, musicians, and other celebrities. Miss Maxwell is the arbiter of the cafe society of New York City.

One writer classifies contemporary New York society into four groups:

> The smart international set, led by Vincent Astor; the Newport group, last embattled remnants of the old 400, led more or less by the Vanderbilts; the fast but well-connected Long Island set who go in for horses, women and an occasional cock-fight; and cafe society, an amazing polyglot group which is willing to accept authors, motion picture stars and almost anyone who wears good clothes and talks well.[34]

In addition there are the wealthy German Jewish set, the remnants of the older Knickerbockers, and the many suburban groups. No one of these constitutes "the fashionable set," and in their philanthropic and recreational activities there is much overlapping.

The Social Register

Although there were a number of earlier directories having similar purposes, the Social Register has occupied a specially esteemed position among the plutocracy. Founded by Louis Keller, a member of the Calumet Club in 1887, its publication was undertaken as a means of enhancing his livelihood. It met an important need among the wealthy. Clearly printed, without advertising, more careful in its inclusions than earlier publications, and containing data as to residence, telephone, names and residences of unmarried children, club memberships, and the names of universities, summer residences and yachts, it was welcomed by the New York plutocracy and has enjoyed its esteem ever since its first publication. He later expanded the business into the Social Register Association, publishing directories in Washington, Philadelphia, Chicago, Boston, St. Louis, Pittsburgh, Cleveland, Cincinnati, Dayton, San Francisco, Baltimore, and Buffalo.[35] Admission to the Social Register is accomplished through personal application accompanied by the recommendation of individuals already included. An investigation is made by the staff which is under the direction of the former secretary of Keller. The Register includes primarily families whose income is from business, or from the professions. The tendency is to include the more established families and the very wealthy new families, and families of ancient lineage despite their economic status. It is naturally difficult for very new wealthy families, or families outside of respectable business circles to gain entrance to the Social Register, since they lack in the necessary contacts among those already included. Once contact is established with families already included, through business, philanthropic, or club contact, admission can readily be gained if desired. Actors and journalists, and individuals in less reputable businesses, which would include those involving too close contact with the production and the sale of commodities, are admitted with greater difficulty. In general it might be said that its policy represents the more conservative social tradition of Juliana Cutting, Emily Post, and other articulators of the norms of this class.

To the established family, enjoying at least relative social security the Social Register performs the service of a convenient selected directory of information; to the social-climbing family it represents a goal to be struggled for. And to a certain extent the *parvenu* is right, since in the absence of a commonly accepted set enjoying the highest social esteem, and in a situation of innumerable smaller sets ranked variously according to the judgments of individuals and small groups, inclusion in the Social Register means that one has risen socially one stage beyond mere economic or professional success. The very absence of commonly accepted hierarchization grants great influence to the Social Register, which in the mind of the busy and preoccupied New York socialite, supplies at least a minimum of selectiveness on the basis of which contact and friendship may be admitted. Since its founding the Register has increased in size from year to year. The depression caused a drop, but the years since 1932 have marked a gradual increase. The rate of increase, tremendous before and shortly after the war, has gradually been lessening.

The Register also plays a mildly moralistic and punitive role. On rare occasions it administers social rebukes by dropping names because of socially unacceptable marriages, or misbehavior. It is a weapon rarely used, and its effects are sometimes exaggerated.

Remaining Citadels of Exclusiveness

Although the general tendency in the decades since the war has been toward the destruction of exclusiveness within the plutocracy there are, nevertheless, a number of important exclusive groups to which are admitted only the older families among the wealthy. As has been pointed out these "citadels of exclusiveness" have been pushed into the background because of the tendency to combine social activity with philanthropy and charity, and because of the great size and heterogeneity of the wealthy class. Such clubs as the Union, the Knickerbocker, and the Racquet and Tennis are commonly accepted as the most exclusive clubs of the city to which are admitted only the "blooded stock." For women the Colony Club enjoys a similar position. The Junior Assembly conducts a series of dances to which are admitted only the debutantes of the "Golden Caste of Verc de Vere." Wecter refers to the very exclusive metropolitan "Sub-debutante" dancing class, which is dominated by the older families, and follows a more sober and old-fashioned tradition of social entertainment.[36] And the Tuxedo New Year Ball has also traditionally been limited to the older and more established families. The ancestral associations listed at length in earlier chapters admit and exclude entirely on the basis of birth. Certain families still occupy positions of special esteem among the plutocracy. Mrs. Cornelius Vanderbilt, Sr., is viewed by many as the dowager of New York society. The families of Astor, Vanderbilt, Mills, Fish, Iselin and Oelrichs, and many others still give exclusive private entertainments which large numbers of the less fortunate plutocracy strive to enter. These events, however, have been pressed into the background by the pressure of numbers, and by the changed orientation of social life. There are exclusive groups and institutions among the New York plutocracy at the present time, but there is no commonly accepted fashionable set of the type approximated in the decades before the World War.

In summary, the society of the era of the closed frontier—the era of intensified pressure from the lower classes—underwent two major transformations. The first was the increase in charitable activities and the frequent justification of social and cultural entertainment by associating them with philanthropic purposes. This may be interpreted as an effort to appease public opinion by identifying pleasure with some constructive objective. The second transformation was the destruction of an acquiesced-in exclusive society, due to the emphasis upon charitable activity, to the pressure of the international crisis in 1917–18, and to the pressure of the lower classes over the whole period.

Notes

1. Frederick J. Turner, "Social Forces in American History," *American Historical Review*, XVI (1911), 217.

2. Joseph Schafer, "Turner's America," *Wisconsin Magazine of History*, XVII (1933–1934), 447.

3. Turner, *op. cit.*, p. 224.

4. *Ibid.*

5. Abram C. Dayton, *Last Days of Knickerbocker Life in New York* (New York: G. W. Harlan, 1882).

6. Frederick Townsend Martin, *The Passing of the Idle Rich* (London: Hodder and Stoughton, 1911), p. 13.

7. See copy of Charles W. De Lyon Nicholls *450 Ultra-Fashionables in America* (New York: Broadway Publishing Co., 1912) in New York Public Library.

8. Martin, *op. cit.*, pp. 135–36.
9. Henry Collins Brown, *Brownstone Fronts and Saratoga Trunks* (New York: E. P. Dutton Co., 1935), pp. 334–335.
10. *New York Tribune*, February 11, 1897, p. 7.
11. *Ibid.*, February 14, 1897, p. 4.
12. Henry Demarest Lloyd, *Wealth against Commonwealth* (New York: Harper Bros., 1894); *Lords of Industry* (New York and London: G. P. Putnam's Sons, 1910); *Men the Workers* (New York: Doubleday Page and Co., 1909).
13. Martin, *op. cit.*, p. 104.
14. *Ibid.*, p. 109.
15. *Ibid.*, pp. 113–14.
16. *Ibid.*
17. *Ibid.*, pp. 115–16.
18. *Ibid.*, p. 122.
19. *Ibid.*
20. *Ibid.*
21. *Ibid.*, pp. 125–26.
22. *Ibid.*, p. 158.
23. *Ibid.*, p. 168.
24. *Ibid.*, p. 243.
25. Dixon Wecter, *The Saga of American Society* (New York: Charles Scribner's Sons, 1937), p. 336.
26. *Ibid.*, pp. 340 ff.
27. *Ibid.*, p. 342.
28. *New York Times*, December 2, 1917, Section 8, p. 2.
29. *Ibid.*
30. *Ibid.*
31. Society pages of the *New York Herald Tribune*, January, 1930 to November, 1931.
32. Based upon an analysis of the society columns of the *New York Herald Tribune* for the year 1935.
33. Wecter, *op. cit.*, p. 240.
34. Stanley Walker, *Mrs. Astor's Horse* (New York: Frederic A. Stokes Co., 1935), pp. 6–7.
35. Wecter, *op. cit.*, pp. 232 ff.
36. Wecter, *op. cit.*, p. 229.

12

Political Reactions to Crises

ALTHOUGH THE WEALTHY CLASSES as a rule did not personally engage in politics after the achievement of democracy, exceptional periods and stimuli precipitated increased political action in these classes. These exceptional periods were occasions on which the interests of the plutocracy were endangered. Three types of dangerous situations were noted as causing increased political action in the wealthy classes. These were political corruption, war, and lower class unrest. In normal periods the American social structure presented a situation in which the personnel of the economic controlling class and the governmental office-holders diverged. Periods of crisis forced in varying degrees a convergence between these two groups, bringing the plutocracy into an active political role.

Political Reform

By political reform we understand political activity designed to eliminate corrupt and deleterious governmental practices and to improve, in the sense of rendering more economical and efficient, the mechanism of government. Great corruption is viewed by the established elements of the wealthy classes as not only destructive and wasteful, but as a threat to stability, law, and order, and the cause of high taxation. Upper class reform movements are designed to eliminate corrupt elements and practices, to render government a better mechanism, but they do not contemplate any governmental changes which would seriously alter the prevailing distribution of property and opportunities. Exposures of great political corruption have been the occasions for large-scale risings and political vigilantism of elements of the wealthier classes.

The various governments, federal, state, and local, had important favors to dispense—public lands, charters from the state government for engaging in banking and insurance activities, franchises for street railroads and gas supply, ferry franchises and leases, wharf leases, contracts for removing dead animals, and many others. Both the already wealthy and those who sought wealth were keenly interested in gaining these rights and privileges, since the rate of growth of New York City and its constantly increasing commercial importance made these real estate grants, franchises, charters, and leases of great and continually increasing value. The professional politicians—those who managed to control the parties and the public offices—distributed these rights and privileges among themselves, or in return for bribes and economic and political services.

Many of the great New York real estate fortunes were built in the Pre–Civil War Era. John Jacob Astor acquired much land from the city at such cheap prices as to raise the presumption of fraud and favoritism. The Goelets, the Rhinelanders, Schermerhorns, Havemeyers, Vanderbilts, Robert Lenox, William Dodge, and many others also acquired much of their valuable real estate through city grants.[1]

Charters for banks and insurance companies, street railway and gas-lighting franchises, ferry franchises, and various leases were granted through the state legislature and the Common Council. The principles by which these charters, franchises, leases, and rights were granted were not the size of the bid and the standards of service, but the size of the bribe offered to the legislators and councilmen. Four Sachems of Tammany, Samuel B. Romaine, Michael Ulshoeffer, Peter Sharpe, and Abraham Stagg were prominent "charter dealers" in Albany. They lobbied charters for insurance companies and banks through the legislature and demanded corporation offices or money for their services.[2] Three of these charter dealers, Romaine, Ulshoeffer, and Sharpe, were in Beach's $100,000 or over class.[3] A grand jury and other investigations in 1852–1853 revealed a prosperous charter and franchise business in the city hall. Tremendous sums were distributed among the aldermen at the time of the granting of the charter for the Eighth Street Railway. Solomon Kipp, one of the grantees of the Ninth Avenue Railroad, admitted to the Grand Jury that he had spent more than $50,000 in gaining this franchise from the aldermen. Various other street railroad franchises were also sold for profitable sums. The chief bribers in the Third Avenue Railroad scandal were Elijah F. Purdy and Myndert Van Schaick, both wealthy merchants. Leases and franchises for the ferries were also sold to the highest briber.[4]

Election corruption on a great scale was characteristic of this era. It was practiced not only by Tammany and the Democrats but by the aristocratic Whigs as well. Possibly the most outstanding fraud was perpetrated by the Whigs in 1838. The Whigs in this case were aided by conservative renegade Tammanyites such as Moses Grinnell and Robert Wetmore who were anxious to fight the progressive anti-monopolists who had won control of Tammany. The Whig inner circle imported some two or three hundred "toughs" from Philadelphia to vote repeatedly in the various wards, and thereby acquired a margin of votes ensuring their election.[5] The wealthy Whigs who took part in this fraud according to Glentworth's confession were James Bowen, quoted by Beach as worth $200,000; Simeon Draper Jr., an auctioneer, quoted as worth $100,000; James F. Freeborn, a shipping merchant worth $150,000; Dr. Samuel R. Chilas, worth $100,000; H. L. Pierson, an iron merchant worth $125,000; and Henry W. Havens, a commission merchant quoted as worth $150,000.[6]

Another common corrupt political practice in which the rich participated was the avoidance of taxation by fraudulent assessments. The story is told that the Merchants Bank was taxed at $6,000, though it was worth at least twice as much, and the Merchants Exchange was evaluated at $115,000, though it was known that the land and building had cost $300,000.[7] Many of the merchants of that day established their residences outside of the city, thereby avoiding higher taxation.

It would, of course, be an exaggeration to say that all of the wealthy were implicated in these fraudulent practices. The generalization is possible that these corrupt practices were more characteristic of the newer fortunes, while the established families generally remained politically passive, or in some cases actively fought against the corruption for short periods of time. Many influential groups throughout this era deplored the corruption of the city and state governments, but no effective organized movement for a reformist party took place until after the exposures of the Grand Jury investigation of the fraudulent practices of a large number of city councilmen in February of 1853. Charges of sale of franchises and leases were made and substantiated by many of the recipients of these favors. In response to this publicized corruption a City Reform Party was organized, aided considerably by Horace Greeley and his *New York Tribune*. Wrote Greeley in his editorial column:

> When Government becomes rotten, when our rulers become corrupt, every valuable interest drifts from its moorings. We are exposed to constant perils. Our security is endangered. Property, life, public order are placed in jeopardy. It is time, therefore, high time, that all good citizens without distinction of party, should turn their serious attention to the existing state of our municipal government, and begin to consider measures for a radical and thorough reform.[8]

Political corruption, thus, was defined as a challenge to public order, property, and life, to the most meaningful symbols of the established or propertied classes. Political corruption was also defined as economically threatening, resulting in higher taxation, and lack of faith in the credit of government, which endangered the interests and values of the propertied classes. An appeal was made to the working classes on the ground that the high taxation incident to political corruption raised the rents of the workingmen.

On the eve of a mass meeting called for March 5, 1853, by a number of the respectable citizenry Greeley wrote:

> Our city is fearfully misgoverned, and despoiled, and corruption has been growing worse and worse for years, mainly because her substantial citizens, who do her work, accumulate her wealth, and don't want to make money out of politics, have too generally neglected or slighted their public duties. Every citizen is under moral obligation to do his fair share toward securing upright and capable rulers and magistrates, and holding them to a strict and wholesome accountability; yet a majority of our thrifty, comfortable citizens have shamefully repudiated that duty. Some of them have not even voted half the time; others have barely voted, leaving to the contract-jobbers, office-seekers, grog shop-keepers, and husky rowdies, the substantial control of our elections.[9]

At the mass meeting of March 5, 1853, a City Reform Committee of 44 members was appointed. This committee included 15, or 34 percent, who were listed in Beach's *Wealthy Citizens*.[10] They included the shipping merchant Moses Taylor ($500,000), the iron manufacturer James Boorman ($1,500,000), the linen merchant Thomas Suffern ($600,000), the iron manufacturer Peter Cooper ($1,000,000), and the publisher John Harper ($300,000). The reform committee also included 12 individuals engaged in wholesaling, retailing, and jobbing; 9 lawyers, 7 manufacturers, 4 shipping merchants, 3 in the building contracting business, 2 publishers, 1 *rentier*, 1 insurance company executive, and 1 railroad director.[11]

As a first move the City Reform Committee proposed to amend the city charter. Among the reforms suggested was the prohibition of city leases for longer than ten years duration, to be given to the highest bidder. A two-thirds vote was to be required to pass over the mayor's veto. High punishments were recommended for accepting bribes. The judicial powers of aldermen were to be removed, and the power of the aldermen to appoint policemen was to be taken away. A Board of Councilmen sitting as a separate body was to be substituted for the Board of Assistant Aldermen. Aldermen were to serve for two years and councilmen for one year. All revenue and appropriation measures were to be initiated by the council. The widespread agitation of the city reformers resulted in an espousal of their charter amendments by Tammany, eager to head off the revolt of the respectable classes. Some of the charter reforms passed the legislature and were voted on favorably by the city population.

Fearing that unless suitable measures were taken the professional politicians would negative these legal reforms, the Reform Committee participated in the following city election in the hope of breaking the control of the political organizations. They resolved in a mass meeting late in June of 1853 to take active part in the elections in order that the charter reforms might not be destroyed by the election of party "hacks."

During the summer preceding the November city election mass meetings were held in many of the wards for the purpose of choosing reform candidates from the Whig and "soft and hard shell" factions among the Democrats. These meetings culminated in a mass meeting on November 1, held in Metropolitan Hall for the purpose of approving the candidates selected in the ward meetings. An appeal had been made to the workingmen, with the result that 19 worker representatives appeared and were chosen as vice presidents of the mass meeting. Forty vice presidents were chosen from the middle and wealthy classes. Besides these 19 worker representatives, the 59 vice presidents included 23 individuals whose fortunes were evaluated as $100,000 and over by Moses Beach. The vice presidents of the mass meeting included even a larger representation of the very wealthy than the City Reform Committee itself. The China and India merchant George Griswold ($500,000), the shipping merchant William Earl Dodge, Jr. ($500,000), and the department store owner A. T. Stewart ($2,000,000) among others, had been added to the group of active and wealthy reformers. The movement, thus, had gained considerable momentum among the wealthy classes.[12] The chairman, Peter Cooper, sanguinely anticipated:

> Your committee believe that a large majority of their fellow citizens are ready and determined to take the regulation of city affairs out of the hands of the political managers, and to select for themselves the men who are to govern, and to tax them. The unprecedentedly loud call of the tax-gatherer, now abroad, has gone forth to strengthen and extend this feeling. Our people feel that they are made to pay most exorbitantly for the very small return which they enjoy in safety, comfort, cleanliness, and good order, and they are determined, that hereafter their taxes shall be reduced, if possible—but at any rate, that they shall be applied in some manner to the public service, and not squandered by the very trustees who are appointed for their protection.[13]

The aims of the reform movement as formulated by Peter Cooper in 1853 sound very familiar in the light of the programs and aspirations of contemporary reform movements. The main planks in the program were (1) non-partisan municipal elections, (2) the elimination of spoils politics for subordinate officials, (3) no removal from office for opinion, and (4) economic administration.

In the revivalist atmosphere of the mass meeting William Earl Dodge confessed the political guilt of the wealthy and resolved to do better in the future.

> Before entering upon these remarks, as I stand here to represent the mercantile class, I will make a confession, for myself and for them. I confess before my fellow citizens, as a citizen, I have neglected my duty. For many years I was content with croaking and finding fault with the city government, but yet went, like a sheep to the slaughter, voted with my party, without knowing the men or feeling my responsibility.[14]

He then went on to pledge watchful and constructive action in the future. The mass meeting approved the selections of candidates proposed by the Reform Committee. Interestingly enough, out of a total of 63 aldermanic and council candidates recommended, only one, the lawyer Daniel D. Lord, was listed in Beach's *Wealthy Citizens* as being worth $100,000 or over. The wealthy, thus, were willing to take political action, but apparently not to an extent that would interfere with business and other interests. Many of the aldermanic and council candidates were on the Whig and Democratic slates, but were viewed as good reform men. As a group the candidates were from the middle class, less wealthy elements of the population. They included 24 domestic merchants—retailers, wholesalers, commission merchants, and the like—none of whom were in the very wealthy group. None of the shipping merchants ran for office. Only 4 lawyers were candidates. The balance of the candidates included 11 manufacturers and mechanics, 3 builders, 2 physicians, 2 tailors, 1 dentist, 1 barber, 1 broker, 1 bank teller, and 1 clerk.[15]

The reform slate won a victory by a small margin in the election in November. Their victory was due to a certain amount of popular enthusiasm and the fact that the Democrats were split. They elected 12 out of 22 aldermen, and 27 out of 61 councilmen. In the council the other parties were broken into small factions, and the reformers had the largest group in that body. Of the 12 reform aldermen, however, 6 were actually party men who had espoused reform principles and were recommended by the Committee. Five of the 12 new aldermen were reform Whigs, and 1 was a reform Democrat.

Thus, though the City Reformers had won a numerical victory, the ultimate success of their ambitious objectives depended upon consistent action and watchfulness. And it was precisely in this respect that the reformers failed, as they were to fail many times in the future. Tammany, led by Fernando Wood, successfully conspired to divide the reformers. The reform Whigs gradually separated from the reformers, and, according to Myers, Tammany nominated sham reformers for the less important city and state offices.[16] Wood, the candidate of the "soft shell" Democrats, received the support of the liquor dealers and the so-called disreputable classes. He succeeded in winning the mayoralty as a result of this support, and the division of his opposition, by a very small plurality. With the election of Fernando Wood the City Reform movement may be said to have come to an end. Its quietus was read by the disappointed Horace Greeley in the spring of 1854.[17]

The rise and fall of the City Reformers in 1853–1854 illustrates the general causes of the rise and decline of reform movements in American plutocratic democracy. Aroused by scandalous political corruption, shocking the sense of decency of the respectable wealthy business and professional classes, these classes experience a wave of vigilantism which lasts for a short while, taking them from the security of their business, social, and philanthropic life. But the wealthy and respectable group as a rule are unwilling seriously to engage in politics for various reasons—preoccupation with business and other affairs, the dislike of associating with professional politicians, and the lower classes, and the fact that the fear of corruption on the part of the wealthy classes varies with its seriousness and dramatization and that their fortunes and social positions are not seriously endangered. Then too a reform program identified with tax saving and divorced from more fundamental social reforms cannot adequately seize and hold the imagination of the general population. The effort to recruit the culturally and politically developed elements of the working classes ordinarily fails or achieves only a partial success, since the reformist program does not express the needs and aspirations of the lower classes. For these reasons the reformist movement of the 1850s like many of those which were to follow achieved a measure of political reform, but spent itself rapidly as is ordinarily the case with bursts of vigilantism. The professional politicians were able to dispel the fears for order and property engendered by exposures of corruption by verbal adherence to reformist ideals; and the old situation of a politically passive upper class and an active group of professional politicians controlling the votes of the masses by virtue of favors and services reasserted itself.

The impression should not be gained that the City Reform Committee activities of 1853–1854 were the only reform movement of the Pre–Civil War Era. It took the largest proportions and achieved the greatest success. There were other reform groups previous to this one and after it. The scandals of the Fernando Wood administration in 1860–1861 resulted in another reform movement, called the "People's Union," consisting of reform Democrats and Republicans. They succeeded in electing the banker George Opdyke to the mayoralty in 1861, but the Common Council was still in the control of Tammany and Mozart Hall, the latter being Fernando Wood's headquarters. The Charter provision for a mere majority to override the veto negatived the value of the election of a reform mayor. In the succeeding elections in 1863 and in 1865 the Tammany mayoralty candidates were again elected over Republican and reform opposition.

Following upon the Civil War an era of great industrial construction began in which New York City played a highly influential role. Railroad financing and construction were especially marked by the corruption of public office-holders. The struggle for the Erie Railroad between the "Erie Ring" (Gould, Fisk, and Drew) on the one side and Vanderbilt on the other is one of the outstanding cases of industrial struggle involving the corruption of politics and politicians. In the first stage of the struggle Vanderbilt, the loser of several million through the Ring's issuance of fraudulent stock, had a judge under his control issue an injunction. The Erie Ring on the other hand bought action from favorable judges canceling the order issued by Vanderbilt's judge. After this preliminary skirmishing, the Erie Ring in Albany tried to bribe the legislature to pass a bill legalizing the issuance of

Erie stock. Gould is said to have distributed $500,000 among the legislators, a sum larger than that distributed by Vanderbilt. The Erie Ring succeeded in getting their bill passed, legalizing the issuance of stock and forbidding the merger of the New York Central and the Erie, which had been Vanderbilt's objective.[18] For the great services afforded the Erie group by the Tweed Ring, in gratitude Gould and Fisk elected William M. Tweed and Peter B. Sweeney, the central figures of the Tweed Tammany Ring, to the board of directors.

> This formidable combination [wrote Adams] sent out feelers far and wide; it wielded the influence of a great corporation with a capital of $100,000,000. It controlled the politics of the first city of the New World; it sent its representatives to the senate of the state, and numbered among its agents, the judges of the courts. Compact, disciplined and reckless, it knew its own power, and would not scruple to use it.[19]

Adams, in 1869, appreciated the significance of this close tie-up between the "leviathans of capital" and the "leviathans of politics":

> Now their power is in its infancy; in a few years they will re-enact on a grander scale, with every feature magnified, the scenes which were lately witnessed on the narrow stage of a single state. The public corruption is the foundation on which corporations always depend for their political power. There is a natural tendency to coalition between them and the lowest strata of political intelligence and morality; for their agents must obey, not question. They exact success, and do not cultivate political morality. The lobby is their home, and the lobby thrives as political virtues decay. The "Ring" is the symbol of power and the "Ring" is the natural enemy of political purity and independence. . . . The existing coalition between the Erie Railway and the Tammany Ring is a natural one, for the former needs votes, the latter money.[20]

Of the five years following the Civil War Adams wrote that the

> rapidly developed railroad influences have declared war, negotiated peace, reduced courts, legislatures, and sovereign states to an unqualified obedience to their will, and boldly setting forth law and public opinion at defiance have freely exercised many other attributes of sovereignty.[21]

The dominant figures in the Tweed Ring were Sweeney, the City Chamberlain; John T. Hoffman, later governor; Richard B. Connolly, comptroller; and A. Oakey Hall, district attorney. Tweed himself was a member of the County Board of Supervisors and a deputy street commissioner. In 1868 the Ring elected John T. Hoffman as governor and it thus was in the zenith of its power, controlling the city, county, and state governments. It was in this political atmosphere that the manipulations of Vanderbilt, Gould, and Fisk flourished and the Erie Ring scandals were accomplished.[22]

The Tweed Ring frauds were discovered, that is, discovered in detail, through a leakage of information in the office of the County Supervisor in 1871. For some few months information describing the Tweed Ring activities was published in the *New York Times*. One of the immediate consequences of this exposure was the refusal of the financial community to accept city bonds, resulting in the suspension of salary payments. Previous to this, while the *New York Times* exposures were appearing, pressure was brought to bear against the *Times* to prevent it from publishing its information.

> During the ten months of continuous warfare against the Ring by the New York Times [wrote the biographer of Andrew H. Green] which preceded its publication of the crushing array of figures, the business of the newspaper suffered because there were large advertisers, as there were large property owners, in New York who did not care to be noted as unfriendly to the ruling powers by giving support to their relentless assailant. The certificate signed by a committee of which John Jacob Astor, Moses Taylor, and Marshall D. Roberts were members, setting forth the correctness of Comptroller Connolly's accounts, was only one of the many evidences of how successfully the Ring had hoodwinked some of the best men in New York.[23]

Whether they had been hoodwinked or not, these three bulwarks of respectability (Roberts had sold rotten ships to the government during the Civil War) did lend the power of their names to the Tweed Ring. A large number of the wealthy subscribed money for a statue to be erected in Tweed's honor.

The refusal to accept municipal bonds by the financial community and the issuance of an injunction against the payment of claims against the city by Comptroller Connolly brought the city's affairs to a standstill. Tweed and his followers were disposed to wait until the scandal would blow over, but the situation became increasingly critical. Angry crowds of laborers were demanding their back pay. There was a danger that the police would mutiny. "There was imminent danger of the city being compelled to face the sinister problem of an army of ten to fifteen thousand laboring men turned adrift from their work at parks, streets and boulevards, conscious only that somebody had cheated them out of their hard-earned money."[24] There was general fear that if this situation continued for a long while there would be riot and disorder in the streets. Also the response of the European and American press to the scandals hurt the pride of many New Yorkers. The situation was one of acute crisis—a threat to law and order.

As the plot unfolded Connolly began to realize that Tweed, Sweeney, and the others were going to use him as a scapegoat. Fearing their treachery he went to the reform Democrats Tilden and Havemeyer and asked their advice. They advised him to appoint as deputy controller with full powers Andrew H. Green, in return for "the mercy of the court." This was done immediately. Green thus was in a key position to discover the magnitude of the Tweed frauds. The Citizens' Committee of Investigation appointed in 1871 discovered tremendous frauds and urged in its report that claims ought not to be paid while the Ring remained in office.

The exposures of the magnitude of the Tweed Ring frauds and the consequent threat to the name and standing of New York City resulted in a wave of vigilantism in the business community. A great mass meeting was held on September 5, 1871, a meeting of

> real indignation, passionately expressed. Men of all parties and all ages assembled under the call very early in the evening. Nearly an hour before the time appointed for the opening speech no standing room remained in the hall. The immense and enthusiastic audience was composed in every sense of substantial men, who came there with the purpose of giving free, full, emphatic and unequivocal expression to sentiments long since formed, and to opinions now confirmed by the presentation of full proofs of the frauds of the Tammany leaders.[25]

Havemeyer, a prominent sugar refiner and a Democratic reform leader, warned the business men gathered in the Cooper Union that the "shackling and burdening of trade" by the corrupt administration might result in a loss of commerce by New York City. "This city," said Havemeyer in conclusion, "so magnificent in extent, so liberal in its welcome and hospitality, and boundless in its charities, now calls her people to their duty in this time of her humiliation."[26]

A Committee of 70 was appointed to direct the strategy of the anti-Tweed forces. Of the 58 members of this Reform Committee whose occupations was known, 18 were bankers and brokers, 10 were merchants, 9 were lawyers, 6 were manufacturers, 5 were lawyers and political office-holders, 4 were wholesalers, 2 were publishers and editors, 2 were retailers, 1 a physician, and 1 a teacher.[27] The large majority of the Committee of 70 thus were wealthy bankers, merchants, manufacturers, and wholesalers.

The reform groups succeeded in electing Havemeyer to the mayoralty in 1872. With Andrew H. Green in the comptroller's office and Havemeyer in the mayoralty, the Ring was checked at least temporarily. But as the *Allgemeine Zeitung* of Augsburg, Germany, wrote:

> The great danger of seeing the government of the City of New York again in the keeping of dishonest people is by no means over. If we correctly read the signs a new Ring is being formed from the remnants, mainly, of the old, and only needs the removal of the present Comptroller Green to be speedily completed. . . . The former corruption in many of the departments is by no means eradicated. It is deep rooted, and we fear, alive, although it may not appear above the ground.[28]

While the "heat" was on, the corrupt influences remained in the background. By 1874, however, the reform fire had burned out. In that year

Tammany elected to the mayoralty its own candidate, William H. Wickham, who, though a respectable business man, headed a ticket mainly of old Tammany "Wheelhorses." Out of the ashes of the old Tweed Ring arose "Boss" John Kelly, who managed Tammany's forces. Kelly did not operate with the same openness as the Tweed group. He succeeded in making Tammany relatively respectable again by electing as Sachems such prominent business men, lawyers, and statesmen as Augustus Schell, Samuel J. Tilden, Charles O'Conor, Horatio Seymour, Sanford E. Church, and August Belmont.

By 1874 Kelly's rule of Tammany and the city were consolidated. From 1876 to 1880 Kelly filled the position of city controller. Renewed corruption resulted in the splitting off of groups of Democrats from Tammany. The Irving Hall Democracy broke away in 1875, and the New York County Democracy, a reform element led by Abram Hewitt, broke away in 1880. The establishment of minority factions in the Democratic Party made the older situation of almost open corruption impossible. Kelly was forced to operate with more caution and on a smaller scale. In 1878 and in 1880 Tammany collaborated in the election of Edward Cooper and William R. Grace, both wealthy business men and reform politicians. Again in 1884 the County Democracy and Irving Hall combined to elect the shipping magnate Grace to the mayoralty.

The period of 1884–1886 was marked by the discovery of almost unbelievable corruption in the Board of Aldermen. Two surface railway companies were competing for the franchise for a surface railway on Broadway. Some $500,000 were distributed by one of these companies among the aldermen, each alderman receiving $22,000.[29] The bill was vetoed by Mayor Grace and then repassed over his veto. Following upon the exposure of this bribery six of the guilty aldermen fled to Canada, 3 were jailed, 3 turned state's evidence. Ten others were indicted, but never brought to trial, since public indignation had gradually subsided. Kelly had a nervous breakdown during these exposures and died in 1886.

After the death of Kelly four leaders of Tammany rose to prominence. These were Richard Croker, Hugh Grant, Thomas P. Gilroy, and W. Bourke Cochran. Croker gradually concentrated power in his hands, and by 1888 was virtually the "boss."[30] In that year the Tammany leader Hugh Grant was elected over the reform candidate Hewitt. In 1890 there were again exposures of corruption and fraud in the Tammany-controlled city departments. A citizens' reform movement was organized, calling itself the People's Municipal League. Their nominee for mayor was defeated by the Tammany candidate for re-election, Grant. Again in 1892 Tammany won the mayoralty.

In 1894 the exposures of the Lexow Committee, especially of frauds in the police department, resulted in the appointment of another Committee of 70. The reform groups were led by Reverend Parkhurst, the City and Good Government clubs. The dry goods merchant and reform candidate William Strong was elected. But by 1897 Tammany was strong enough to defeat the Citizens' Union and Seth Low. The Tammany candidate Van Wyck was elected to the mayoralty. The Citizens' Union was more fortunate in 1901 when they succeeded in electing Seth Low. From 1903 to 1913 the Tammany Democrats were in power, with McClellan and Gaynor in the mayoralty. In 1913 a fusion reform movement succeeded in electing Mitchell to the mayoralty. From 1917 again until 1932 Tammany candidates Hylan and Walker held the mayoralty. The Hofstadter Committee Investigation of the Walker administrations in 1932 discovered graft, extortion, and racketeering from "top to bottom," resulting in Walker's removal from office. These scandals resulted in the rise of a fusion reform movement which succeeded in electing the Republican La Guardia to the mayoralty.

There was a general tendency in the latter half of the nineteenth century toward the bureaucratization of political reform activities. In the Pre–Civil and immediate Post–Civil War eras, reform was of a spontaneous and vigilantistic character, resulting in great mass meetings and increased personal political activity on the part of the wealthy classes. Gradually a number of reform organizations were formed, supported by the contributions of the wealthy classes. Thus in the early 1880s the City Reform Club and the Civil Service Reform Association were established. A Municipal Tax-Payers Association had been active in the 1870s. In the 1890s there were two city clubs and one Reform Club, a City Improvement Society, and a Civic League. A number of "good government" clubs were also organized during this period. These reform groups were largely controlled by lawyers and influential business men.

The success of reform movements, especially in the earlier period tended to bring some of these wealthy individuals into municipal office. Thus under the Strong administration in 1985 the merchant Smith Ely, and the real estate man S. Van Rensselaer Cruger served as park commissioners. The police commissioners included Theodore Roosevelt, the lawyers Avery D. Andrews and Andrew D. Parker, and Frederick D. Grant, son of the former president and Civil War general. The civil service commissioners included the lawyers Everett P. Wheeler, W. Bayard Cutting, and J. Van Vechten Olcott, and the wholesale druggist William J. Schieffelin. The Strong Board of Education included William Greenough, a woolens dealer; the lawyers John E. Eustis, E. Ellery Anderson, and John G. Agar; and the banker James Speyer. The Rapid Transit Railroad Commission consisted of the banker and merchant Alexander E. Orr; the dry goods dealer Woodbury Langdon; the lawyer George L. Rives; and the transport owner J. H. Starin. Most of these were wealthy business men and corporation lawyers, and a large proportion were Social Registerites.

The 1901 Seth Low administration resulted in the appointment to administrative office of the Social Registerite E. R. L. Gould as city chamberlain. J. Hampden Dougherty, a lawyer, was appointed commissioner of water supply, gas, and electricity. The socialite lawyer George Lockhart Rives was appointed Corporation Counsel. The civil service commissioners included the woolens dealer W. S. Ogden, the lawyers A. T. Mason and W. N. Dykeman, and the finance capitalist Cornelius Vanderbilt. The Board of Education included well known bankers, brokers, corporation lawyers, real estate owners, and other prominent business and professional men.

Fewer wealthy, influential, and professional men took office in the Mitchell fusion administration in 1913. And even fewer of the very wealthy held or hold appointive offices in the 1933 and 1937 La Guardia administrations. The La Guardia administration, however, rests upon classes of the population and a program differing greatly from the earlier reform administrations. It has combined a program of social legislation with that of pure technical and mechanical reforms, and hence relies for support not only upon the wealthier elements of the population but upon the trade unions and the lower classes generally.

It may be generally concluded from this all too brief and sketchy review of the history of reform politics in New York City that reform politics previous to the La Guardia administration have tended to be a special type of plutocratic political activity. Corruption, we have seen, has been commonly viewed as a threat to public order and the security of property. Because of their larger need for the maintenance of public order and property, the plutocracy has generally been aroused in periods of great corruption into political activity. This type of crisis tends to result in a situation in which the leadership in actual economic and social power tends to converge with the formal governmental leadership. Social crises, it may be said, tend to make apparent the actual power situation.

The Wealthy Classes and War Situations

War crises tend to increase the volume of upper class participation. Generally speaking, wars of great magnitude make for a general subordination of the economy to military necessities. The general population tends to become politicized, the lower classes as well as the upper. But the upper classes play a special political role in war crises. They participate by giving financial aid and by holding office in the *ad hoc* agencies set up to control the economy. The increased political participation of the upper classes in war situations is motivated partly by the threat to their position involved in defeat, the possible aggrandizement of their position involved in victory, by the social and moral pressures specially operative during wartime, and by the great prospects for profit due to the increased governmental consumption of credit and commodities.

In war situations a typical function of the wealthy classes is the floating of government loans and the purchase of government bonds. New York bankers have generally taken an important part in the support of government credit during wars. In the War of 1812 a number of New York bankers subscribed heavily to the Federal Loan of 1813 and 1814. Among these were Henry de Rham, quoted in Beach as worth $100,000 in 1836, Robert Chesebrough, worth $250,000,[31] Benjamin Bailey, Isaac Clason, Lucius Bleecker, and Peter Schenck.

The Civil War, however, was the greatest political and military crisis the Republic had endured, and the typical political activities of the plutocracy during wartime are well illustrated. Because of close association with the cotton states many in the merchant and banking classes in New York City were active southern sympathizers before the final breach. Shortly after the Republican victory of 1860 and the decision of South Carolina to secede, a group of Democratic politicians and business men held a meeting in New York for the purpose of discussing a plan whereby the Southern states might be mollified. They resolved to send a committee to the South to urge the Southern states to remain in the union, until they (the Democrats) could defeat the Republicans in the succeeding election. Prominent in this group were William B. Astor, Royal Phelps, Wilson G. Hunt, James W. Beekman, William H. Aspinwall, Edward Cooper, and J. H. Brown. All of these were wealthy bankers, merchants, and manufacturers. The mission of this group was a dismal failure, since the South viewed them as a minority group, and refused to take them seriously.

The firing on Fort Sumter temporarily stilled these compromise movements. A vast mass meeting was held in New York City for the purpose of supporting the federal government. Some hundred thousand are supposed to have attended the meeting in Union Square, which was presided over by John A. Dix, Secretary of the Treasury in the first Lincoln administration. Eighty-seven vice presidents were "selected from the solid men of the community."[32] Thirty-two of these were listed in Beach's directory of 1855 as owning $100,000 or over.[33] The rest were also wealthy and well-to-do bankers, merchants, manufacturers, and lawyers.

Out of this meeting came the formation of the Union Defense Committee which took the lead in collecting private contributions for the aid of the government and its new army. The committee functioned for a year, until April, 1862, aiding in the raising, equipping, and arming of troops. Many financial contributions were made toward the raising and equipping of the army. Thirteen New York banks contributed nearly $500,000; and a number of wealthy individuals contributed sums of $1,000. A. T. Stewart, Isaac Bell, W. H. Aspinwall, and Cornelius Vanderbilt were among this group.

The organization of the Union Defense Committee was followed by the establishment of the Women's Central Association of Relief, which was influential in the later establishment of the United States Sanitary Commission. The association collected money for medical aid. The women in the committee were from the old and new wealthy families—the Fishes, Aspin-walls, Roosevelts, Astors, Stuarts, Bayards, Stuyvesants, and many others.

In 1863 a number of wealthy citizens formed the Union League Club in New York. The nucleus of this organization was a group of members of the old Union Club who demanded a stronger pro-union policy than that club was prepared to indorse. The Union League Club was supported entirely by wealthy Republicans. They organized a propaganda agency called the Loyal Publication Society which issued 88 pamphlets during this period on subjects connected with the war and with the issues of the 1864 campaign. The club also raised three Negro regiments in New York.

The threat to the Union was responsible for bringing into occasional political activity a fairly large proportion of the wealthy classes. For the great majority this action was short-lived, being limited to attendance at a few meetings, financial contributions, and the like. An outstanding exception was John A. Stewart of the United States Trust Company, who served as Assistant Treasurer to the United States during the progress of the war. On the other hand, the Civil War provided great opportunities for merchants, shipowners, and manufacturers to realize tremendous profits. The demand for arms, munitions, clothing, and food resulted in a great price rise. A congressional investigation in 1862 revealed graft, bribery, and fraud on a tremendous scale. It seems to have been a general practice for the merchants and manufacturers of New York as well as elsewhere to charge the government fantastic prices for goods which in many proven instances were inferior in quality. A few cases may suffice to illustrate: Cornelius Vanderbilt, who had so virtuously contributed $1,000 to the government early in the hostilities, chartered 5 of his ships to the government at rates that gave him the cost of running them four and five times over. The merchant Russell Sturges served as agent in New York to buy ships for the government. Sturges demanded and received a percentage from shipowners before he would buy their ships. He thus charged the government outrageous prices, and split the winnings with the sellers. Marshall O. Roberts was the owner of two vessels which had been pronounced by naval authorities before the Civil War as unfit for service. Nevertheless he sold these ships to the government through corrupt agents for $100,000 each. One of these vessels sank on her first voyage.

But of all the profiteering merchants and manufacturers the young J. P. Morgan, then fresh from his father's banking office, was involved in what seems to have been the worst scandal. The story goes that in 1857 the government arms inspector had recommended the sale of a certain type of carbine because they were of poor make and dangerous. A dealer who loaned money for the transaction from J. P. Morgan bought these arms from the government in New York for $3.50 per rifle, and resold them to General

Fremont in St. Louis for $22.00. The government refused to pay the whole amount, but J. P. Morgan pressed his case before the courts and finally collected the entire profit. Whether or not J. P. Morgan knew of this piece of highway robbery when he loaned the money is uncertain, but the facts had all come out when he insisted on full payment through the courts. He was, thus, clearly one of the most cynical and determined of all the profiteers who plagued the government during the Civil War. Marcellus Hartley, a prominent gun dealer in New York, also was implicated in these profiteering sales. Manufacturers and merchants in the clothing trades reaped tremendous fortunes through government contracts. So widespread and malodorous were these swindles in New York City that the whole group of New York profiteers were snubbed by the older families as "shoddyites," after the inferior cloth furnished by merchants on government contracts.

The bankers during the Civil War crisis made great fortunes through government business. Writes Myers:

> [T]he bankers were allowed to get an annual payment from the government of six percent interest in gold on the government bonds that they bought. They could then deposit those same bonds with the government and issue their own bank notes against ninety percent of the bonds deposited. They drew interest from the government on the deposited bonds, and at the same time charged borrowers an exorbitant rate of interest for the use of the bank notes, which passed as currency.[34]

This was a legal business as was that of floating the government loans. Both were tremendously lucrative, and solidified many a banker's fortune. Among the New York bankers active in the flotation of government loans were Richard Henry Winslow, Moses Taylor, and Henry Clews.

It may be said generally that the wealthier classes performed important organizing and economic functions, but an examination of the facts makes the common evaluation of altruistic patriotism a palpable piece of sycophancy. In the early days of the war there was a considerable amount of fervent patriotism. But the bureaucratization of the war found the merchant, banking, and manufacturing classes seeking profits in many cases through any means that lay at hand. As far as service in the army and government was concerned, there were cases of disinterested patriotic activity. But although the figures are not available it seems likely that the wealthy group as a class less frequently engaged in military service than the other classes. The compulsory draft had a provision permitting individuals to purchase substitutes for $300. This was one of the causes of the destructive draft riots of 1963 in New York. This obvious piece of class legislation was justified by the historian of New York's riots with the following casuistry:

> The objection that a rich man, if drafted, can buy a substitute, while the poor man with a large family depending on him, must go, if of any weight at all, lies

against the whole structure of society, which gives the rich man at every step immunities over the poor man. When pestilence sweeps through a city, the rich man can flee to a healthy locality, while the poor man must stay and die; and when the pestilence of war sweeps the land, must one attempt to reverse all this relation between wealth and poverty? When Society gets in that happy state, that the rich man has no advantages over the poor, there will be no need either of drafting or volunteering. Yet, after all, it is not so unequal as it at first sight appears. War must have money as well as men, and the former the rich have to furnish and if they do this, it is but fair that they should be allowed to furnish with it the men to do their fighting. Besides there must be some rule that would exempt the men that carry on the business of the country.[35]

The necessity for mobilizing the entire economy after the entrance of the United States into the World War resulted in a degree of regulation of economic life never before experienced in America. This development naturally brought into temporary public and semi-public service the leaders of the various industries. The increased number of tasks performed by the government also necessitated large increases in public personnel. In the capacity of "dollar a year" men, many wealthy men from all over the country became temporary public officials. The large number of war charities and philanthropies brought into semi-public service the women of the wealthy classes.

The Advisory Commission of the Council of National Defense, an overall body formed in 1916 to coordinate and mobilize industrial life, had as one of its members Bernard M. Baruch, a New York banker. The Council directed the activities of a number of auxiliary organizations including the Aircraft Production Board, the General Munitions Board, and various other industrial coordinating committees.[36] This body was followed by the later organization of the War Industries Board under the chairmanship of Baruch. An analysis of the occupations of individuals from New York City employed by the War Industries Board shows that a fairly large number of the more influential economic classes in New York City were engaged in this type of public war work. Bernard Baruch, banker and stock broker, served as chairman. Among his assistants were the New Yorkers Clarence Dillon, a member of a banking firm, and Harrison Williams, officer of 11 utility companies. Industrialists, bankers, managers, professional men and technicians were drawn into positions as experts in the War Industries Board.[37]

Ultimately the powers of the War Industries Board rested upon the powers of the president in wartime. The exercise of its powers in determining what was to be produced, according to what standards, and at what wholesale prices sales were to be made to the government was never legally challenged. A study of the operation of the board indicates that it was a case of self-regulation of industry in an emergency situation. It was not a case of an unfriendly government regulating economic enterprise. It was generally understood that Baruch was an agent for the more prominent finance capitalists. The operation of the Industries Board assured a high profit to producers generally. The War Industries Board type of regulation of industry was a case of self-regulation of industry at a high and assured rate of profit. The same may be said of the War Trade Board and the War Shipping Board. Between these agencies there was a high degree of interlocking control.[38] Government control over economic life in the World War amounted to little more than self-control in which economic policy was shaped mainly by the more powerful bankers and industrialists.

Lower Class Unrest

Of the three types of crisis affecting plutocratic political activity that of depression and unemployment results in the greatest and most immediate danger to the powers and privileges of the wealthier classes. The study of the relationship between the economic and political process is of the utmost importance for an understanding of political movements and changes. It may be said that depressions affecting the whole economic structure, resulting in widespread unemployment and distress, generally precipitate lower class unrest and organization. In an ideological environment which has increasingly discarded older religious and supernatural forms of coping with economic and political crises, lower class protest in times of crisis has come to assume increasingly political forms. Each widespread crisis has the effect of developing within the lower classes movements aimed at the seizure of political power, movements designed to interfere with and regulate the economy. Historically in America organized protest among the lower classes has been checked and diverted by the open frontier and by the periods of prosperity succeeding periods of depression. Hence until modern times this type of danger to the upper classes has been spasmodic and was relatively easily met by ordinary political means—by the shifting and concentration of the support of the wealthy classes to the party defending property rights, by dividing the opposition, and by increased propaganda. The passing of the frontier and the stabilization of the economy presents a situation of more or less constant danger to the wealthier classes. What protective policy will be followed by the plutocracy in this situation is difficult to foretell. It may follow a policy of submitting to gradual governmentalization of the economy, or, if the attack upon the plutocracy is of a rapid frontal character, it may have the consequence of precipitating a violent defense of the established order.

Generally speaking, the wealthy support the party most consistently favoring property rights. In the period before the Civil War the great majority of the wealthy in New York City supported the Whigs. But even though Tammany in its origin was an anti-aristocratic organization, the controlling influences for considerable periods of time were conservative merchants and bankers in alliance with professional politicians.

Tammany controlled the votes of the lower classes of the population. Third party democratic movements robbed Tammany and not the Whigs of votes. Hence Tammany was forced to espouse the programs of protest movements to avoid defeat. In the absence of active protest movements such as the Workingman's Party of 1829 and the Equal Rights Party of the 1830s, the Tammany professional politicians worked hand in glove with the conservative classes. The Tammany merchants and bankers voted for and supported Tammany as long as its program did not affect their interests. When the Equal Rights Party in 1835 gained enough votes to divide the normal Tammany votes and gave the victory to the Whigs in the city elections, Tammany was forced to join hands with the Equal Rights men or "Loco Focos," as they were called. The response of the Tammany conservatives in this situation was to give their support to the Whigs, and hence to defeat what was called "purified Tammany."

The success of Tammany in winning elections brought these merchants and bankers desirous of franchises and other favors into the Tammany organization. This working relationship between merchants and bankers and the professional Tammany politicians was workable only as long as Tammany remained in control of the corrupt and conservative political leadership. When lower class movements forced Tammany to the left, the Tammany conservatives deserted to the Whigs, a desertion which was ordinarily capable of defeating it. An outstanding illustration of this kind of desertion was the implication of renegade conservative Tammanyites in the Whig election scandal of 1838.

In the municipal sphere there were but few strong political efforts on the part of labor organizations and groups to gain control of the municipal government. This was due largely to the fact that the city government did not enjoy the powers necessary to advance the lot of workingmen. The efforts of the growing labor movement were directed toward influencing the state and federal governments in the interests of social and labor legislation. In the latter part of the nineteenth and in the twentieth century progressive and socialist parties participated in municipal campaigns with little prospect of victory. The outstanding exceptions were the two Henry George campaigns, the first in 1886 and the second in 1897. The aim of the Henry George group in their municipal campaign was not to gain control of the municipal administration for its own sake. George and his followers were naturally aware of the fact that it was not within the sphere of municipal power to carry through the reforms the single tax movement contemplated. It was rather their intention to build a stable national party by achieving political success in the municipal sphere.

The George campaign in 1886, coming during the depression of 1885–1886[39] achieved proportions which frightened both the Republican Party and the conservative Democratic factions. The dominant Democratic factions nominated Abram Hewitt, a wealthy iron manufacturer with a record for philanthropy and political reform. The Republicans nominated the young Theodore Roosevelt. Hewitt based his campaign on his reform record, on his progressive labor policy in his own factories, and on the danger of introducing the class issue into politics. W. Bourke Cochran, a Tammany Sachem, in placing Hewitt as a candidate before Tammany, emphasized his activity in political reform and his own progressive labor policy.[40]

Hewitt defined the campaign issue as a struggle between the proponents of good government, represented by himself, and the followers of the doctrines of the Paris Commune of 1870. He foresaw violence and bloodshed in the doctrines of Henry George:

> A new issue, however, has been suddenly sprung upon the community. An attempt is being made to organize one class of our citizens against all other classes, and to place the government of the city in the hands of men willing to represent the special interest of this class to the exclusion of the just rights of the other classes. . . . The ideas they propound are not new. They have even been reduced to practice for a short time at long intervals in the history of the world. The horrors of the French revolution and the atrocities of the Commune offer conclusive proof of the dreadful consequences of doctrines which can only be enforced by revolution and bloodshed, even when reduced to practice by men of good intentions and blameless private life. . . . Between capital and labor there never is and never can be any antagonism. They are natural and inseparable allies. . . . The other side proposes a radical departure from the existing methods of free government by political parties composed of citizens in every walk of life, and ask us to substitute not merely new ideas as to the nature of property, but new modes of government through the organization of social classes of the community. The issue is thus between the democratic idea of the founders of the Republic and the socialistic views of mere theorists who have never had any experience in the practical business of life, generated in an atmosphere foreign to our habits and modes of thoughts, and based largely upon grievances which have no existence under our form of government. . . . If I have not exaggerated the situation, it behooves the people of this city to pass sentence of condemnation in no uncertain tones upon the effort to array class against class and to unsettle the foundations upon which its business and security rest.[41]

George in response to these remarks wrote an open letter to Hewitt pointing to the fact that Hewitt was supported by the corrupt elements of New York City politics and that his concept of class was incorrect, that actually the laboring classes constituted the overwhelming majority of the population.[42]

Carl Schurz attempted to arouse the German business community against the dangers of a George success. At one meeting he was quoted as saying,

> As Mayor, he [George] says that he would not expect to cure any of these evils. In that he is wise, for he could not do it. But he does expect to inaugurate a

movement that shall give power to one class in this community. Men of business, what will be the effect of such a revolution? Will it not undermine the foundations of confidence and put you back into the business slough from which you have recently escaped?[43]

And in the same meeting Frederick R. Coudert cried, "Those who want democratic prosperity and freedom must bury in their birthplace the hell-born doctrines of the anarchist, and I would that in trumpet tones I might warn the voters in every street in this city—don't unchain the tiger!"[44]

The strategy of the wealthy classes and the Tammany and democratic leadership in the George campaign was temporarily to unify the main camps of the Democratic Party—Tammany and the opposition reform group, the County Democracy—and to raise the fears of bloodshed and violence by reference to the Paris Commune, and to stress the danger to business and prosperity in the radical Henry George program. The corrupt Tammany group nominated a man known for his reformist attitude and his liberal philanthropies, thereby to draw general conservative, middle class, and workman support. Their strategy was successful despite the large vote polled by Henry George.

Again in 1897, during the 1894–1898 depression,[45] Henry George took up the fight for the mayoralty, this time supported by a party called the Jeffersonian Democrats. Opposed to him was the Croker supported Van Wyck and the Citizen's Union Reform candidate Seth Low. George died during the campaign. His son Henry George, Jr. took over the campaign, but the death of the elder George robbed this progressive group of its leadership and morale. Van Wyck was elected.

No left municipal movement after the 1897 campaign arose in New York City until the candidacy of La Guardia in 1933. Nominated and elected by the Republicans and the Fusion Reform groups, La Guardia made so excellent a record in municipal administration that despite his identification with the New Deal Democrats and with progressive aspirations his Republican supporters were at a loss as to what program to follow in the 1936 election campaign. La Guardia's progressivism in his first term had won him the support of the smaller income class majority. His record bound him to the Roosevelt group in Washington. His identification with progressivism tended to alienate him from conservative Republican support. Kenneth Simpson, Republican County Chairman, described the quandary of the Republican voters in the second La Guardia campaign in a letter to the Fifteenth District Republican Club. He referred on the one hand to the avowed radicalism of La Guardia and on the other hand to his excellent record as mayor and administrator:

> Mayor La Guardia, both in public utterance and in private conversations, had made it clear that he is an avowed radical. He has let it be known that in his opinion the national election in 1940 will witness a new political alignment. On

one hand, in his opinion, there will be a constitutional party, representing a union of Republicans and Democrats; on the other side will be a party dedicated to the ideal of a collectivist state, a party of Lewis, Dubinsky, the New Deal wing of the Democratic Party, La Follette and himself. He has made it clear that his allegiance will be to this group and its collectivist purposes. If and when that alignment takes place there will be no question that the Republican voters of the country will be on the side of the Constitution, and against collectivism. They will have to be against Mayor La Guardia. It is a serious question whether the Republican voters of New York City have a right, by reelecting him to the mayoralty, to put him in a position of power from which he can more efficiently work in 1940 for the defeat of the principles which they hold to be fundamental.[46]

The strategy of the conservative Democrats in the primary campaign—Alfred E. Smith and the Tammany group—was to run Royal S. Copeland for the Democratic nomination. The strategy of the less conservative New Deal Democrats placed Jeremiah T. Mahoney, a reform Tammany leader, in nomination. The conservative Democrats, in collaboration with the Republican leadership of Charles Hilles and Ogden Mills, also entered Copeland in the Republican primary. This illustrates the tendency for the conservative elements of both parties frankly to set aside party loyalty and principles in a situation of threat. Their strategy failed because of the general liberal and progressive attitude of the New York population, La Guardia winning the Republican nomination and Mahoney the Democratic. The popularity of La Guardia was remarkably attested to by the fact that 55,000 registered Democrats wrote in La Guardia's name in the Democratic primary. The strategy of the conservative party bosses failed, and the popularity of La Guardia and his progressive program proved sufficient to defeat the Democratic New Deal candidate.

In the sphere of municipal politics the struggle between economic and social classes is not so clearly defined as in the sphere of national and state politics. The scope of municipal power does not include the making of policy affecting the power of the various classes of the population, with the exception of the use of judicial and police power in industrial conflicts. The effort to control the city and its patronage has an important indirect bearing upon the class conflict, a bearing abundantly appreciated by political strategists. Henry George frankly described his effort to control New York City as intended to supply a basis for the formation of a national party. Hilles, Mills, and Simpson were equally aware of the dangers of La Guardia's continued incumbency in the mayoralty from the same point of view.

The influence of lower class unrest upon plutocratic political participation is more clearly revealed in the sphere of state and national government. It is before these bodies that the pressure agencies of the various economic interest groups are most active to urge or obstruct legislation affecting their interests. It is upon the members of state and national legislative bodies that the pressure groups of the wealthier classes bring the might of their money and propaganda power to bear. And a constant struggle is going on, with the weight of success until the present almost consistently on the side of the upper economic groups, for the domination of the higher state courts and the federal judiciary and the policy-making levels of the executive services.

Organized political movements on the part of labor and agrarian groups aiming to control or share in the control of the policy-making agencies ordinarily receive a great impetus in situations of economic crisis. It is difficult to arouse a movement of protest in a normal economic situation. Economic crises have become more severe since the closing of the frontier, increasing industrialization and urban concentration, and the rise of what seems to be a large permanently unemployed group due to technological developments. The great decrease in the rate of economic expansion due to the fact that economic opportunity has declined since the closing of the frontier and to the partial loss of the foreign market, has resulted in a greatly decreased rate of vertical social mobility in America. The consequence of this development is the increasingly fixed character of economic and social classes. The political consequence of these economic developments has been the development, particularly since the crisis of 1929, of increased class struggle politics. The social psychological influences operative here are the growth of a sense of common political destiny among classes of the population, a growing political class consciousness, illustrated by the development of state labor parties, and movements directed toward the reconstruction of the two party system dominated mainly by motives of seizing and holding offices and their perquisites into left and right combinations.

This situation of increased pressure from the left upon the wealthier classes has resulted in countermovements led by permanent and vigilantistic conservative pressure groups and by the plutocratically owned newspapers. These countermovements have arisen especially in the Post-War Era during World War I and the Bolshevik scare and since the depression of 1929. Among the vigilantistic pressure groups were the American Defense Society and the National Security League. Both of these had functioned as patriotic societies during the World War and continued to operate during the twenties as defenders of America against alien radicals, pacifists, and other "dangerous" elements. These vigilantistic pressure groups commonly receive their financial support from the plutocracy which naturally feels itself more threatened in these crises, and hence tends to be specially susceptible to this type of hysteria.

In 1919 the National Security League numbered among its officers the statesman and corporation lawyer Elihu Root, the former Democratic presidential candidate Alton B. Parker, and the corporation lawyer and Social Registerite James W. Gerard—all New Yorkers.

In 1926 the Security League numbered 20 New Yorkers as officers and directors. Ten of these were listed in *Poor's Register of Directors* for 1928;[47] 12 were included in the New York Social Register. Table 12.1 lists

TABLE 12.1 Corporate Offices and Social Status of Officers and Directors of the National Security League from New York City in 1926*

Names of Officers	Corporate Offices	Social Status and Principal Club Memberships
Franklin Q. Brown	Vice President, Chairman of Board of American Beet Sugar Company; Director American Light and Traction Company; and director and officer of 15 other corporations	Social Register; Union, New York Yacht, Racquet, and 11 other clubs and societies
Theodore Roosevelt	—	Social Register; Brook Club
George H. Putnam	President and Director G. H. Putnam's Sons; and 4 other corporations	Social Register; Century and Authors clubs
James M. Beck	—	Social Register; Metropolitan; Sons of the American Revolution; and 2 other clubs
Lewis S. Clarke	Chairman Board American Exchange Securities Corp.; Director American Locomotive Co.; Director American Smelting and Refining Co.; officer of 31 other manufacturing, insurance, and banking companies	Social Register; Automobile Club; Lotos, Metropolitan, National Arts clubs; Union League; and others
R. E. Condon	—	—
Frederic R. Coudert	—	Social Register; University, New York Yacht, Century, and 7 other clubs and societies
Joseph P. Day	Officer and director of 17 real estate, building, banking and insurance corporations	—
Thomas C. Desmond	Director and officer of 6 real estate and housing corporations	—
T. Coleman Du Pont	—	Social Register
Lindley M. Garrison	—	—

(continues)

TABLE 12.1 *(continued)*

Names of Officers	Corporate Offices	Social Status and Principal Club Memberships
Samuel T. Hubbard	—	Social Register; New York Yacht, Downtown, Republican clubs; St. Nicholas Society
De Lancey Kountze	Treasurer and Director Devoe and Reynolds Company	Social Register; Knickerbocker, Metropolitan, Brook, and other clubs
Lewis W. Stotesbury	Director Schenectady Airport and 5 manufacturing, real estate, and other corporations	—
Charles Strauss	Director Underwood Typewriter Company and 4 other banking and manufacturing companies	—
Russell R. Whitman	—	—
Benjamin L. Winchell	Chairman Board of Remington Rand, member Advisory Committee Chase National Bank, and officer of 6 other corporations	—
Louis M. Josephthal	—	—
Henry W. Marsh	—	Social Register; Union League; University and Downtown clubs
Newbold Morris	Director of 4 charitable and educational institutions	Social Register; Metropolitan, Fencers, Riding, Turf and Field, Republican clubs; Sons of Revolution; and other clubs

*Names of officers from New York City were taken from pamphlets of the National Security League for March and May, 1926; data on directorships were taken from *Directory of Directors in the City of New York* (New York: The Audit Company of New York, 1927); data on social status from *Social Register New York* (New York: The Social Register Association, 1926).

the corporate connections, Social Register inclusion, and club memberships of the New Yorkers holding office in the Security League.

The Liberty League, formed in the first Roosevelt administration to fight its liberal tendencies, had a large number of wealthy New Yorkers on its advisory council and among its principal financial supporters. Table 12.2 shows the economic and social affiliations of those New Yorkers who served in the National Advisory Council of the American Liberty League. Of the 26 officers and members of the Advisory Council 19 were listed in *Poor's Register of Directors* in the United States and the *Directory of Directors of New York City,* and 17 were listed in the Social Register. The balance, it may be assumed, also were in the upper income classes.

The analysis of the Senate Lobby Committee, listing the contributors and contributions during 1935–1936 to a number of anti–New Deal and anti-radical organizations, shows 90 percent to have been contributed by a few central groups of large finance capitalists. The Du Pont family, and associates who have New York representatives, contributed some $350,000 to a total of a little over a million. The Pitcairn family, although primarily of Philadelphia in locality, but having New York representatives, contributed approximately $100,000. The J. P. Morgan and Rockefeller groups contributed another $100,000 between them; and the Hutton group of New York contributed over $40,000.

A detailed analysis of the contributors to these pressure organizations brings out a number of interesting points: the National Economy League had 119 New York contributors, of whom 100, or 92 percent, were Social Registerites. The American Liberty League had 118 New York contributors, 55, or 48 percent, of whom were Social Registerites. The Crusaders had a 56 percent Social Registerite group of New York contributors. With minor variations the tabulation shows each of these pressure groups to have received financial support mainly from the esteemed wealthy circles (cf. Table 12.3).

The data on the New Deal Era are of special interest, since they reveal the volume of this type of indirect propagandistic pressure in a period during which reformist, but certainly not revolutionary, elements control the federal government. If we were to project this line of increasing attempts on the part of liberal and progressive elements to control the economic order, it is entirely fair to assume that the volume of this indirect political activity on the part of the wealthy classes will increase.

In general conclusion to this necessarily brief discussion of plutocratic political activity in crisis situations, it may be said that crisis tends to increase the political activities of the plutocracy. The crisis of political corruption threatens the plutocracy materially in their tax costs and in the safety of their investments in public bonds, as well as in their sense of moral decency, and results in organized efforts on the part of the plutocracy to introduce reform

TABLE 12.2 Economic and Social Status of Members of the National Advisory
Council of the Liberty League from New York City in 1936*

Names of Members	Principal Corporate Offices	Social Status and Principal Club Memberships
John W. Davis	Trustee Mutual Life Insurance Co.; Director National Bank of Commerce, U.S. Rubber Co.	Social Register; University, Century, Piping Rock, Creek, The Pilgrims, Metropolitan, and Chevy Chase of Washington, Colony
Grayson M. P. Murphy	Director American Ice Co., Bethlehem Steel Co., Cuba Cane Sugar Co., Goodyear Tire and Rubber Co., Guaranty Safe Deposit Co., and 16 others	Social Register; Union, Racquet, Brook, Army and Navy, Rockaway, Hunting, Turf and Field, Downtown, and 8 others
Joseph M. Proskauer	Jonas and Naumburg Corporation	Not in Social Register
Alfred E. Smith	President and Director Empire State Inc., Chairman Board Lawyers Trust Co., Director New York Life Insurance Co., and 5 other corporations	—
Edwin M. Allen	Executive Vice President and Director, National Surety Corporation	Not in Social Register
Mrs. Cornelius Newton Bliss	(Data on Mr. Bliss) Director Bankers Trust Co., Associated Dry Goods Corp., New York Life Insurance Co., Otis Co., United States Trust Co., and 5 others	Social Register; University, National Golf Links, India House, Union League, Racquet, Turf and Field, Colonial Dames of America
William C. Breed	Director Ansco Photo Products, Inc., Castra, Inc., Dictaphone Corporation	Social Register; Sons of the American Revolution, Union League, University, Metropolitan, Racquet, Downtown, 7 others
R. E. Desvernine	President and Director International Marble Co., and 2 other corporations	Social Register; Riding; Metropolitan
Mrs. Wm. Emmet (Cornelia B. Zabriskie)	—	Social Register; Colony

(continues)

TABLE 12.2 (*continued*)

Names of Members	Principal Corporate Offices	Social Status and Principal Club Memberships
Mrs. Arthur Fowler	(Data on Mr. Fowler) President and Director of Rogers, Brown and Crocker Bros., Director Corn Exchange Bank, Equitable Life Assurance Society, New York Fidelity-Phoenix Fire Insurance Co., Northern Insurance Co., and others	Social Register; Knickerbocker, University, Downtown, India House, Turf and Field, Metropolitan of Washington, and 2 others
Mrs. Christian R. Holmes	—	Social Register
Edward F. Hutton	E. F. Hutton Co., Director Chatham, Phoenix, National Bank and Trust Co., Coca Cola Co., Chairman Board Postum Co., and others	Social Register; Union League, Turf and Field, India House, Links, Creek, and 7 others
Arthur Curtiss James	Director Chicago, Burlington and Quincy R.R., President and Director Curtiss Southwestern Co., Phelps Dodge Corp., and many others	Social Register; Metropolitan, Century, Downtown, Colony, Colonial Dames of America, and others
Cornelius F. Kelley	Director American Brass Co., President and Director group of Anaconda companies, director and officer in some 30 mining, banking, railway and manufacturing companies	Social Register; Metropolitan, Links, Riding, Creek, India House
George M. Moffett	Vice President and Director Corn Products Refining Co., Director Commercial Solvents Co., Allis Chalmers Mfg. Co., and others	Social Register; Metropolitan, Turf and Field, Racquet, Riding, Creek, and others
Mrs. McGinley Moore	—	Not in Social Register
Mrs. William C. Potter	President and Director of Guarantee Trust Co., Director Agricultural Products Corp., American Congo Co., Atchison Topeka and Santa Fe R.R. Co., Electric Bond and Share Co., and 21 other banking, railroad, manufacturing, utilities, and securities corporations	Social Register; Racquet, National Golf Links, Links and Piping Rock

(*continues*)

228

TABLE 12.2 (*continued*)

Names of Members	Principal Corporate Offices	Social Status and Principal Club Memberships
Herbert S. Pratt	Director Bankers Trust Co., President and Director Standard Oil Co. of New York, and others	Social Register; National Golf Links, Downtown, Sons of the Revolution, Links, Turf and Field, Creek, many others
Dr. Alexander Hamilton Rice	—	Social Register; New York Yacht, Turf and Field, Racquet, May-flower Descendants, and many others
George Emlen Roosevelt	Roosevelt and Son, Director Atlas Assurance Co., National Bank of Commerce, Bank of Savings in the City of New York, Buffalo, Rochester, and Pittsburgh, Ry., and others	Social Register; New York Yacht, Piping Rock, Metropolitan, Links, Downtown, Turf and Field, and others
Elihu Root	Director American Smelting and Refining Co., Investment Managers Co.	Social Register; Union League, Knickerbocker, Century, University, and others
Alfred P. Sloan, Jr.	President and Director of General Motors, Director Chase National Bank, various Chevrolet companies, E. I. Du Pont de Nemours Co., and director in 26 corporations	Not in Social Register
Dr. Walter E. Spahr	—	—
Mrs. Edmund Stout	—	—
Mrs. Coffin Van Rensselaer	—	—
William J. Walter	Director Lawyers Mortgage Co.	—

*Members of the Executive Committee from New York City. Adapted from the *Report of the Senate Lobby Committee, List of Contributions,* Part I (Washington: Government Printing Office, 1936). For data on directorships and social status, *Directory of Directors in the City of New York* (New York: The Audit Company of New York, 1927); *Social Register New York* (New York: The Social Register Association, 1926); and *Poor's Register of Directors in the United States* (Babson Park, Mass.: Poor's Printing Co., 1937).

TABLE 12.3   New York Contributors to Anti–New Deal, Anti–Radical Pressure
Groups During 1935–1936[a]

Pressure Group	Number of New York Contributors	Social Registerites Among Contributors Number	Percent[b]
National Economy League	119	100	92
American Liberty League	118	55	48
Crusaders	50	27	56
Farmers Independence Council	14	11	79
American Taxpayers League	13	7	54
Southern Committee to Uphold the Constitution	9	5	55
New York State Economic Council	9	5	55
Sentinels of the Republic	8	3	37
American Federation of Utility Investors	6	—	—

[a]Adapted from *Report of the Senate Lobby Committee. List of Contributions,*
Part I (Washington: Government Printing Office, 1936); and *Social Register New
York* (New York: Social Register Association, 1936).

[b]In computing percentages of Social Registerites the corporate contributors have
been excluded.

and efficiency in governmental activity. The crisis of war places great pressures upon the entire social economy demanding a centralization and governmentalization of control. In this type of crisis the policy-making levels of economic life assume for the duration of the crisis a more formally political character. The crisis of depression and lower class unrest tends to evoke defensive activities on the part of the plutocracy, well illustrated in the recent formation of the Liberty League, and the League to Uphold Constitutional Government, designed to re-establish a safe political situation.

Of crisis generally it may be said that in the measure that it threatens the general powers of the plutocracy, it initiates countermovements intended to defend their share of social power. These countermovements are efforts at safeguarding the powers and prerogatives of the plutocracy through influencing or altering the existing governmental personnel, and through shaping public opinion.

Notes

1. Gustavus Myers, *Great American Fortunes* (Chicago: Charles H. Kerr Co.,
1903), I, 148.

2. Myers, *History of Tammany Hall* (New York: privately published, 1901), p. 91.

230   *Political Reactions to Crises*

3. Moses Yale Beach, *The Wealth and Biography of the Wealthy Citizens of New York* (New York: the Sun Press, 1846).

4. Myers, *Great American Fortunes,* pp. 198–99.

5. James B. Glentworth, *A Statement of the Frauds in the Election in the City of New York, 1838 and 1839* (New York, 1839).

6. Beach, op. cit.

7. Myers, *Great American Fortunes,* I, 185.

8. *New York Tribune,* January 3, 1853.

9. *New York Tribune,* March 5, 1853.

10. Beach, *op. cit.*

11. See *Trow's New York City Directory* (New York: J. F. Trow, 1853).

12. See Beach, *op. cit.*

13. *New York Tribune,* November 2, 1853.

14. *Ibid.*

15. *Trow's New York City Directory.*

16. Myers, *Tammany,* p. 207. For general historical data on Tammany see also M. R. Werner, *Tammany Hall* (New York: Doubleday Doran and Co., 1928).

17. *New York Tribune,* March 3, 1854.

18. Charles Francis Adams, "Chapter of Erie," from *High Finance in the Sixties,* edited by Frederick C. Hicks (New Haven: Yale University Press, 1929), p. 116.

19. *Ibid.,* p. 3.

20. *Ibid.,* pp. 116–17.

21. *Ibid.,* p. 156.

22. See Dennis Tilden Lynch, *Boss Tweed: The Story of a Grim Generation* (New York: Boni and Liveright, 1927); Samuel J. Tilden, *The New York City King* (New York, 1873) for further details.

23. John Foora, *The Life and Public Services of Andrew Haswell Green* (New York: Doubleday Page and Co., 1913), p. 115.

24. *Ibid.,* p. 95.

25. *New York Tribune,* September 5, 1871.

26. *Ibid.*

27. *Trow's New York City Directory* (New York: J. F. Trow, 1870).

28. Foord, *op. cit.,* pp. 143–44.

29. Myers, *Tammany,* p. 316.

30. *Ibid.*

31. Beach, *op. cit.*

32. James Grant Wilson, *Memorial History of the City of New York* (New York: New York History Co., 1893), III, 487. For a comprehensive survey of the activities of citizens of New York State during the Civil War see *New York in the War of the Rebellion,* compiled by Frederick Phisterer (5 vols.; Albany: J. B. Lyon, 1912).

33. Beach, *op. cit.*

34. Myers, *Great American Fortunes,* II, 300.

35. H. J. T. Headley, *The Great Riots of New York City* (New York: E. B. Treat, 1873), pp. 139 ff.

36. James M. Jensen, "New War Time Administrative Agencies" (Unpublished Master's thesis, Department of History, University of Chicago, 1919).

37. See Bernard M. Baruch, *American Industry in the War,* A Report of the War Industries board (Washington: Government Printing Office, 1921), pp. 298–316.

38. These conclusions are based upon an article in a manuscript on "War Planning" by Clifford Hynning.

39. Robert R. Doane, *The Measurement of American Wealth* (New York: Harper Bros., 1933), chart 1, frontispiece.

40. *New York Tribune,* October 12, 1886, p. 5, col. 2.

41. *New York Daily Tribune,* October 17, 1886, p. 2, col. 1.

42. Letter to Hewitt in the *New York Herald,* October 19, 1886.

43. *New York Herald,* October 30, 1886.

44. *Ibid.*

45. Doane, *op. cit.*

46. Jay Franklin, *La Guardia* (New York: Modern Age Books, 1937), pp. 151–152.

47. *Poor's Register of Directors of the United States* (Babson Park, Mass.: Poor's Printing Co., 1937).

13

General Perspectives

THE POLITICAL ORDER of the American colonies and states roughly until the early decades of the nineteenth century was of an open plutocratic type. That is, the franchise was accorded automatically in most cases to all those reaching a set minimum wealth level. Less than half of the population of New York State, for example, enjoyed political rights during the late eighteenth and early nineteenth centuries. And of these only a minority were genuinely politically active. This minority was made up of the larger landholders, the wealthier merchants, and the lawyers. The wealthier landholders and merchants could actively engage in politics because they—especially the landholders—were free to leave their occupations. The large landholder was only occupied seasonally, and even in the active season could leave his property to an overseer. The wealthy merchant had his apprentices to whom he could leave his business temporarily. The lawyer was a special case. His training and work fitted him specially for politics. He was accustomed to speak, and was familiar with law and public agencies. As an entrepreneur he could leave his regular occupation and return to it. Indeed, achieving a position of public prominence, enhanced the lawyer's future earning power, making him a public figure with a reputation for knowledge of the ins and outs of law and government. Although in the colonial era and in the early decades of independence the landholder and the merchant played an important role in politics, the future of politics was to the lawyer.

Thus government in New York in the early days before the democratization of the franchise was in the hands of the notables—individuals of wealth and social honor—capable of serving without pay or with small pay, and economically independent enough to leave their work. With government in the hands of a limited group, similar in background and social position, and in many cases personally known to one another, politics was an informal, gentlemanly occupation. Instead of a regular party headquarters and permanent staff, parties met at private houses or in a "gentleman's tav-

232

ern." There were no permanent party officials and workers. Patronage was small, and the class eligible for patronage was limited. Corruption, in the strict sense of that term, was not possible since the class capable of buying advantages was the class enjoying direct political control.

Their relatively secure control over politics tended to shape a balanced existence for the wealthy class. Aside from the general adherence to religious norms characteristic of that era which tended to restrict and channelize consumption, and aside from the fact that wealth was not so easily acquired nor so great as that of the later era, the political responsibilities and functions of the wealthier classes tended to encourage balance, sobriety, and culture in the plutocracy. Since politics was the exclusive function of the wealthy notables, it served as the main channel through which prestige and social distinction were to be won. The "Society" of the era of plutocratic political control was preeminently political society for which social life assumed the proportions of recreation and culturally oriented association.

The breakdown of the exclusive political controls of the plutocracy resulted from the interplay of a number of factors. The Revolutionary War and the post-Revolutionary expropriations had seriously diminished the numbers of the wealthy class. And those lost through exile and expropriation were naturally the most conservative of the defenders of the obtaining political order. At the same time the Revolution was fought in the name of the democratic ideals of the eighteenth century which posited the political equality of mankind. However seriously this doctrine was intended by the dominant classes, it morally weakened the defense when the lower classes presented their reckoning a decade or so later. At the same time the unfranchised of the cities and the countryside had been given a slogan and a sense of moral strength which came from having fought for values which were now being withheld from them by the very leaders who had preached them with such enthusiasm at an earlier time. But more important than the diminution in the numbers of the plutocracy and these ideological and moral factors was the settlement of the frontier by a small independent farmer class, eligible for the franchise, and by social origin and position sympathetic with the demands of the unfranchised smaller landholders and renters and city dwellers. It was upon these independent agrarian elements and the less numerous mechanics in the cities that the national and local leaderships of Democratic-Republican party relied for support, and whose strength finally defeated the Federalists.

In New York State the year 1821 may be set as the date of the final thoroughgoing defeat of the Federalists, and what is more of their policy of a "democracy" limited to property holders in which political initiative and control rested with the more powerful and esteemed of these. From then on the wealthier classes tended to adapt themselves to a democratic situation, directing their efforts politically toward maneuvering within the new party organizations for control.

It may well be asked how it came about that so thorough and rapid a political transformation was accomplished with so little violence and so ineffective a resistance. The answer to this is to be found not only in the changed economic structure and ideological atmosphere of New York and other American states but in the changing social composition and attitudes of the plutocracy itself. The loss of the pro-English party represented a serious diminution in the numbers and strength of the conservative party. The early decades of the nineteenth century were marked by a great development of the commercial activity and wealth of the eastern seaboard. This increased commercial activity brought to New York City a large class of *parvenus* from the lower classes of England, Scotland, and Germany, and from the lower classes of the New England states. They arrived in an era when the control of wealth over politics was already being seriously challenged, so that it was impossible for them to be gradually assimilated to a securely powerful oligarchy. On the contrary they were so numerous that it was their pattern rather than that of the older wealthy elements which tended to become dominant. Coming generally from the lower farming and trading classes of the New England states and abroad, the new elements of the plutocracy were the bearers of a religious-commercial tradition, a tradition which did not generally view political activity as a privilege of wealth.

The influx of a great number of *parvenus* in the early nineteenth century resulted in a stratification of the wealthy class into the older families on the one hand, and the *nouveaux riche* on the other. The older strata maintained a social and cultural life to which the *parvenus* were not generally admitted. It was in this class of descendants of the old notables—primarily Dutch and English in nationality origin—that there developed an attitude of contempt for American institutions and a slavish admiration for the aristocracies of England and the continent. As Tocqueville pointed out, "it is easy to perceive that the wealthy members of the community entertain a hearty distaste for the democratic institutions of the country."[1]

The newer wealthy accommodated themselves more readily to democratic institutions. It was from this *parvenu* group particularly that from generation to generation the great corrupters of the democratic process in America were recruited. Elements in the newer plutocracy saw clearly the wealth and privileges which were to be gained by connections with the politicians and the political parties. Pursuing on the whole narrowly commercial goals, any means calculated to achieve the ends of gain were admissible. Primarily Protestant in religious composition, and in great part recruited from the more narrow sects, the first generation was incapable of developing a worldly social and cultural tradition. Rather they developed on an impressive scale a large number of religiously oriented philanthropies, hospitals, orphan asylums, homes for various categories of dependents, missions, and the like. In considerable measure the social life of the newer plutocracy of the Pre–Civil War Era was also religiously oriented.

For the New York plutocracy the first half of the nineteenth century was an era of transition and latency. Its old world had been crushed, and its new world was to be born. The old world of a politically dominant plutocracy had given way to a new one in which the political function of the plutocracy took the form of maintaining an indirect control over politics by maneuvering within the parties, by control over politicians, and over public opinion. The elaboration of social life which was to serve as the central prestige-gaining value of the plutocracy of the later nineteenth century was restrained by religious and economic norms.

The Civil War and the great industrial development in America following it resulted in a great influx of wealthy *parvenus*. The economic character of the wealthy classes underwent important transformations. From having been a primarily merchant and smaller industrial wealthy class the era of industrial and financial giants was beginning. Of especial importance for the shaping of the attitudes and activities of the New York plutocracy was the development of a class of *rentiers,* who lived off the income from inheritances, or the profits of securities transactions, in other words a class of the population not bound to daily work for their incomes. It was this class of *rentiers* in alliance with admissible *parvenu* elements which set the pace for the "Gilded Age" and which influenced the ideals and standards of the entire wealthy class. This group came to be known as "society." The attention of the wealthy classes all over the United States was directed toward this New York–Newport set. Its standards influenced plutocratic social life throughout the United States. Dissociated from active economic life and unwilling to share in political life on a formally equal basis, this dominant element of the wealthy classes sought to objectify its superior position by a great elaboration of recreational activity. Prestige in the wealthy class was won by engaging in social competition, by great expenditures for spectacular purposes, by inventiveness in entertainment, clothing, and housing styles. Having no formal and acquiesced in special status in American society it differentiated itself from the rest of the population by its social activities, by cultural patronage, and by intermarriage with and engaging in the social life of the European aristocracies. With noteworthy exceptions the cultural activities of the "golden caste of Vere de Vere" arose not out of a genuine feeling for beauty and knowledge, but as an expression of social and economic power, and out of a desire to imitate the patterns of the more secure older aristocracies.

Within the wealthy class the special bearers of the "gaudy tradition" achieved the greatest social prominence. During the latter half of the nineteenth century in New York, Mrs. William Astor was the leader of this ultra-fashionable set. The older Knickerbockers occupied a distinctly secondary position. They were marked by a greater sobriety, were more tradition-bound, and tended to be more frequently identified with cultural and philanthropic activity. The newer elements of the wealthy classes in part imitated the patterns of the "gilded set," in part were narrowly commercial in their aspirations, and in part were active in the rapidly developing cultural life of New York City. But the fashionable group around Mrs. Astor placed its mark upon the whole age. Unanchored politically and economically, dissociated from the currents and aspirations of American life, drawing extravagantly from resources which they assumed to be limitless, careless and unaware of those whom they exploited and of posterity, they lived in a child's world of continual self-indulgence.

The failure of the wealthy classes to strive for a more personal control in politics in this and later eras may be understood in terms of the objective conditions of political competition and industrial activity and the subjective incentives for political activity. On the one hand under democracy politics became a practically full-time occupation. On the other hand economic activity became much more time and energy absorbing than it had been in the earlier era. This would apply of course only to those actively engaged in business. The failure of the *rentiers,* or the semi-employed to engage in politics may be interpreted only in terms of incentives. From the point of view of incentives these may be classified as motives of power and prestige, or motives of fear and defense. Power and prestige in politics were only to be gained by achieving the higher offices—the executive offices in the three levels of government and the higher judiciary. The holders of these offices tended to be recruited most frequently from among the wealthy business men and corporation lawyers. In most cases the wealthy holders of these offices did not work up from the ranks, but were nominated because of their prestige and respectability, or because of party contributions. But this type of public office-holding tended to decrease as time went on. The public offices in the national, state, and municipal legislative bodies were rarely held by wealthy individuals.

These more numerous political offices were held by the smaller entrepreneurs and lawyers. The types of entrepreneurs most frequently represented among the professional politicians were either those whose business involved frequent and continued contact with large numbers of people—saloon-keepers, real estate and insurance dealers, and other types of entrepreneurs—individuals who were strategically located among the masses, or individuals whose business could specially profit from good political connections—various types of building contractors, wagoners, and truckers, printers, and the like. The rank and file of the politicians thus were from the middle classes, and in a place like New York City were in great part recruited from among the newer immigrations. Within their own communities these politicians constituted a kind of class of notables. As lawyers, or entrepreneurs, their poorer and less well-informed compatriots had constantly to turn to them for advice and aid. It was upon relations of this type that the power of these politicians was based.

The dominance of politics by these middle class newer nationality types had the consequence of lowering the prestige level and pulling power of the public service. It must of course be clearly understood that the classes of the population who came to bear this negative attitude toward politics were the wealthier and professional elements of the population, numerically a minority but the dominant classes as far as the shaping of public opinion is concerned.

Democratization had thus brought two new social phenomena into being: a "society"—a special unproductive grasshopper element which sought in this existence to objectify its superiority to the democracy—and a special class of professional politicians who engaged in politics as a business enterprise, profit oriented, and hence safe as far as the plutocracy was concerned, since profits were to be gained mainly by working along with the wealthy business interests.

Although in the great majority of cases the professional politicians were conservative and of no danger to the wealthier elements as a class, special interest groups in the capitalist class sought for reasons of defense or the acquisition of advantages to exercise special influence over politics. This resulted in the rise of special political agents representing the interests of the plutocracy. These agents frequently were corporation lawyers, although a number of wealthy business men went into politics themselves, conducting their business directly, so to speak. The conclusion may not be drawn, however, that all wealthy individuals in politics were there for purely business reasons. The mayoralty, the governorship, and federal cabinet, and diplomatic positions appealed to the desires for honor and for public service among the upper business elements.

A type of political institution which arose in the democratic period to give the wealthier classes contact with politics and politicians was the special upper class political club. Political clubs such as the Union League, the Manhattan, the National Democratic, and the National Republican clubs were convenient and necessary points of contact between the upper levels of the politician group and the politically interested industrialists, merchants, and financiers. These upper class political clubs were among the important points at which upper class pressure for legislative issues and the selection of candidates was exercised. These clubs served the politician by giving him access to "money bags" for the financing of his machine. Another instrument by means of which the wealthier elements as a whole, or special interest groups within them, endeavored to safeguard or aggrandize their positions took the form of money contributions to the various party organizations. The volume of this type of political activity varied directly with the safety or threatening character of the political situation.

The maintenance of this type of social structure the main characteristics of which have been briefly described was conditioned upon a generally expanding economy and conditions of peace. The latter half of the nineteenth century with minor fluctuations was a period almost without comparison of rapid industrial and financial development. The great vertical and horizontal social mobility restricted the "politicization" of classes. The frontier both in an agricultural and an industrial sense functioned as a safety valve. However, the development of crises of various types temporarily altered the political and social position of the wealthier classes.

These crises were of three types: revelation of political corruption, war, and depression resulting in lower class unrest.

Political corruption, although in considerable measure elements of the upper business classes were involved in it, when exposed, endangered the position of the wealthier classes in both a material and a moral sense. The exposure of municipal corruption for example lowered the value of municipal securities, the great holders of which were the wealthier classes. Then too, widespread political corruption was viewed as a threat to public law and order, the maintenance of which was a pre-condition of the security of the wealthier classes. The history of the plutocracy of New York City is full of vigilantist reactions in response to exposure of the corrupt practices of the political machines, especially Tammany Hall. These eras of corruption precipitated political action in the wealthy classes. They resulted in the formation of reform civic clubs and associations, and *ad hoc* non-partisan political movements which in a number of cases succeeded in temporarily bringing into public office wealthy business men and civic and philanthropic leaders. Generally, however, these vigilantist risings lasted only for short periods of time. The wealthy groups, after the immediate danger was overcome, withdrew again from political activity, thus permitting the development of a new political machine; and a new cycle of corruption, vigilantism, and disinterest followed.

A second type of crisis affecting the political attitudes and activities and the social attitudes and activities of the wealthier classes is the war situation. The greater the severity of the war, the greater the transformation of the normal functions and attitudes of the plutocracy. Particularly in the era of the "Total War" has the wealthy class become politicized in war crises. This development is of course due to general politicization of life consequent upon modern warfare. Since this era of the "Total War" has begun with the World War, we have only World War experience for purposes of illustration of this type of crisis politicization of the economic controlling classes. However, in the American Civil War there were adumbrations of this later role. The wealthy classes enter into political activity during war periods in military and civil capacities for moral-patriotic, and material-profiteering motives. The necessity for the subordination of the economic order to military ends resulted in the establishment of *ad hoc* regulatory agencies in which many of the larger industrialists and financiers served. War crises also tend to diminish the emphasis upon differences in the population. Temporarily "society" gives up its elaborate social life for military-philanthropic activities.

The third type of crisis which tends to influence the volume and direction of the political and social activity of the plutocracy is depression and its consequent social unrest. As far as the social life of the plutocracy is concerned philanthropic activities take precedence over purely social activities in depression periods. The various strata of the plutocracy, based upon differences in religion, social, and nationality origin, and tastes and interests tend to unite temporarily in the face of serious depression.

The consequences of depression for the political attitudes and activities of the plutocracy vary with the movements precipitated in the lower classes by unemployment and need. Where lower class unrest resulted in dangerous political movements the plutocracy could struggle against this danger by maneuvering within the political parties, by financing safe political elements, by propaganda control, and by techniques of dividing the dangerous movement. These modes of action sufficed in the era of general expansion to check the danger of such left movements as the "Loco-Focos" in the 1820s and 1830s, the Henry George campaigns in 1886 and 1897, and in the national arena in the Bryan campaigns and the era of the first Roosevelt.

More recently, however, these normal methods of political defense have not sufficed. The general labor unrest following upon the World War, and the unrest during the present depression have resulted in the formation of *ad hoc* vigilantist groups which have engaged in anti-liberal and anti-radical propaganda. In these two campaigns individuals in the New York plutocracy have been extremely active.

The increase in lower class protest and organization consequent upon the passing of the frontier, and the general stabilization of the American economy and social structure have had important influences upon the social life and activities of the plutocracy. These influences have transformed the content of upper class social life, and have practically destroyed the organization of exclusive society. The emancipation of women has also played an important role in these developments. The purely pleasure-oriented society of the "set" around Mrs. Astor has given way to a society whose pleasurable activities have come to be justified by philanthropic objectives. Competition for prestige in society thus is no longer a matter of giving spectacular private functions within the home, but has taken the form of social-philanthropic competition, a situation which makes impossible the maintenance of an exclusive group. This is due to the fact that the objective of philanthropic activity is the collection of the largest quantity of money, a type of activity inconsistent with the setting of exclusive standards.

It seems abundantly clear that American politics of the present and future is now and will continue to be animated by an intensifying struggle between the wealthy classes and those elements seeking a greater share in the fruits of our economy and technique. This historical review of the major transformations in the plutocracy of New York makes possible a number of insights into the future character of this struggle.

Such a recent writing as Ferdinand Lundberg's *America's 60 Families* tends to create a misunderstanding as to the qualities of the American plutocracy. On the one hand it exaggerates the degree of its political power and control. The claim that American democracy is a mere facade behind which the machinations of the plutocracy take place does not square with the hysteria of reactionary and conservative interests at the present time. Such hysteria could not arise in a plutocracy in secure political control. On the other hand the impression is conveyed of a plutocracy universally and self-consciously anti-democratic. Thus Lundberg mistakenly claims that the social life of the plutocracy has become even more spectacular, extravagant, and wasteful in recent times.[2] That extravagant expenditure still continues is beyond question and not the issue here. The twentieth century saw in the plutocracy the tendency toward the subordination of pleasurable functions to philanthropist values. However poorly calculated this philanthropy is to cope with modern needs, or however genuine the philanthropic motive, is not under discussion here. That the transformation has occurred is beyond denial.

From a political point of view the point must also be made that there is a concession group as well as a die-hard group in the plutocracy. Important elements in the plutocracy have not resisted the passage of recent social legislation; and in some cases have been positively identified with it.

We have also seen in this review of plutocratic experience that roughly for the last century the plutocracy in America has not enjoyed a formally prior political position. George Counts[3] sees in this absence of a tradition of political precedence a force in favor of the survival of democracy. To be sure, this precludes the possibility of an attempted regaining of formal political power on the part of the plutocracy. But the lack of such a tradition in Germany did not prevent the financing of the National Socialist Party by industrialists and bankers. In fact the political tradition of the American plutocracy has been that of defense by financial and propaganda support to political elements willing to safeguard their interests. Such a political attitude seems to make for a greater likelihood of the rise of fascist tendencies in America. We have no reason to believe that the wealthier classes confronted by great and immediate danger will not support in greater measure those vigilantist and fascist-like groups which elements among them are supporting at the present time. A strong argument can be made for the fact that the plutocracy has never in any genuine sense been democratic, that is, willing to take the consequences of political equality. It has always sought by whatever means were most effective to defend its superior position. Should it be confronted by the choice on the one hand of a serious loss of economic power, or on the other of maintaining its position by alliance with anti-democratic elements, the past history of the plutocracy makes the latter seem to be a likely future policy. The saving factor in American democracy, at least temporarily, seems to be the fact that in the mass of the population the assumptions of formal democracy are taken for granted. No political group of decisive political importance in contemporary America opposes democracy in principle. And it will take a great crisis to destroy this attitude in enough people to make a genuine and complete fascism possible.

Notes

1. Alexis De Tocqueville, *Democracy in America*, trans. by Henry Reeves (New York: A. S. Barnes and Co., 1862), I, 192.

2. See Ferdinand Lundberg, *America's 60 Families* (New York: The Vanguard Press, 1937), p. 408.

3. George S. Counts, *The Prospects of American Democracy* (New York: The John Day Co., 1933), pp. 274 ff.

Bibliography

This bibliography does not claim to be exhaustive. It includes all sources specifically referred to in the endnotes to the text, and most of those sources not directly referred to but which were used for theoretical and general background purposes.

Biographical Compilations and Sources of Biographical Data

Appleton's Cyclopedia of American Biography. Edited by James Grant Wilson and John Fiske. New York: D. Appleton Co., 1888.

Beach, Moses Yale. The Wealth and Biography of the Wealthy Citizens of New York. 1842–1855. New York: The New York Sun.

Blake, E. Vale. History of the Tammany Society. New York: Souvenir Publishing Co., 1901.

The Centennial History of the Protestant Episcopal Church in the Diocese of New York, 1785–1885. Appendix A. Edited by James Grant Wilson. New York: D. Appleton and Co., 1886.

Chamber of Commerce of the State of New York. Catalogue of Portraits. New York: Chamber of Commerce, 1924.

Dictionary of American Biography. Edited by Dumas Malone. New York: Charles Scribner's Sons, 1928.

Folsom, George. Historical Sketch of the New York Historical Society. New York: New York Historical Society, 1841.

Hall, Henry. America's Successful Men of Affairs. 2 vols. New York: The New York Tribune, 1895–1896.

Hamm, Marguerita Aulina. Famous Families of New York. 2 vols. New York: G. P. Putnam's Sons, 1902.

Keep, Austin Baxter. History of the New York Society Library. New York: The DeVinne Press, 1908.

Kelby, Robert Hendre. The New York Historical Society, 1804–1904. New York, 1905.

King, Moses. Notable New Yorkers of 1896–1899. New York: M. King, 1899.

Lanman, Charles. Biographical Annals of the Civil Government of the United States. Washington: James Anglin, 1876.

_____. Dictionary of the United States Congress. Washington: Government Printing Office, 1864.

The National Cyclopedia of American Biography. New York: James T. White and Co., 1906.

New York Red Book, 1892. Albany: J. B. Lyon Co., 1892.

Stevens, John Austin. Colonial New York. New York: J. F. Trow and Co., 1867.

Weeks, Lyman Horace. Prominent Families of New York. New York: The Historical Co., 1897.
Who's Who in America. 1899–1937. Chicago: The A. N. Marquis Co.
Who's Who in Our American Government, 1935. Washington, 1935.
Who's Who in Commerce and Industry, 1936. New York: New York Institute for Research in Biography, Inc., 1936.
Who's Who in Finance and Banking. 1911–1926. New York: Who's Who in Finance, Inc.
Who's Who in Government. New York: Biographical Research Bureau, 1930.
Who's Who in Jurisprudence. Brooklyn: John W. Leonard Corporation, 1925.
Who's Who in New York City. 1904–1929. New York: Who's Who Publications, Inc.
Who's Who in the East. Washington: Mayflower Publishing Co., 1930.
Who's Who in the Nation's Capitol. Edited by Stanley H. Williamson. Washington: Ransdell, Inc., 1934.

Directories, Yearbooks, Almanacs, and Reports

Chamber of Commerce of the State of New York. Annual Report of the Corporation. 1870, 1901, 1935.
Directory of Directors in the City of New York. 1898–1927. New York: The Audit Company of New York.
Elite Catalogue of Clubs. New York: New York Publishing Co., 1890.
The Evening Journal Almanac. New York: Evening Journal Almanac, 1870.
Junior League of New York. Annual Report, 1935.
Knickerbocker Club. Yearbook. 1872, 1932.
Manual of the Corporation of the City of New York, 1842–1870. Compiled by D. T. Valentine. New York: the City of New York.
Metropolitan Club of New York. Yearbook. 1892, 1935.
Minutes of the Common Council of the City of New York, 1784–1831. Analytical Index. Prepared by David Maydole Matteson. New York: M. B. Browne Co., 1917.
New York City Common Council. Minutes, 1675–1776. New York: Dodd Mead and Co., 1905.
New York City Directory, 1932. New York: R. L. Polk, Inc.
New York Civil List, 1855. Albany: Secretary of State's Office, 1855.
New York Clearing House Association. Annual Report. 1894, 1935.
New York Directory. 1786–1835. New York: Trow City Directory Co.
New York Merchants Association. Annual Report. 1906, 1931.
New York Secretary of State. Manual for the Use of the Legislature of the State of New York, 1890. Albany: Weed Parsons and Co.
Poor's Register of Directors of the United States. 1928–1937. Babson Park, Mass.: Poor's Printing Co.
Presbyterian Church in the United States. Digest of Records. Philadelphia: printed for the Trustees, 1820.
The Scrapbook of the Tontine Coffee House. New York: The Tontine Society, 1796.

Social Register New York. 1889–1935. New York: Social Register Association.
Social Season of 1882–1883. New York: New York Tribune, 1883.
The Tribune Almanac, 1838–1868. New York: New York Tribune, 1868.
Trow's General Directory of the Boroughs of Manhattan and Bronx. New York: Trow Directory Printing and Bookbinding Co., 1900.
Trow's New York City Directory. Compiled by H. Wilson. New York: John F. Trow, 1870.
Union Club. Yearbook. 1871, 1900, 1935.
World Almanac. 1892–1936. New York: the New York World and the New York World Telegram.

Newspapers

New York Herald, 1886.
New York Herald Tribune. 1930–1931 and 1935.
New York Times. December, 1917.
New York Tribune. 1853–1854, 1871, 1886, 1890, and 1897.

Books

Adams, Charles Francis. "A Chapter of Erie," from High Finance in the Sixties. Edited by Frederick Hicks. New Haven: Yale University Press, 1929.
Baruch, Bernard M. American Industry in the War. A Report of the War Industries Board. Washington: Government Printing Office, 1921.
Beard, Charles A. The Economic Basis of Politics. New York: A. A. Knopf, 1922.
_____. An Economic Interpretation of the Constitution. New York: The Macmillan Co., 1913.
Becker, Carl. The History of Political Parties in the Province of New York, 1760–1776. Bulletin of the University of Wisconsin, No. 286, History Series, Vol. II, No. 1. Madison: University of Wisconsin, 1909.
Berle, Adolph A., Jr., and Means, Gardiner C. The Modern Corporation and Private Property. New York: The Macmillan Co., 1933.
Bishop, Joseph Bucklin. The Chamber of Commerce: A Chronicle of 150 Years. New York: Charles Scribner's Sons, 1918.
Bonner, William T. New York, The World's Metropolis, 1623–1923. New York: R. L. Polk and Co., 1924.
Booth, Mary Louise. History of the City of New York. New York: W. R. Clark and Meeker, 1863.
Breen, Matthew Patrick. Thirty Years of New York Politics Up-to-Date. New York, 1899.
Brown, Henry Collins. Brownstone Fronts and Seratoga Trunks. New York: E. P. Dutton and Co., 1935.
_____. In the Golden Nineties. Hastings-on-the-Hudson: Valentine's Manual, Inc., 1928.
Browne, Junius Henry. The Great Metropolis: A Mirror of New York. Hartford: American Publishing Co., 1869.

Bryce, James. American Commonwealth. 2 vols. New York: The Macmillan Co., 1891.

Chambers, Walter. Samuel Seabury: A Challenge. New York and London: The Century Co., 1932.

Counts, George S. The Prospects of American Democracy. New York: John Day Co., 1938.

Davenport, John Isaacs. The Election Frauds of New York City and Their Prevention. New York, 1881.

Dayton, Abram C. Last Days of Knickerbocker Life in New York. New York: G. W. Harlan, 1882.

De Tocqueville, Alexis. Democracy in America. Translated by Henry Reeves. 2 vols. New York: A. S. Barnes and Co., 1862.

Doane, Robert R. The Measurements of American Wealth. New York: Harper Bros., 1935.

Earle, Alice. Colonial Days in Old New York. New York: Charles Scribner's Sons, 1897.

Edwards, George William. New York City as an Eighteenth Century Municipality, 1731–1776. New York: Columbia University Press, 1917.

Ellington, George. The Women of New York. New York: The New York Book Co., 1870.

Fairfield, Francis G. The Clubs of New York. New York: H. L. Hunter and Co., 1873.

Fay, Bernard. The Revolutionary Spirit in France and America. New York: Harcourt Brace and Co., 1929.

Fine, Nathan. The Collapse of the Seabury Investigation. New York: Rand School Press, 1932.

Finegan, James Emmet. Tammany at Bay. New York: Dodd, Mead and Co.

Foord, John. The Life and Public Services of Andrew Haswell Green. New York: Doubleday Page and Co., 1913.

Fox, Dixon Ryan. The Decline of the Aristocracy in the Politics of New York. New York: Longmans Green and Co., 1919.

Francis, John W. Old New York. New York: W. J. Middleton, 1886.

Franklin, Jay. La Guardia. New York: Modern Age Books, 1937.

Glentworth, James B. A Statement of the Frauds in the Elective Franchise in the City of New York. New York, 1841.

Grund, Francis J. Aristocracy in America. London: R. Bentley, 1839.

Hammond, Jabez Delano. The History of Political Parties in the State of New York. 2 vols. Buffalo: Phinney and Co., 1850.

Harrington, Virginia Draper. The New York Merchant on the Eve of the Revolution. New York: Columbia University Press, 1935.

Headley, H. J. T. The Great Riots of New York City. New York: E. B. Treat, 1873.

Hill, Robert Tudor. The Public Domain and Democracy. Columbia University Studies in History and Public Law, Vol. XXXVIII, 1910. New York: Longmans Green and Co, 1910.

Hodder, Alfred. A Fight for the City. New York: The Macmillan Co., 1903.

Ivins, William. Machine Politics and Money in Elections in New York City. New York: Harper and Bros., 1887.

Josephson, Matthew. Robber Barons. New York: Harcourt Brace and Co., 1934.

Klein, Henry H. Bankrupting a Great City. New York, 1915.

_____. Politics, Government, and the Public Utilities in New York City. New York: Isaac Goldmann and Co., 1933.

Lamb, Martha Joanna R. History of the City of New York. New York: A. S. Barnes and Co., 1877.

Lasswell, Harold D. Politics. New York: Whittlesey House, McGraw-Hill Book Co., 1936.

_____. World Politics and Personal Insecurity. New York: McGraw-Hill Book Co., 1935.

Lavine, Emmanuel H. "Gimme": or How Politicians Get Rich. New York: The Vanguard Press, 1931.

Leonard, John William. History of the City of New York. New York: The Journal of Commerce, 1910.

Lewis, Alfred Henry. The Boss and How He Came to Rule New York. New York: A. S. Barnes and Co., 1904.

Lincoln, Charles J. Constitutional History of New York. 2 vols. Rochester, New York: Lawyers Cooperative Publishing Co., 1906.

Lloyd, Henry Demarest. Wealth Against Commonwealth. New York: Harper and Bros., 1894.

_____. Lords of Industry. New York and London: G. P. Putnam's Sons, 1910.

_____. Men the Workers. New York: Doubleday Page and Co., 1909.

Lundberg, Ferdinand. America's 60 Families. New York: The Vanguard Press, 1937.

Lynch, Denis Tilden. "Boss" Tweed: The Story of a Grim Generation. New York: Boni and Liveright, 1927.

Martin, Frederick Townsend. The Passing of the Idle Rich. London: Hodder and Stoughton, 1911.

Merriam, Charles E. New Aspects of Politics. Chicago: University of Chicago Press, 1931.

Merriam, Charles E., and Gosnell, Harold F. The American Party System. New York: The Macmillan Co., 1928.

_____. Four American Party Leaders. New York: The Macmillan Co., 1926.

McAllister, Ward. Society as I Have Found It. New York: Cassell Publishing Co., 1890.

McCarthy, James Remington. Peacock Alley. New York: Harper and Bros., 1931.

McGuire, James K. The Democratic Party of the State of New York. New York: United States History Co., 1905.

Michels, Roberto. Political Parties. New York: Hearst's International Library Co., 1915.

_____. Umschichtungen in den Herrschenden Klassen nach den Kriege. Berlin: W. Kohlhammer, 1934.

Minnegerode, Meade. The Fabulous 40's. New York: G. P. Putnam's Sons, 1924.

Myers, Gustavus. History of the Great American Fortunes. 3 vols. Chicago: C. H. Kerr and Co., 1909.

_____. History of Tammany Hall. New York, 1901.

Nevins, Allan. Abram S. Hewitt. New York: Harper and Bros., 1935.

New York in the War of the Rebellion. Compiled by Frederick Phisterer. 5 vols. Albany: J. B. Lyon, 1912.

Nicholls, Charles W. D. The 469 Ultra-Fashionables of America. New York: Broadway Publishing Co., 1912.

Northrop, William Bacot. The Insolence of Office. New York: G. P. Putnam's Sons, 1932.

Overacker, Louise. Money in Elections. New York: The Macmillan Co., 1932.

Parkhurst, Charles H. Our Fight with Tammany. New York: Charles Scribner's Sons, 1895.

Peel, Roy Victor. The Political Clubs of New York City. New York: G. P. Putnam's Sons, 1935.

Pollock, James K, Jr. Party Campaign Funds. New York: Alfred A. Knopf, 1926.

Pulitzer, Ralph. Society on Parade. New York and London: Harper and Bros., 1910.

Richmond, John Francis. New York and Its Institutions, 1609–1872. New York: E. B. Treat, 1872.

Riordan, William L. Plunkett of Tammany Hall. New York: McClure Philips and Co., 1905.

Rochester, Anna. Rulers of America. New York: International Publishers, 1936.

Scoville, Joseph (pseudonym Walter Barrett, Clerk). Old Merchants of New York. 5 vols. New York: Thomas R. Knox, 1885.

Seldes, George. Freedom of the Press. Garden City, N.Y.: Garden City Publishing Co., 1937.

_____. Lords of the Press. New York: Julian Messner, 1938.

Seymour, Charles, and Frary, Donald P. How the World Votes. 2 vols. Springfield, Mass.: C. A. Nicholls Co., 1918.

Sherman, Philemon T. Inside the Machine, 1898–1899. New York: Cooke and Fry, 1901.

Singleton, Esther. Dutch New York. New York: Dodd, Mead and Co., 1909.

_____. Social New York at the Time of the Georges, 1714–1776. New York: D. Appleton Co., 1902.

Sorokin, Pitirim A. Social Mobility. New York: Harper Bros., 1927.

Speier, Hans. "Democracy and Social Stratification," in Political and Economic Democracy. Edited by Max Ascoli and Fritz Lehman. New York: W. W. Norton Co., 1937.

Stead, William Thomas. Satan's Invisible World Displayed: or Despairing Democracy. London, 1897.

Stoddard, Theodore L. Master of Manhattan: The Life of Richard Croker. New York: Longmans Green and Co., 1931.

Taussig, F. W., and Joslyn, C. S. American Business Leaders. New York: The Macmillan Co., 1932.

Thomas, Norman Mattoon. What's the Matter with New York? New York: The Macmillan Co., 1932.

Tilden, Samuel J. The New York City Ring. New York, 1873.

Tuckerman, Bayard (ed.). The Diary of Philip Hone. 2 vols. New York: Dodd Mead and Co., 1889.

Turner, Frederick Jackson. The Frontier in American History. New York: Henry Holt and Co., 1920.

Valentine, David Thomas. History of the City of New York. New York: G. P. Putnam and Co., 1853.
Van Pelt, Daniel. Leslie's History of Greater New York. 3 vols. New York: Arkell Publishing Co., 1898.
Van Rensselaer, Mariana. History of New York in the 17th Century. 2 vols. New York: The Macmillan Co., 1909
Van Rensselaer, May King. The Goede Vrouw of Mana-ha-ta. New York: Charles Scribner's Sons, 1898.
_____. The Social Ladder. New York: Henry Holt and Co., 1924.
Walker, Stanley. Mrs. Astor's Horse. New York: Frederick A. Stokes Co., 1935.
Weber, Max. Gesammelte Politische Schriften. Munich: Drei Masken Verlag, 1921.
_____. Wirtschaft und Gesellschaft. Abt III. Grundriss der Sozialökonomik. 2 vols. Tübingen: J. C. B. Mohr, 1925.
Wecter, Dixon. The Saga of American Society. New York: Charles Scribner's Sons, 1937.
Werner, M. R. Tammany Hall. New York: Doubleday Doran and Co., 1928.
White, Leonard D. Prestige Value of Public Employment in Chicago. Chicago: University of Chicago Press, 1930.
_____. Further Contributions to the Prestige Value of Public Employment. Chicago: University of Chicago Press, 1932.
Wilson, James Grant. The Memorial History of the City of New York. 4 vols. New York: New York History Co., 1893.

Magazine Articles and Pamphlets

Bayles, W. Harrison. "Old Taverns of New York," Journal of American History, XXIII to XXVIII (1930 to 1934), series of articles.
Bureau of Municipal Research. Purposes and Methods of the Bureau of Municipal Research. New York, 1907.
City for the People. Issued by the Committee on Press and Literature of the Citizens Union, 1897 and 1903.
National Security League. Miscellaneous pamphlets. March and May, 1926.
New York City. Mayor's Committee for the Relief of the Unemployed and Needy of the City of New York. 1930–1931, and 1932–1933.
Report of the Senate Lobby Committee. Part I, List of Contributions. Washington: Government Printing Office, 1936.
Overacker, Louise. "Campaign Funds in the Presidential Election of 1936," Political Science Review, June, 1937.
Schafer, Joseph. "Turner's America," Wisconsin Magazine of History, XVII (1933–1934), 447.
Sereno, Renzo. "The Anti-Aristotelianism of Gaetano Mosca and Its Fate," International Journal of Ethics, July, 1938.
Sorokin, Pitirim A. "American Millionaires and Multi-Millionaires," Social Forces, May, 1925.
Speier, Hans. "Honor and Social Structure," Social Research, February, 1935.

Turner, Frederick Jackson. "Social Forces in American History," American Historical Review, XVI (1911), 217.

Unpublished Material

Jensen, James M. "New War Time Administrative Agencies." Unpublished master's thesis, Department of History, University of Chicago, 1929.

Index